THEOLOGICAL APPROACHES TO CHRISTIAN EDUCATION

Edited by
Jack L. Seymour and Donald E. Miller

ABINGDON PRESS

Nashville

THEOLOGICAL APPROACHES TO CHRISTIAN EDUCATION

This book is printed on recycled acid-free paper.

Library of Congress Cataloging-in-Publication Data

Theological approaches to Christian education/Jack L. Seymour, Donald E. Miller.
   p.   cm. Includes bibliographical references.
   Contents: Openings to God/Jack Seymour and Donald E. Miller—Tradition and education/Melanie A. May—Tradition and sacramental education/Marianne Sawicki—Feminist theology and education/Mary Elizabeth Mullino Moore—Education in the quest for church/Charles R. Foster—The church in a racial-minority situation/Fumitaka Matsuoka—Education in the image of God/Susanne Johnson—Education and human development in the likeness of Christ/Romney Moseley—Christian education in a world of religious pluralism/Choan-Seng Song—Ecumenical learning in a global perspective/David Merritt—Latin American theology and education/Robert T. O'Gorman—Teaching as practical theology/Richard R. Osmer—Living into a world of confessional pluralism/Donald E. Miller and Jack Seymour.
   ISBN 0-687-41355-9 (alk. paper)
   1. Christian education—Philosophy. I. Seymour, Jack L. (Jack Lee), 1948– . II. Miller, Donald Eugene.
BV1464.T46   1990   0-35784
268'.01—dc20   CIP

95 96 97 98 99 00 01 02 03 04 — 10 9 8 7 6 5 4

MANUFACTURED IN THE UNITED STATES OF AMERICA

Acknowledgments

Since 1982, the reception to *Contemporary Approaches to Christian Education* has been gratifying.[1] Critical comments by colleagues in scholarly journals, as well as the attention by educators to actual approaches used in local churches, has encouraged us to continue the conversation about directions for Christian education.

When we sought in 1982 to describe the differing emphases present in the literature of the field, it seemed that further reflection was needed, both on foundational assumptions and on the patterns of education which emerge within the ministry of the church. To describe ideal types for Christian education was never our intention. The task we addressed, and the one we believe will provide direction for the field, is to struggle with the role of education in communicating and understanding the meaning of the presence of God in human life. We hope this volume contributes to that conversation.

We are reminded by H. Richard Niebuhr, in his contemporary classic *Christ and Culture*, that the Christian church is always one generation away from extinction.[2] Without specific efforts to teach the traditions of the faith to the next generation in such a way that persons are included within the life of faith, the church loses its power to transform human life and cultures. Education is crucial to the future of the faith.

We thank colleagues at our institutions, Garrett-Evangelical Theological Seminary and Church of the Brethren, who have encouraged us in our work. Also we thank colleagues in the academic field of Christian education who graciously responded to our inquiries as we shaped this book—Ronald Cram, Gloria Durka, Craig Dykstra, H. Edward Everding, Maria Harris, Susanne Johnson, James Michael Lee, Charles Melchert, David Merritt, William Myers, Robert O'Gorman, Richard Osmer, James Reed, Marianne Sawicki, Kieran Scott, Grant Shockley, Joanmarie Smith, David Steward, Edward Trimmer, and Linda Vogel. Their advice was helpful.

In particular, we thank our co-authors in *Contemporary Approaches*—Sara Little, Charles Foster, Allen Moore, and Carol Wehrheim. By describing an approach, each risked identification with that description. In fact, in a few cases they found it necessary to defend themselves against such "typing." They sought to contribute to dialogue in the field, and they accomplished that purpose. Those of us in Christian religious education need more people who will attend, as they did, to the development of theory for the field and the discipline. Their gracious and substantial efforts in the first project and their advice on the second are greatly appreciated.

We also thank Sue Snyder of Church of the Brethren, who helped to see that details of this present project were accurate, and the editors and staff at Abingdon Press, who have supported us in both projects.

To

Anne and Laura

and

Natasha,

who carry the faith into the future

Contents

Part III—*Person*

Part IV—*Mission: The Church in the World*

Part V—*Method*

CHAPTER 1

Openings to God:
Education and Theology in Dialogue

Jack L. Seymour and Donald E. Miller

Education is a fundamental issue in United States culture. Having heard the public's concern about the educational skills necessary to function in society, state legislators have passed laws requiring basic-education tests of students as they progress through the grades, and tests of the teachers who guide them. Candidates for President have vied to be known as the "education president." Business has even taken the lead in the conversation about education. Its leaders worry about the effectiveness of education to produce a population with the technical and scientific skills to compete in a world market, as well as the multicultural and geographic skills necessary to understand and communicate with people whose culture differs from their own. Moreover, recent tests have suggested appalling gaps in the historical knowledge of United States' high school students—a knowledge necessary for the development of values and commitments consistent with the "American experience."

Clearly, there is overall concern about education, and differing groups compete for their agendas to be legislated into school curriculum. This struggle reflects the fact that education is critical to a society. Clarifying the values and skills necessary in a constantly changing world is crucial to a people. Increased pluralism; apparent confusion about national directions; significant and rapid social changes; and the increased demand for multicultural, multiethnic, and interreligious communication and understanding, as well as the seemingly constant threat of repression and international military conflict, call upon educators to assist persons in preparing to engage public life and develop appropriate strategies to respond to social challenges.

Within the attempts to reshape education is the recognition that education is fundamental to human discourse and human community. Education defines a people. It involves the processes by which a community, society, or nation clarifies and communicates the values and commitments (the *paideia*, or ideals) fundamental to itself as a people. Education also involves the way these commitments engage and "take on" new life in the midst of changing social circumstances. A people builds a community to sustain itself, to share and order its living (defining the rights of individuals and groups), and to communicate values and commitments to new generations and to strangers. These tasks are the content and process of education. Simply put, education is about *passing on* a tradition and *participating in* the re-creation of that tradition.

However, educational conversation in United States culture cannot be carried out, though it seems that everywhere there are such efforts, without religious reflection. Religion is concerned precisely with the depth issues of the way a people defines itself. Basic issues of the vision of a society, of the vocation of that society in the world, of which institutions carry the tasks of meaning-making and understanding, and of how members will participate in decisions that affect their lives—these concerns are discussed in theological issues known, in turn, as those of eschatology (the realm or "kingdom" of God), of mission, of church, and of anthropology.

The very issues that call education to respond also call theology to reform the way it participates in public dialogue about the fundamental meanings of a society. The possibility of the end of creation in a nuclear disaster transforms the way theology is conducted.[1] Conversation about the nature of human beings and the brokenness they experience, as well as about possibilities and visions for transformation, are intensified by these issues. That theology has a public duty to communicate the possibilities brought forth into the world by God is clear when the reality and intensity of brokenness is encountered. Fundamentally, the questions of the future are theological questions of the destiny of the creation, and of humans in light of the eternal.

Theologically, the dialogue of education and society is summarized in the question of God, or of how our experience with transcendence, the Holy One, shapes our response to living—for example, how we are changed, what we are called to do and be, how we live together as children of God, and together, how we shape meanings and structures that define meaning. Discerning God's presence and call and following God into the action of making history are fundamental tasks of education. *Therefore, any book about religious education is about knowing God and learning to live faithfully in relation to God. Moreover, for Christians, that knowing is described in the incarnation and continuing revelation of Jesus of Nazareth, the Christ.* These issues are not the private property of the church. They have public implications.

However, theological and religious discourse can contribute to the cultural conversation only when attention is given to praxis—that is, concrete activities through which cultural analysis and criticism occur and meanings are shared. Here the questions of religious education are generated. Religious education attempts to understand and contribute to the processes by which a society touches its deepest and most fundamental resources for meaning (its ultimate concern) as it makes decisions about clarifying and embodying its vision. A task of religious education is to examine and understand these cultural processes of engaging the vision of God with the possibilities of human experience.

Because of the significance of these concerns, the role of religious education is being reassessed. For example, a fundamental reassessment of religious education seems to be occurring in theological studies. Christian education is no longer seen as merely a technical and applied practical area within the theological encyclopedia. Rather, it is recognized

9

that it has to do with basic questions of the meaning of the Christian faith, the meaning of theological education, and the role of the church in the education of the public.[2]

In turn, within the field of Christian religious education, there is new effort to ground the discipline in theological and educational questions: How is education an expression of Christian experience and revelation in the world? How does Christian education arise from the reality of the church in the world?[3] The unity of theological and educational issues has been recognized.

This book, *Theological Approaches to Christian Education*, is an attempt to integrate and probe the conversation of those in education and theology about the processes by which Christian faith is embodied, communicated, and re-formed within the culture. It addresses, from the perspective of a *Christian* religious education, some of the crucial theological issues central to the educational task.

The format is much like that of our previous effort, *Contemporary Approaches to Christian Education*. Educator/theologians consider five crucial issues which have been historically important for Christian education: the nature of the tradition (knowledge about God), the role of the church, the nature of human beings, the mission of the church in the world, and the method of theology. Through these essays the authors clarify the field of Christian religious education by describing its goals, suggesting patterns of teaching and learning, and defining ways to carry religious education into the culture. After these issues have been addressed, the editors suggest directions for Christian religious education. The goal is to assist students and professionals to reflect on tasks and options within the educational ministries of Christian faith.

Contemporary Approaches to Christian Education

In *Contemporary Approaches*, we sought to map the literature of the field. It was an attempt to relate what was being said about Christian education by Christian educators.[4]

We now hope to move beyond that "mapping" of literature to address issues fundamental to the dialogue of education, religion, and culture.

As a text for the field, *Contemporary Approaches* provided one set of organizing principles, among others, to reflect on and clarify the state of the church's education.[5]

In translation, the book has introduced the literature of the field to Korean and Japanese churches.[6] And the map it offered has been of assistance to those wishing to examine church education. The book was used as an interpretive framework during the tenth-year consultation of Joint Educational Development, when directions for the future and curriculum of JED were discussed.[7] In addition, in "Christian Education Effectiveness: A National Study of Protestant Congregations," a study being conducted by the Search Institute for several denominations, the approaches provided one interpretive lens for examining the practice of church education.[8] Moreover, an independent study of African-American Christian education in the United States has discovered patterns similar to those in the book in the strategies being embodied in local congregations.[9]

In 1982, it seemed to us that five primary metaphors were being used in the field: religious instruction, community of faith, development, liberation, and interpretation.[10] Each put emphasis on contrasting "strategies" for engaging in education. The issues raised by these approaches continue to be significant, and they deserve further exploration with attention to major theological issues.

Religious Instruction

Educators who use this metaphor often are concerned about content. *What* needs to be taught? Sara Little argued persuasively that religious instruction is concerned with thinking, understanding, deciding, and believing. She defined religious instruction as "the process of exploring the church's tradition and self-understanding in such a way that persons can understand, assess, and therefore respond to the truth of the gospel for themselves."[11] God's self-revelation and the way that "inheritance" is being re-created is central to any teaching.

While the teaching/learning interaction takes place in many settings, the task of the teacher is to present the content of the tradition in such a way that the pupil encounters and engages it. Such engagement must be intentional and structured, and the structuring of both content and process is a significant responsibility; the teacher will participate in another's life to affect that life. Teachers are thus agents of the tradition and the content they teach. In fact, it could be said that in the act of teaching, teachers are the tradition.

A primary instrumentality for teaching is, of course, the school. Yet there are many other settings for religious instruction—families, camps, youth groups, home studies. As instructional agencies, the distinguishing characteristic of these settings is their structure, which can present and engage the content of the faith.

Fundamentally, what is the tradition that is to be taught, understood, and believed? What is the tradition upon which one can stake one's life and decision making? This very question has been central to reflection in contemporary theology: George Lindbeck's *Nature of Doctrine*, Sallie McFague's *Models of God*, Edward Farley's *Theologia*, and Gordon Kaufman's *Theology in a Nuclear Age*. All ask, in their own way, what do we teach and how do we teach it—through community life, ordered learning, or metaphor?[12]

Farley's *Fragility of Knowledge*, shows that all knowledge is the result of human striving to know or to control, and thus end all confusion and paradox. As such, knowledge is corruptible and fragile. Moreover, in the contemporary world the separation of "disciplines" of knowledge from one another and from the "culture of professionalism" has resulted in the fragmentation of the search for knowledge. Each of the "sciences" competes with the others for what is regarded as truth.[13]

12

In relation to religious faith, Farley argues that "ordered learning" is necessary. Because religious faith purports to speak about reality and therefore truth, the necessary teaching is theological (that is, a reflective wisdom), through which persons continually seek to understand the meaning of the faith in the world and decide how to organize their lives in relation to it. People need to be engaged with the processes of thinking, understanding, deciding, and believing. As Farley says, this theological approach would require a "comprehensive reconstruction" of church education:

> A cumulative, rigorous educational process and post-Enlightenment tools of analysis and interpretation (historical, literary, social, psychological, philosophical) will have to be introduced into church education. A very different kind of church teacher will be called for. Directors of religious education will have to be more than administrators of educational programs. The educator on the church staff will have to be a theologian-teacher.[14]

What is the content to be taught? How can the tradition be taught so that it is learned?

Community of Faith

The nature of the church (ecclesiology) is a primary question for Christian education when examined from this metaphor. In his inaugural address at Princeton Theological Seminary, Craig Dykstra helpfully framed the question: "What difference does it make that the *church* does Christian education?"[15] Dykstra noted something happens to education when it is conducted within the church. Education itself is transformed by the context of the community of faith.

Those writing from a community-of-faith perspective grounded their work in the insights of sociology and anthropology, which acknowledges that communities do in fact shape (educate) the way people see the world, value it, and live in relationship to others. That shaping occurs through the

13

strategies of education woven throughout the fabric of the community. One simple evidence of this reality is dialect: Persons from a particular region of a country speak with a particular style, and often with regionally meaningful collo- quialisms.

The Christian community of faith is no different. As a "culture" within which persons interact and experience great life transitions of birth, marriage, illnesses, and death, the meanings attached to these experiences are formed by participation in the community of the church. The worship, rituals, educational conversations, and actions experienced in the church profoundly affect a person in an explicit and intentional fashion, as well as in a "hidden" fashion.

Yet, beyond anthropological reflection, those who recom- mend this approach turn to theological reflection on the nature of the church itself. Dykstra, in his address, defines the church as a context of participation in the redemptive activity of God.[16] Moreover, in *Contemporary Approaches*, Charles Foster explicitly examined the nature of the community of faith. To him, the church is the corporate identity of the Body of Christ which participates in "Christianity's historical embodiment" (the tradition), in relationships that bond people together (the particular customs and events of the community which communicate the meaning of being children of God), and in spontaneous experiences where the power of the Spirit is encountered.[17]

The goal of this view is to understand and embody the meaning of being a people of God and a community of faith. To do so provides particular strategies of teaching and learning rooted within the life and experiences of the church. People learn through participation in the event called church.[18] The instrumentalities for education are the customs, rituals, roles, and patterns of communicating and of thinking of the church as a community of faith. The fundamental question then is: What is the church? How is the church affected by participa- tion in particular cultures, and how does it unite differing cultural experiences?

14

Development

Since its origins, the church has been educating. However, the self-conscious discipline of Christian religious education was born only at the turn of the twentieth century when the concern for human development helped to give birth to this "new" discipline. Beginning in the last decades of the nineteenth century, increased attention was given to child study and psychology. Attempts were made to discover how children "developed" through a nurturing environment to become adults. Since that time, developmental concerns have permeated the field. The religious education movement (1903–1940) saw people as perfectible and searched for the processes of human religious development. The hope was to coordinate church curriculum with these natural processes of development. In contrast, the later neoorthodox Christian education movement (1935–1960) began with the reality of human brokenness (the doctrine of sin) and sought to discover how a theology of revelation and salvation could be "taught" through the church.

As Donald Miller clarified in *Contemporary Approaches*, the concern for human development was stimulated in the 1960s and 1970s with the popularization of the work of the great developmentalists—Jean Piaget, Erik Erikson, Lawrence Kohlberg, and James Fowler. The result has been the focusing of education on the learner.[19] The concern has been to discover ways to help learners participate in the faith tradition in order to become mature Christians.

The interaction of teaching and learning consists of those developmentally appropriate activities, usually individualized, which guide or sponsor a person into a more complex form of maturity. The instrumentalities of education are many, both formal and informal. In each, however, attention is given to understanding the individual, to defining his or her needs and potentials, and to providing stimuli to ongoing processes of development.

Within each definition of development is both a definition of who the human being is and a goal for human maturity. Theologically, these are summarized in the doctrine of the nature of human beings (theological anthropology). Miller evidenced this theological grounding when he challenged the concepts of development by attending to the meaning of conversion and the communal nature of a person within the Christian faith.[20] These theological issues have been sharpened in recent critical reviews of developmentalists' work.[21] One example is the critical attention of feminists to the processes of women's development, which has tended to be excluded from traditional developmental theories.[22]

Moreover, concern for development has been enjoined by concern for spirituality. For segments of the Christian community, the person has traditionally been understood through the processes of spiritual guidance. Christian education also can be defined as a process of spiritual direction, by which an individual moves through life seeking to more faithfully discern and engage the vocation to which God is calling. A splendid educational description of this process is provided in Parker Palmer's *To Know as We Are Known*. For Palmer, education is a mode of spiritual formation through which persons are shaped in terms of the image of God.[23] The definition and goal of education then become the image of God and Christian vocation, rather than maturity and the ability to deal with cognitive complexity.

At stake in these conversations is the understanding of the person. Without attention to the theology of human nature, church education becomes captured by psychological views of human beings. The importance of theological conversation is evidenced in James Fowler's *Becoming Adult, Becoming Christian*.[24] He includes the psychological concern for maturity by summarizing the research on adult development, yet he sets that conversation within the context of "becoming Christian." The theological roots of his understanding of human beings are made explicit. By grounding adult

16

development in a theology of vocation, Fowler explains how the Christian story defines maturity in the faith.

Liberation

The movement of liberation theology has brought to awareness the reality that all theology and education are rooted in a social context. As the Brazilian liberation educator Paulo Freire is teaching us, no form of education is neutral:

> We cannot discuss churches, education or the role of the churches in education other than historically. Churches are not abstract entities, they are institutions involved in history. Therefore to understand their educational role we must take into consideration the concrete situation in which they exist.[25]

All education then participates within the historical process of shaping or maintaining social existence. This process itself is essentially political. To teach through the church is to be concretely involved in shaping the world, in participating in God's mission.

In *Contemporary Approaches* Allen Moore argued that "Christian education must recover its historical relation to Christian social action." Prophetic education, as he defined it, moves beyond our typical concern with *personal psychological* structures of living to action for the transformation of *political* structures of living. Life-style is the crucial goal of education—a life-style that embodies a new Christian consciousness of radical participation with efforts to transform and humanize the world.[26]

In a similar way, Freire calls for a "prophetic" church—a church that critically participates within the making of history by analyzing the social structures within which humans are formed, including a class analysis, and by engaging that world from the perspective of the prophetic vision.[27] Fundamental to this conversation about education is the question of the "mission" of the church in the world. Here

17

mission refers to the activity of the church in shaping the history of the world in light of God's call for humanization.

The interaction of teaching and learning in this approach occurs as people participate in action and reflection to engage the structures of their world. The instrumentalities for education are precisely those structures. Social action, guided by an integrated reflection on God's vision for the world and on the structures that shape the world, is a task for Christian religious education.

Interpretation

This metaphor evidences a concern with the field of Christian religious education for the way persons discover and construct meaning from the experiences of their lives. Jack Seymour and Carol Wehrheim argued in *Contemporary Approaches* that the "natural process of interpreting experience and understanding its meaning provides important clues for the process of Christian education." Christian religious education seeks to use this process to help people "make meaning in light of the revelation of the Christ of God and live faithfully in terms of that meaning."[28] The connection of the faith-story to experience is the key.

A profound illustration of this process appears in Andrew Greeley's analysis of religious imagination:

> The purpose of religious discourse is . . . to stir up in the other person resonances of experiences similar to that which the religious storyteller himself or herself has had. Thus the telling each year in Holy Week of the story of the death and resurrection of Jesus, complete with all the profoundly resonating liturgical imagery, is not designed primarily to communicate doctrinal propositions but to rekindle memories of death-rebirth experiences that have marked the lives of the hearers and to link those to the historic experience of Christians through the ages, leading back to the founding experience itself. . . . Religion as story leaps from imagination to imagination, and only then, if at all, from intellect to intellect.[29]

18

Therefore the goal of interpretation is to assist persons to learn the skills of "connecting" the faith tradition to their actual experiences of daily living. How do persons attend to the sources of knowledge, integrate these into a meaningful system, then decide and live faithfully as a result of that integration? These are key questions. Many concerns of this perspective are similar to those of instruction: concerns for thinking, understanding, and deciding overlap. The difference, however, is that interpretation focuses more exclusively on process.

The interaction of teaching and learning then attempts to stimulate in the learner the processes by which interpretation (reflecting and deciding) occurs. The faith tradition is included as an aspect in that interpretation, and the use of imagination, story, ritual, and artistic expression are primary strategies. As in other approaches, there are many settings for interpretation, the primary one being the faith community within which people come to name the meanings that guide them as they participate in the great events of living.

Underneath this reflection is the fundamental theological concern for the processes by which religious understanding occurs—the concern for theological method. Increased attention is being given to this issue. Greeley, for example, argues that the communication of images, rather than doctrinal conversation, is the key to religious communication. Here religious educators have contributed to the dialogue. Thomas Groome's *Christian Religious Education*, James Poling and Donald Miller's *Foundations for a Practical Theology of Ministry*, and Maria Harris's *Teaching and Religious Imagination* are examples of attempts to examine the ways meaning in theology and religion occur.[30] Moreover, in base communities (small-group churches) in Latin America and around the world, the empowering of the people as agents of theology unites the processes of theological method, Christian education, and social action.[31]

19

CONTEMPORARY APPROACHES TO CHRISTIAN EDUCATION

RELIGIOUS INSTRUCTION

GOAL

To assist learners in encountering God's self-revelation and the tradition. Understanding, thinking, believing, and deciding about that content.

TEACHING/LEARNING INTERACTION

Ordered learning. Teacher provides the content of the tradition in an intentional and structured way so that the pupil encounters and engages that content.

INTRUMENTALITIES FOR EDUCATION

Many, including school, families, camps, youth groups, where content and process have been intentionally structured to engage the content of faith.

COMMUNITY OF FAITH

GOAL

To help people understand and embody the meaning of being a people of God and a community of faith in the world.

TEACHING/LEARNING INTERACTION

Strategies of teaching and learning are rooted within the life and experiences of the church. People learn by participating in the event called church.

INSTRUMENTALITIES FOR EDUCATION

Customs, rituals, roles, and patterns of communication of the church as a community of faith.

DEVELOPMENT

GOAL

To help learners participate in the faith tradition in order to become mature Christians.

TEACHING/LEARNING INTERACTION

Developmentally appropriate activities, usually individualized, including spiritual direction, which guide or sponsor the person into a more complex form of maturity.

INSTRUMENTALITIES FOR EDUCATION

Many, formal and informal, where attention can be given to understanding the person, to defining personal needs and potentials, and to providing stimuli to the ongoing processes of development.

LIBERATION

GOAL

To help people embody a life-style of Christian participation in efforts to transform and humanize the world.

TEACHING/LEARNING INTERACTION

Persons participating in action and reflection to engage the structures of their world.

INTRUMENTALITIES FOR EDUCATION

Activities that engage *and* stimulate reflection on social structures in light of God's vision for the world.

INTERPRETATION

GOAL

To assist persons in learning the skills of "connecting" the faith tradition with the actual experiences of daily living.

TEACHING/LEARNING INTERACTION

Teaching and stimulating the processes by which interpretation (reflection and deciding) occurs, including the use of imagination, story, ritual, and artistic expression.

INTRUMENTALITIES FOR EDUCATION

Many settings, the primary one being the faith community within which persons learn to name the meanings that guide their lives as they participate in daily living.

Through the examination of these approaches, five theological issues appear crucial to the present conversation in Christian religious education: (1) the content for the faith—the nature of the tradition; (2) the nature of the community of faith and how the church provides and transforms the activities of education; (3) the nature of human beings and the processes of personal transformation; (4) the mission of the church in the world and the relationship of education to social transformation; and (5) theological method—the processes by which religious and theological meanings are made.

Theology and Education

The definition of the church's teaching ministry has encountered a strange shift in meaning since the Englightenment. Prior to the professionalism of knowledge, church leaders primarily were driven to find ways to give shape to the faith so that it could be taught and lived. In contrast, in the modern period, teaching has been defined as a way to translate the "propositional, or dogmatic, content" of the faith. The result has been a separation of teaching and systematic theology, with theology defining the content and education applying it. One consequence has been the separation of the clergy and the people, with the clergy or scholars as agents of theology and the people as recipients.

Christian education thus tends to become a ministry to support and build up the church, rather than a theological discipline that struggles to understand how the faith is to be communicated so that it can be lived. This shift in education tends to ignore basic issues about the nature of the church and the teaching necessary for the faith to be lived in a secular public world. Therefore, the problem of the nature of doctrine is itself a problem of the nature of teaching—of what is to be taught and how.

We hope to reclaim the dialectic between theology and teaching that has been reflected throughout the history of the church. We believe that a more fundamental understanding of education is needed—one that sees teaching as a theological activity—that is, empowering the people of God to be agents within the public world of God's presence. In fact, teaching of God's Word was what was meant by the Hebrew concept of Torah and the original meaning of the term *doctrine.* Teaching was a theological task of seeking to discern and understand God's revelatory activity in the lives of persons. In this view, education is changed from an activity of church maintenance to one process of the continual re-forming of the church—in other words, of participating in the dynamic process of understanding, interpreting, and living in relation to the Holy One, the horizon of being.

The fundamental issue for Christian religious education is our response to God in Jesus Christ—that is, the issue of revelation, how God's will is to be made known. Our plan in this manuscript is to begin with the five theological issues that the praxis of Christian religious education has raised, and then consider teaching in light of that fundamental issue, God's revelation. We thank the significant and diverse group of teachers/theologians concerned about the church and education, who have agreed, through the chapters of this book, to participate in the conversation.

Throughout its history, the teaching ministry has engaged in several theological tasks. Early in the church's life the task was that of apologetics, communicating the reality of the Christian gospel in cultural thought-forms. At that time, teaching also was concerned with how people were to be informed and initiated into the faith community. *Catechetics* sought to understand what was essential for belief and to help people define their own vocations and those of the churches. Finally, throughout the history of the church, teaching has been concerned with critical reflection on faith and culture. Through criticism, the church was reformed and engaged in cultural re-formation as well. These tasks of communicating, initiating, and critically reforming are still crucial to teaching.

Theology is an activity of the people of God. Whenever people teach within the congregation, they becomes agents of the theological tradition which seeks to communicate the faith so that it can be understood and lived. *We define theology as reflection by the people of God within the community of faith, seeking to understand and respond to what it means to be accepted, sent, and called by God into the brokenness of the world.* This is a task for the whole people of God as we seek to transmit the tradition, initiate people into the faith community, relate faith to culture, and continue the constructive and critical process of reunderstanding and re-forming the tradition. It is these tasks that are at stake in Christian religious education as a theological enterprise.

Part I—Tradition

Foreword

What is the content of Christian teaching? How are we to have access to the events that birthed and formed the Christian faith? Do the expressions of the faith shaped over time—that is, the tradition—clarify what is to be taught by churches? Moreover, how does a tradition which was developed within particular cultures communicate across cultures?

In his recent *Nature of Doctrine*, George Lindbeck raised the question of the content of Christian faith. He located the content (doctrine) within the believing community. For Lindbeck, doctrine is the language within the community that gives the community meaning and vocation.[1] With this understanding, education, then, is a form of socializing people into the meanings of a particular community.

Others, however, have argued that a community definition of truth is not sufficient; Christian truth, to be truth, must speak persuasively to persons who are not insiders. Education, then, is speaking the truth to strangers. These positions suggest two ways the church has sought to answer the question of the content of teaching: apologetics and dogma (catechetics).

Apologetics, the public defense of the faith, was born early in the Christian era as faithful persons tried to communicate the Christian faith within the religious pluralism of the Roman Empire. Apologists sought to teach the faith through careful reflection, so that it was plausible to strangers from other faith systems. Apology was open to the pluralism.

25

Another form of teaching (catechetics) attempted to define and limit the faith. As conflict emerged within the Christian community, the need arose for a strategy to provide limits to Christian expression. Definitions of orthodoxy were established in catechisms, which prescribed the meaning of the faith for new Christians, and in creeds, formulated by councils to define the faith. Catechisms and creeds defined doctrine (or teaching), and doctrine became tradition. With increasing social and political power came the church's concomitant power to enforce orthodoxy. Tradition became dogma (enforced teaching).

Until recently, despite the splintering of the church, theology has been related to this power. Theology was an activity that defined the authoritative content of the faith. The role of education, in turn, was to discover ways to teach definitions of truth embedded in the traditions of the various denominations. Education was a derivative of theology.

Today we know that even the content of the faith has been shaped by the act of teaching. The effort to express the faith linked it to cultural thought-forms. Education was not derivative, for teaching was an act by which the faith was expressed and defined. But how are we to have access to the events that birthed and continued the Christian religion? Furthermore, we need to be concerned with ways the tradition is being dynamically reshaped in present reflection and communication.

Melanie A. May, Marianne Sawicki, and Mary Elizabeth Mullino Moore provide direction for these questions. Writing from her experience in world ecumenical dialogue, May focuses on the unity and diversity of tradition. She describes its development and how it is received within the growing pluralism of world Christianity. Sawicki, in turn, focuses on one aspect of tradition, the sacraments. For her, the task of the tradition is to provide access to Jesus Christ as Risen Lord. Sacraments teach tradition through both verbal and nonverbal levels, and therefore provide a strategy for sacramental education. Moore focuses on tradition which is transmitted to a new generation through interaction between the community of faith and the world. Through an examination of feminist theology, she illustrates how theological questions are re-formed in the dialogue. For these authors, teaching is seen as a "traditioning" activity.

CHAPTER 2

Tradition and Education

Melanie A. May

Christians across the continents acknowledge the Bible—the Hebrew Scriptures and the New Testament—as a unique source for understanding their faith. But the range of perspectives on the authority and meaning of Scripture is as rich as the confessional and cultural circumstances in which Christians live their faith today. Some Christians regard the Bible as the Word of God directly and literally authored by God. Others regard it as a more human witness to the living Word spoken by God to God's people during diverse historical periods and in varied places. Still others see the Bible as the bearer of words that may or may not be meaningful amid the turbulent world today, a world characterized by complexity and change, and held in thrall by present powers and principalities.[1]

This range of perspectives has been particularly rich among Protestants. This is not surprising, since the Protestant Reformation was propelled on the basis of the authority of Scripture. Protestant reformers Luther and Calvin, for example, believed that God cannot be known adequately apart from the Bible. Both were clear that, as a book, the Bible is not God's self-revelation. Both taught that Scripture, apart from the Spirit of God, was not God's Word, that the Word lives by the power of the Spirit and, accordingly, life in the Spirit must be tested through Scripture. God speaks to God's people as Word and Spirit are conjoined.

For Protestants, the Bible has a particularly significant place in Christian tradition. Many agree with the Reformers'

27

affirmation that Scripture, as distinct from the tradition of the church, is the primary source of knowledge of God. This conviction means that the Word of God present in Scripture has an authority that transcends both ecclesiastical office and tradition. Tradition is appropriately secondary, as its power is readily abused by those in authority. Indeed, Protestants in the stream of the Radical Reformation would say that Scripture *is* tradition. In their formative experience, Scripture was the sole trustworthy source of the knowledge of God, since the perpetrators of their persecution wielded "Holy Tradition" as a weapon against them.

The first note of this twofold thesis is that the peculiar Protestant predisposition to assume a separation of Scripture and tradition is neither tenable nor desirable. Transmitting the faith from one generation to another always involves tradition—indeed, traditions—cultural as well as ecclesial. Moreover, every text is embedded within a context and expresses that context's particular perspective. In the words of Robert Coote and David Robert Ord, "No text has any meaning whatever except through interpretation. The question is, in relation to what, or in terms of what, is it to be interpreted?"[2] That is, we inevitably rely on something other than the text, to understand its message and meaning. Scripture and tradition are extraordinarily entangled.

The second aspect of this thesis addresses the implications of the Christian confession that the Word became flesh, that God's living Word cannot be fixed forever in any deposit of faith. There are at least two implications of this confession. First, the form in which the faith comes to persons and communities will not sustain the faith throughout its future. As following generations receive and recast the faith, making it their own, the faith of a people is fulfilled in previously unfamiliar forms. Thus simultaneously and secondly, faith lived in others' contexts, situations, and cultures must be cast and conveyed in forms utterly different, sometimes even alienated from the forms familiar to earlier generations.

Thus the ability to acknowledge and appreciate difference is a critical part of educating for the future.

The Word of God: Scripture and Tradition

Israel's faith was founded upon the understanding that God's presence, power, and self-revelation is remembered and made present in the spoken word. At the heart of the Hebraic account of creation, reverberating throughout the account is the refrain, "And God said . . . " (Gen. 1:3ff). God spoke with the Hebrew people, saying to Abram: "Leave your country, your people and your father's household and go to the land I will show you" (Gen. 12:1). God spoke with Moses "face to face" (Exod. 33:11) and later called prophets to be the bearers of God's authority, speaking God's Word to the people. The "Words of life," the Torah instructions which God gave to Moses to direct the life of Israel as God's convenanted people, were written in stone so they would not be erased or forgotten.[3]

In time, the oral traditions surrounding God's Word were augmented by the understanding that written words, or Scriptures, were God's Word. This conviction did not originate with Christianity. By the first century of the Common Era, a canon of Hebrew Scriptures existed, although this was not formally fixed until the Jewish Council of Jamnia around 90 B.C.E.[4] Teachers in Israel knew well both the oral traditions and the written Scriptures, basing their understanding and instructions on their common God-given legacy.

Jesus also knew the Hebrew Scriptures; his teachings are rife with reinterpretations. Throughout the Sermon on the Mount, for example, he refers to the Scripture's teachings, and continues with this refrain: "But I tell you . . . " (Matt. 5:22ff). Jesus states his method clearly: "Do not think that I have come to abolish the Law or the Prophets; I have not come to abolish them but to fulfill them. I tell you the truth, until heaven and earth disappear, not the smallest letter, not the least stroke of a pen, will by any means disappear from the Law until everything is accomplished" (Matt. 5:17-18).

29

The Gospel writers present Jesus as basing his entire life and teaching upon Scripture; indeed, Israel's fulfillment, promised in Scripture, *was* Jesus' life and ministry. Consider the account of his teaching at the synagogue in Nazareth. Having read from the prophet Isaiah, Jesus rolled up the scroll, sat down to teach, and began by saying: "Today this scripture is fulfilled in your hearing" (Luke 4:21).

Accordingly, from the beginning of Christian history, the church claimed the Hebrew Scriptures as its own. The point was not that Christians held the Hebrew Scriptures in common with Jews. The claim was that, rightly interpreted, those Scriptures testify to Jesus Christ. Early Christians read the writings with an eye as to how they were fulfilled in Jesus; correspondingly, they understood Jesus in light of those writings.

Later, words were written to guide believers in living "as" Christians. Likewise, the ancient church set words about Jesus' life, teachings, and ministry alongside the Hebrew Scriptures. By around 135 c.e., the Gospels' teachings of Jesus carried authority equal to the Hebrew Scriptures, although in some circles more authority was attached to "an oral tradition resting on a living chain of testimony than to anything that was to be found in any book." Even early in the second century, many Christian communities still had oral tradition that was more highly valued than anything written: "The authority still rested in the words of the Lord, not in any of the books containing his words."[5] At the same time, the letters of Paul, addressed to particular people in local communities of faith, as well as the words of other apostles, were increasingly influential in church life and thought. These words were gradually brought together in a tentative way by 200 c.e., although the New Testament canon was not finally formed until the second half of the fourth century at the Council of Carthage.

Thus, however formative the God-given written words came to be, the central confession of the early church was that Jesus Christ is the Word of God become flesh. Jesus himself, the

Word of God incarnate, was the foremost authority; the words of the prophets and apostles were to be understood in light of his life, death, and resurrection. The source of knowledge of God was no longer only, or primarily, the written Word of God.

This double source of authority—written and oral—has a precursor in the Jewish tradition. Jews speak of another part of Torah, the oral part, which was passed on by word of mouth until rabbis ordered and recorded it as the Mishnah in the second century of the Common Era. Consequent interpretation of the Mishnah was compiled into the Jerusalem and Babylonian Talmuds. Torah requires both parts: "The Oral Law depends upon the Written Law, but at the same time, say the rabbis, it is clear that there can be no real existence for the Written Law without the Oral."[6] For rabbis, the oral Torah is not finally fixed, but evolves from generation to generation as the fullness of the teaching given to Moses by God is revealed.[7]

Jesus' teaching was by word of mouth, as was much of the early Christian missionary teaching. Amos N. Wilder, in his study of the language of the gospel, states that the power of the gospel is as spoken word: "The new speech of the Gospel was not a matter of words on a tablet but a word in the heart, not a copybook for recitation but winged words for life."[8] This early Christian speech, says Wilder, was not prepared, but was spoken spontaneously in a specific situation:

> It is naive, it is not studied; it is *extempore* and directed to the occasion, it is not calculated to serve some future hour. This utterance is dynamic, actual, immediate, reckless of posterity; not coded for catechists or repeaters. . . . We find ourselves at first and for a rather long time in the presence of oral and live face-to-face communication. The Gospel meant freedom of speech in this deeper sense. One did not hoard its formulas, since when occasion arose the Spirit would teach one what to say and how to witness and what defense to make. The early Christians lived on the free bounty of God in this sense also. The speech of the Gospel was thus fresh and its forms fluid and novel; it came and went . . . with the freedom of sunshine, wind and rain.[9]

31

This quality of the Gospel language is expressed even when written. Wilder declares that even the written words of the New Testament "are better understood if we keep in mind the primal role of oral speech in the beginning. *Viva voca* communication is more malleable, more personal and more searching."[10]

An appreciation of the primacy of the oral word, on one hand, and the Word become flesh, on the other, leads to an acknowledgment that our present-day preoccupation with the written Word is problematic. It is important to recall that writing was first developed to keep records of taxation. Writing came to consolidate vast power in the hands of an elite whose interests were served by the "formulation, revision, and preservation" of accounts which justified their political position. The written word thus tends to be aligned with and perpetuate a status quo. Coote and Ord remark that writing "set the criteria by which the rule of a few over the masses was justified and applied those criteria for the benefit of the rulers. By projecting a sense of social place onto the people of a society, the literary image produced by writers in ancient courts assisted in the necessary maintenance of law and order."[11]

The predisposition to homogenize and bolster the hegemony of a ruling elite is inherent in the written word. But finally, the written word is indispensable for the transmission of the faith from generation to generation. Next we will consider an understanding of this transmission that may check the propensity of the written word to wield power over others.

Reception: Scripture and Tradition in Church History

The early Christians had no concern for the relative authority of Scripture and tradition. Indeed, until well into the second century, the distinction between oral or written Scripture and tradition was not made. The foundational affirmation for early Christians was that Jesus Christ is the authoritative teacher. The means by which his teachings were transmitted was secondary to living a life patterned after them.

In time, however, the way teachings were transmitted became increasingly important. *Reception*—the way local churches accepted the decisions of the ecumenical councils during the early centuries—became an important dynamic.[12] The emerging ecumenical significance of reception has been helpfully defined by William G. Rusch as

> all phases and aspects of an ongoing process by which a church under the guidance of God's Spirit makes the results of a bilateral or multilateral conversation a part of its faith and life because the results are seen to be in conformity with the teachings of Christ and of the apostolic community, that is, the gospel as witnessed to in Scripture.[13]

Like the French Roman Catholic theologian Yves Congars, I believe the concept of *reception* has a significance beyond either the classical or the ecumenical meaning. *Reception* refers to the way the church and individual Christians appropriate and attest anew, appreciatively and critically, the faith passed to them by a previous generation.[14] Reception is never mere acceptance of or acquiescence to a decision made by someone else. Neither is it a submission of integrity or identity to what has been. The power of reception is its call for change and renewal. Because the concept of reception calls for renewal, it illumines a Protestant perspective on tradition dedicated to all the people of God.

Returning to our narrative, the formation of the canon put the authority of tradition into question, for it did not diminish the threat heretics were perceived to pose. Indeed, distinguishing the concept of tradition from the reality of Scripture occurred during a controversy among Christians over what constituted right tradition. The Gnostics, perceived by orthodox Christians as heretics,[15] based their teachings on Scripture also. In addition to the final fixing of the canon, the

33

question of proper authority was addressed also by linking ministry to the apostolic succession. And soon another dimension was added to the teaching authority of the church—the creeds.

Creedal formulation has its roots in the tradition of the Jewish people. Similar formulations are found in the Hebrew Scriptures—for example, the Shema:

> Hear, O Israel: the LORD our God, the LORD is one. Love the LORD your God with all your heart and with all your soul and with all your strength. These commandments that I give you today are to be upon your hearts. Impress them on your children. Talk about them when you sit at home and when you walk along the road, when you lie down and when you get up. Tie them as symbols on your hands and bind them on your foreheads. Write them on the doorframes of your houses and on your gates. (Deut. 6:4-9)

This early affirmation illustrates certain central characteristics of confessions of faith. They were never matters of the mind alone. A creedal confession of faith claims the whole person and commits the whole of one's life.

Similarly, whatever their use by individuals, creeds are fundamentally communal as to both origin and occasion for use.[16]

The popular consensus is that creeds proper emerged in the context of the celebration of baptism. While not arguing against this assertion, J.N.D. Kelly, in his seminal study of early Christian creeds, cautions against a too-simplistic assent to this consensus. He goes on to list two distinct moments in the celebration of baptism when such a confession of faith might have been expected. One moment comes as the candidates stand before the official and are asked whether they believe in God the Father, the Son, and the Spirit. The other moment would have arrived earlier in the celebration, or even during the course of the candidates' preparation for baptism.

> This time it was not a case of assenting to interrogations, but of reciting a declaratory creed. It is this rite which was technically known as the "rendering" of the creed . . . and which marked the culmination of the catechetical training leading up to the sacrament. At a certain stage in the training . . . the bishop formally "delivered" the creed . . . to the more advanced catechumens. It was then their business to learn and assimilate it, so as to be able to reproduce it as their own spiritual possession on the eve of their initiation.[17]

Kelly concludes that while creeds were part of the baptismal rite, questions of faith were more important to the actual baptism than was a declaratory creed. Moreover, the roots of the creed are primarily and more properly related to the catechetical preparation for the ceremony of initiation.[18] The church's teaching ministry, then, was the most significant source of creedal formulation.

A particularly Protestant consensus asserts that creeds proper emerged in the context of controversy with heretics. Here too Kelly cautions us, since this consensus simplistically ignores other formative factors. While recognizing that early apologists such as Irenaeus and Tertullian were unabashedly polemical in portions of their rules of faith, Kelly argues that such polemicism actually was a resurgence of an earlier "insistence on the public, apostolically authorized deposit of doctrine which had been handed down in the Church from the beginning as the canon or rule of faith." In accounting for the apparent impulse toward more formal and concise confessions of faith, Kelly is inclined to look to the tendency of liturgy, as such, "to assume a fixed shape."[19]

Protestants of Magisterial Reformation churches have tended to emphasize the catechetical use of creeds, along with the teaching ministry of the church.[20] The ancient creeds have been accepted as authoritative guides to the church's interpretation of Scripture and authentic summaries of the faith, as evidenced by the Reformation confessions. Accordingly, the authority of Reformation confessions lies in their claim to be faithful witnesses to Scripture.

Protestants of Radical Reformation churches, in contrast, have emphasized that a fresh reappropriation of the faith in each generation is more adequately demonstrated through right living than by right teaching, and through consensus-building conversation than by catechetical formulations. Radical Reformation churches have viewed creeds in relation to their conception amid controversy with heretics. Radical Reformers readily identified with heretics and "against" the use of creeds as normative instruments of faith, having themselves been identified and persecuted as heretics with the aid of creeds.

Though the use of creeds and confessions is not uniform, most Protestants have ascribed to the Reformation battlecry: *Sola scriptura*. These words have signaled the Protestant conviction that the Bible is both the source for understanding God and for receiving guidance for living as God's people. Following upon Luther's translation of the Bible into vernacular German, these words also embody the conviction that the Bible belongs to the people. Luther invited them to read it for themselves. This act gave dramatic power to his stated conviction that the Magisterium of the Roman Catholic Church no longer controlled the understanding and use of the Bible. The authority of the Word of God stands over against the assumed authority of tradition.

The twentieth-century ecumenical movement has given many Protestants a renewed appreciation that tradition holds great treasures and that we all also live by tradition. Even so, Protestants continue to affirm the Word of God as the only proper tradition—a tradition in which we are called to constant reformation. Reformation was not once-for-all; Scripture's witness to what God does and says is to be constantly translated as guidance for the daily life of people and of communities of faith, in each age and place. This unbroken cloud of witnesses who know and live their faith is, for most Protestants, basic to an affirmation of the unbroken tradition of the church of Jesus Christ.

In other words, for Protestants, tradition is the reception of the faith by each generation to whom it has been passed by a previous generation. In William G. Rusch's words, "Reception is not repristination, but it is the lively process of the church's drawing from the resources of its past to seize and accept the present activities of its loving Lord."[21] And although Protestants have tended to receive Scripture as unaffected by originating and consequent contexts, they recognize that even the canon of Scripture evolved by a process of reception. Thus they expect faith's convictions to be reinterpreted, tested by new generations in their own age and place. A living faith is grounded in a community of believers willing to engage the diversity and controversy in the world within which they are called to be disciples.

Christianity's Wider World: Diversity in Scripture and Tradition

What has been written thus far about a Protestant perspective on Christian tradition has presupposed the Western ecclesial and cultural context, just as most interpreters of the Bible have been Europeans or North Americans. Andrew F. Walls cautions care regarding our limited contextual presuppositions. He reminds us that cross-cultural connections have been integral to the life of the Christian faith from its inception:

It is a feature of Christian faith that throughout its history it has spread through cross-cultural contact; indeed its very survival has been dependent on such contact. This is not true of all the great faiths; not of Judaism, for instance, found throughout the world, but almost entirely in ethnic communities; nor of Hinduism embracing countless millions in the oldest faith in the world, but overwhelmingly concentrated in one nation and people. Buddhism and Islam have indeed repeatedly crossed the cultural divide, but of Christianity we may almost say that it exists today only *because* it has crossed it. For Christian expansion has not been progressive, like Islamic expansion,

37

spreading out from a central point and retaining, by and large, the allegiance of those it reaches. Christian expansion has been serial. Christian faith has fixed itself at different periods in different heartlands, waning in one as it has come to birth in another.[22]

The survival of Christianity as a vital faith depends upon the ability of Christians to acknowledge and meaningfully engage the wider world in which we live. The "heartlands" of Christianity are no longer the centers of global energy. There is a profound shift in the areas where Christianity is growing today—a shift from north to south, from west to east—that is, from the so-called first world to the two-thirds world. By the year 2000, more Christians will be living outside than within the confines of the old Western Christendom.

This shift is not simply statistical; its significance is readily visible in the word *inculturation*. A relatively recent word to theological discourse, it aims to come to terms with the contemporary awareness of the shifting centers of Christian faith and identity. *Inculturation*, according to Aylward Shorter of the Catholic Higher Institute of East Africa, is "the ongoing dialogue between faith and culture or cultures," or more fully, "the creative and dynamic relationship between the Christian message and a culture or cultures."[23] The words of Pope John Paul II are even sharper: "The synthesis between culture and faith is not just a demand of culture, but also of faith. *A faith which does not become culture is a faith which has not been fully received, not thoroughly thought through, not fully lived out.*"[24] It must also be noted, however, that the pope usually adds to his call for inculturation a word of warning against going too far.[25]

It is significant that most of the theological thinking about inculturation has been undertaken by Roman Catholics. By contrast, Protestants have talked more about context and contextualization. But more than text and context is at stake for Roman Catholics. For example, the mass celebrated at St. Aphonese in Kinshasa, Zaire, combines ancient African cultural symbols, with an "emphasis on lay participation in general and women's leadership in particular."[26] At St. Alphonse, there is also a weekly children's mass, where African fables are told to teach the gospel message. Roman Catholics assume that liturgy and Scripture call for immersion in the diverse cultures where Christians live and work. Their experience of inculturation offers all Christians the recovery of an element of the drama of the Christian faith.

The subject matter of inculturation is always Jesus Christ, as Shorter explains:

> It is he who enters into dialogue with human culture. Inculturation is a further and definitive step by which Jesus Christ enters into a living relationship with a cultural tradition. . . . Through inculturation Jesus Christ adopts new forms and new approaches in carrying out his saving mission to the world, the Gospel acquires a new cultural language and the Church is thereby enriched.[27]

A "living relationship with a cultural tradition" is increasingly critical today. The simplistic Protestant assumption that Scripture and tradition are distinct entities set over against each other is inaccurate and inadequate. *Inculturation,* in many ways, is a contemporary word for *incarnation,* pointing to an appreciation of cultural diversity and acknowledging the diversity inherent in Scripture and in Christian tradition.[28]

The work of a number of contemporary scholars helps to clarify the recognition that living traditions are now reshaping the understanding of Scripture in Christian life and faith. Cain Hope Felder, in *Troubling Biblical Waters,* for example, argues against the assumption that "the relation of Black people to the Bible is a post-biblical experience. . . . This book seeks to illuminate the Black story within The Story, so the ancient record of God's Word takes on new meaning for the Black Church today."[29] Aloysius Pieris points to the diversity inherent in the Christian tradition by articulating a crucial question: "Which brand of Christianity seeks to be inculturated—the one framed within a cosmology that is repudiated in the Third World, or the one derived from a Third World hermeneusis of the gospel?"[30] Writing in South Africa, Itumeleng Mosala underscores the contradictory conditions under which biblical texts were produced and understands these sources to be characterized by differences in social class, race, culture, and gender.[31] Eduardo Hoornaert, writing about the early church from his perspective on Christian base communities of the poor in Brazil, cites often overlooked writings of the first Christians, writings that are "vastly heterogeneous" and testify to the diverse life of early Christian communities.[32] These church people and scholars, as other writers, open to us a wider understanding of God's reality present in the Scriptures and traditions of Christianity; we are freed from the stifling security of "stabilized texts . . . that become sacred texts."[33] We are open for the reception of new interpretations and the new words of God.

Educating for the Future

Having explored the twofold thesis that the Protestant separation of Scripture and tradition is untenable and that the Word of God become flesh is a living Word, unable to be fixed forever in any deposit of faith, we come to the educational implications of this perspective on the source of faith's confession. The implications for Christian education are wide-ranging.

First, we take a clue from Jesus' teaching. Actually, as Dodd notes, Jesus did not so much teach as preach—that is, rather than offer systematized instruction, he spoke a significant word to the situation at hand.[34] Similarly, the heart of Jesus' teaching was his eschatological outlook. He did not train his followers in a learned mode that they could use for generations to come. His directness, and "the intense urging with which he spoke to the immediate crisis" and "face-to-face with the hearer," engaged the hearts and spirits as well as the minds of those who learned from him.[35] Jesus' personal and committed posture is a fundamentally important characteristic for all Christian education settings and styles.

Second, throughout this essay we have been aware that the Christian tradition is tangled at its roots with the Jewish tradition. That awareness calls us to reach out in dialogue to Jewish, as well as other religious traditions. Indeed, just as early Christian identity emerged in relation to Jews, in coming years it will be forged in relationship with believers other than Christian. Unlike former experiences, Christians in the future will rarely live in homogeneous communities of faith isolated from the wider world. Our need for interfaith dialogue addresses the need for education to lead us to recognize, acknowledge, and appreciate differences.

Third, the Word become flesh focuses the attention of educators on the particularity and uniqueness of peoples in their various places and periods. God spoke no abstract word from on high; God dwelt with God's people in the world God loves. But as Rebecca Chopp puts it, the Word too often is "separated . . . from its fullness and denied its solidarity with creation . . . its embodiment in incarnation, and its rhythm of resurrection and crucifixion."[36] Educational settings and styles have robbed the Word of its rich resonance in multiple contexts. Specialized, systematized, and abstracted from living communities of faith, the Word fails to bear life abundant and is diminished into "letter of the law." The Word has been bent to serve the interests of powerholders in academic and ecclesial institutions; it is far removed from the people of God.

Let the cry resound: *Semper Reformanda!* Protestants, who broke with the content of "Holy Tradition," have taken a similar posture: They fasten onto a fixed deposit of the faith. The call to reformation, however, is unceasing, that the Word may again always be accessible to the people, as God's Word to and for all. Let God's Word be related to the practice of religion in local communities, which themselves embody the diversity of creation. Let God's Word open out to embrace the fullness of creation, ever enunciating new meanings in new moments!

41

Educational institutions will not be changed simply by adding another course, while the core of the curriculum is still thoroughly Western in perspective and posture. There must be change in the way all courses are taught. Biblical courses, for example, should wrestle with interpretations of Scripture from South Africa, as well as with the historical-critical methods of Western white men. Accordingly, early church history should be taught for church unity, rather than to judge other Christians by its own faith and practice; it should wrestle with Latin American, Asian, and African perspectives on those formative centuries. The changes call for educational settings, and styles that highlight differences and multiplicity rather than hiding behind identity and definition.

Finally, in educating for the future, Nel Noddings directs us to Antionio Gramsci's recommendation that education should "dedicate itself to producing working-class intellectuals." Noddings continues:

> It can succeed only by incorporating into education itself real work—both physical and intellectual—that will be at least partly planned, executed, evaluated, and revised by students and teachers working together. A working-class intellectual is one, or ought to be one, who works and thinks and theorizes. The long-range goal would be to have a society of worker-thinkers and no classes.[37]

Embodiment is of the essence for all education, and assuredly, for any Christian education. For God in Christ is incarnate in and engages the integrity of our human bodies and spirits, as well as our minds, in order to renew and redeem all creation and all peoples.

CHAPTER 3

Tradition and Sacramental Education

Marianne Sawicki

Tradition tells Christians who Jesus was, in such a way that it becomes possible for us to discover who he is. The function of tradition is to provide reliable access to Jesus, who lived long ago and far away, but whose Spirit is alive and working in contemporary communities. Tradition is the basis on which a Christian today discovers that Jesus of Nazareth is the Risen Lord and, moreover, that the power at large in the church is indeed the Spirit of that same Jesus, the Christ.

Access to Jesus as Risen Lord is no simple affair. The church knows three interrelated means of contact with him—through narrative, through sacraments, and through the poor. In fact, church is the name we give to the quest for the Risen Jesus, fulfilled in the active ministries of Word, worship, and care. This chapter explores sacraments as a means of tradition and examines how people acquire the competence to meet the Lord in the liturgy. But sacraments are best understood in context, within the interplay of Word, worship, and care—that is, within the traditioning ministry of the church itself.

Access to the Risen Lord Jesus was already a problem for the churches of the New Testament. Although they did not need to overcome the differences of language and culture we face today, nevertheless they stood with us on the same side of the ultimate barrier to human availability—death. Ordinarily, death is the end of the possibility for personal relationship, whether one has been dead for two thousand years or only for a day.

Yet very shortly after Jesus' death, our ancestors in faith experienced someone they recognized as Jesus alive in their midst. Their accounts indicate that it was relatively easy to perceive that someone was indeed there; the difficulty was to recognize that someone as Jesus, a particular individual whose life had ended in death. Hence the claim that "Jesus is risen" must carry a twofold meaning: not only that the someone at large in their communities was continuing the work of Jesus, but that Jesus himself remained available to them despite death.

As years passed, the task of the young Christian communities was to sustain the power of the Spirit, doing new things in their midst, and also to keep that work tied to the concrete reality of Jesus. For a generation, Christian prophets spoke new words for the Risen Lord as they continued Jesus' work of healing and exorcism and made thanksgiving—Eucharist—in Jesus' name. But about thirty years after Calvary, the profile of Jesus had begun to blur. Christian teachers sensed a danger, that despite the Eucharist and the healings, their link to the real man from Nazareth might be lost in a haze of diverging memories; and with it would be lost the possibility of recognizing whether it was *that* Jesus who was enabling *this* sacrament and *this* care.

Therefore the Gospels were written to define who Jesus had been, to place closure upon the growing collections of his sayings. These texts belonged to the churches—that is, they disclosed the identity of Jesus to people who already knew him by oral witness and by breaking bread with the poor. But if taken in isolation from the life of the church, these texts themselves were dangerous, for they were liable to bury the Lord in the past. A story by itself would give only the kind of access to the pre-Calvary Jesus that we have for other historical figures. In fact, Luke's resurrection story illustrates that narrative alone was not enough to bring people to faith in the resurrection, for when the three women announced that Jesus was risen, "their story seemed like nonsense," and they were not believed (Luke 24:10-11, 22-24 NAB).

The Gospels contain words, but those words were read by churches which already were employing *more than* words to bring people to the brink of resurrection faith. The New Testament presents itself as the verbal component of a traditioning process which also involved certain distinctive actions.

In the earliest written account of the Lord's Supper, Paul tells the church at Corinth, "I received from the Lord what I also handed on to you, that the Lord Jesus, on the night when he was handed over, took bread, and when he had given thanks, he broke it, and said, 'This is my body which is for you. Do this in remembrance of me' " (I Cor. 11:23-24).

Here the memorial of Jesus is a gesture, with a story to explain it. We have in this account the distinctive elements of the Christian theology of "tradition": receiving, handing on, thanksgiving, nourishing, remembering, and intimate contact with the broken body of Jesus the Lord.

Christianity is a tradition. That is to say, it is a process of receiving and of handing on what has been received. Although one can distinguish between the Christian *message* and the *process* which delivers it, nevertheless, neither has ever been independent. For example, since the message offers salvation to everyone, regardless of ethnicity or culture, translation has become an essential component of its delivery process, as meanings are "carried across" languages and continents. The universality of the message calls for enculturation to be part of the process. Moreover, we always receive the gospel from someone else, rather than through an inner experience directly from God. The gospel is not my own private revelation or relationship with God, but a gift given through the hands of others. The mediation of the message of Jesus across the centuries and the oceans, from hand to hand, is a constituent part of that message itself, and we are to be thankful that such is the cause. In God's plan we are not to have direct access to Jesus the Risen Lord, but mediation across space, time, and culture, through human beings, the church.

Both the often-translated words of the Gospels and the often-repeated gesture of Eucharist propagate the presence of the Risen Lord across time and space. But in addition, the Gospels tell of a third means of access to Jesus:

Whoever welcomes one child such as this in my name welcomes me. (Matt. 18:5)

45

"Lord, when did we see you hungry and feed you, or thirsty and give you drink?" . . . "Whatever you did for one of these least brothers and sisters of mine, you did for me." (Matt. 25:37, 41)

These sayings reflect the experience of the first generation of Christian teachers that Jesus the Risen Lord is available in the weak and the poor—not independently of the traditioning process, but thanks to it. These verbal and sacramental remembrances still enable people to recognize who it is who confronts them in the needy "little ones."

Sacraments Work by Signifying

Sacrament, then, is one of the means of Christian traditioning.[1] Together with Word and care, the sacramental liturgy presents the possibility of access to Jesus. In our tradition, sacramental experience places one in position to recognize not only that Jesus is the Risen Lord, but that the Spirit which animates the ecclesial community is the Spirit of Jesus.

A sacrament is a communications phenomenon, a media event, so to speak. It works by signifying. That is, a sacrament opens the door to Jesus as Risen Lord by communicating through both verbal and nonverbal channels, the same channels used by any other variety of human communication. Yet in this particular multichanneled communication, the message conveyed is the Paschal Mystery itself. It is God's offer of reconciliation, along with its definitive human acceptance in Jesus Christ, which becomes available within the ecclesial assembly, effectively interpreted through song, gesture, story, textiles, pottery, architecture, water, fire, oil, bread, and wine. These media project the Paschal pattern onto the lives of those who join in the liturgical celebration of the sacrament.[2]

Human transformation can happen in this way, but not automatically. The person participating must have a certain receptivity and faith.[3] The importance accorded to such subjective factors by Catholic sacramental theology has grown enormously during the years since the Second Vatican Council. It is not enough simply to "place no obstacle" to the availability of the Risen Lord. Individual and community must have active faith and desire, both at the time of celebration and subsequently. Moreover, it is not enough merely .to meet the minimum requirements of rubrics and text. The sacrament is meant to *communicate* God's saving love. This implies that sacramental efficacy, the "delivery" of God's love, depends upon two factors: whether the celebrants use the media appropriately and effectively, and whether the people have been trained to be sensitive to aesthetic communication.[4]

It is the responsibility of Christian teachers to see that people have the competence for sacramental communication, the competence to celebrate. This competence is in some ways like the ability to create or enjoy music, a painting, a novel, or a beautifully handcrafted quilt. Sacramental competence also entails faith—the kind expressed in questions as well as that expressed in answers—and an intense desire to seek and see the Lord. There is also a more specialized competence for each of the sacraments. For the sacraments of initiation—Baptism, Confirmation, Eucharist—a community must be competent to initiate, the candidates prepared to undergo initiation. For the sacraments of reconciliation—Penance, Anointing of the Sick, Eucharist—a community must be prepared to reconcile, and candidates ready for reconciliation. For the sacraments of commitment—Marriage, Orders, Eucharist—a community must be reliable enough to support commitment, the candidates competent to commit themselves.[5]

Therefore there is no simple prescription for teaching in the Christian sacramental tradition. The picture is quite complex, and we need to examine more closely the nature of Christian teaching before suggesting some appropriate goals and methods.

Teaching is a problematic term in Christianity, for it refers to a component of the traditioning process itself. There are longstanding debates among academics about the proper terminology. Many favor the term *education* for naming those deliberate activities which hand down the memories, wisdom, and praxis of the Christian community.[6] The vocabulary of education highlights the kind of concerns the Christian community has in common with society's other traditioning

47

agencies, and it facilitates the sharing of expertise. Usually an adjective modifies *education*. The term *religious* education places Christian traditioning in a class with the instructional efforts of other faith communities. (And it preserves continuity with the religious education movement of early twentieth-century America.) With the addition of a different adjective, the term *Christian* education stresses instead the distinctiveness of what we do, as compared with *Jewish* education or *Islamic* education.

On the other hand, one may object to using the basic term *education* at all. More than *educere*, (to lead out), Christian teaching intends *inducere*, (to lead into or persuade); or even *inire*, (to move into, enter, or begin). From *inire* comes *initiation*, which names both the goal of Christian teaching and that larger process of which teaching forms a part. From this perspective, Christian traditioning is a process unique to Christianity; it is as distinctive as the gospel itself. The nature of the ecclesial process of initiation—initiation into Christ, into the church, into a particular future—distinguishes Christianity from other philosophical or religious ways of life.

In contemporary Catholic sacramental and liturgical theology, and in church documents, a special term refers to Christian teaching done in the context of sacramental initiation, reconciliation, and commitment. That term is *catechesis*.[7] Forms of this Greek word were used by Luke to denote the presumably rather sophisticated instruction given to His Excellency Theophilus (Luke 1:4) and to Apollos the philosopher (Acts 18:25). *Katechein* (to catechize) literally means "to echo down." This aural image, suggesting the faithful replication of sound, resembles the tactile image at work in the Latin *tradere* (to hand over or impart), from which comes our word *tradition*.[8]

The different terms reflect different approaches; each is valuable. The use of *catechesis* in the rest of this chapter signals an emphasis upon the ecclesial nature of Christian teaching, especially as it occurs in the context of preparing people for sacramental celebration. Catechesis is the personal instruction given face to face, which builds up the faith of

48

individuals and constitutes a group as a local ecclesial community, by means of reflective dialogue about their experiences of God's care.[9] Catechesis brings people to the threshold of seeing the identity and significance of the Lord, in the modes of initiation, reconciliation, and commitment.

Experiences that are grist for catechesis include the reading of Scriptures, the assembly's liturgical celebrations, the ministries of church members to those in need, the struggles and joys of Christian life, and the study of theology, church history, and moral law.[10] Material for catechesis comes from the past, but also from the present; from the church's memory of what God did for our ancestors in faith, but also from the church's active participation in God's ongoing care for people and its celebration of intimate communion with Christ Jesus. If theology is faith seeking understanding, then catechesis is faith seeking maturity.

Planning Sacramental Catechesis

Goal-setting is essential for sacramental catechesis. Moreover, it is a theological task, in the deepest sense of the word *theology*. Theory that may look good on paper will meet its real test when we put it into practice. Goal-setting is a step toward making our theoretical beliefs operational. In this process of implementation, our beliefs can be validated, but they can also be clarified and modified. Goal-setting requires a continual reassessment of who we are as church in God's plan.

Parish experience with the Catholic Rite of Christian Initiation of Adults provides an excellent illustration. The RCIA, as the rite is commonly called, has restored the catechumenate for unbaptized people who seek to enter the Catholic Church.[11] They, together with baptized Christians transferring from other churches and those baptized but previously unchurched, receive a year or more of instruction, counseling, and formation, punctuated by ritual celebrations. Because the RCIA mandates personal attention for each candidate, along with activities that require a wide variety of

49

leadership skills, more parishes find that one person alone cannot administer the RCIA process. It takes a team.

When the team members first sit down to plan the catechesis for initiation, they generally presume that somewhere there must exist a curriculum, a master list of all the facts that someone entering the church "ought to know." Of course, the Creed contains such a list, but its function is liturgical rather than curricular.[12] If the team members turn to official church documents, they may be frustrated, then intrigued, for there the goals are defined not as lists of things to know or do, but as a cluster of attitudes and competences. Team members discover that they need to interpret and specify what these competences imply for their own particular parish (or diocesan) setting. They then must devise learning experiences that will foster these competences.

The text of the RCIA lists the following competences as goals for the catechumens, or learners: to turn more readily to God in prayer; to bear witness to the faith; to keep their hopes set upon Christ in all things; to follow supernatural inspiration in their deeds; to practice love of neighbor—all of this amounting to "a progressive change of outlook and conduct."[13]

A content and format, this list resembles that given in the *National Catechetical Directory*, which states that the task of catechesis is "to foster mature faith." Maturity is not a final state, but a direction of growth. The *Directory* profiles mature faith by listing the competences which people of mature faith would possess: They recognize the real and lasting value of human activity in this world; direct their thoughts and desires to the full consummation of the kingdom in eternal life; strive constantly for conversion and renewal; give diligent ear to what the Spirit says to the church; live in communion with God and other people; accept willingly the responsibilities that arise from these relationships; know the mystery of salvation revealed in Christ; know the divine signs and works which are witnesses to the fact that this mystery is being carried out in human history; have an active sacramental and prayer life; test and interpret human events, the signs of the times, in a wholly Christian spirit; spread the gospel zealously in order to make the church known as the sign and instrument of salvation and unity of the human race.[14]

Far from providing the planners of sacramental catechesis with ready-made guidelines, these listings orient team members toward accepting the responsibility for deciding and providing what their people will need in order to participate fully in their own particular worshiping, serving community. This is always the responsibility of the local parish or congregation, although guidance and oversight come from the hierarchy.[15] Therefore team members do the tough theological work of defining what sacramental initiation means for their parish as part of the church universal. This time is itself a precious opportunity for faith formation and catechesis, and parish staff members are wise to allocate a good portion of their own schedules and energies for working with lay planners as they "reinvent the wheels" of sacramental initiation each year. Faced with the challenge of setting objectives within the process of Christian initiation, people quickly see what is at stake—a definition of Christian adulthood itself.[16] The committee meetings of the parish RCIA team thus become an authentic locus of the developing theology of initiation.

Although the specifics of sacramental catechesis must be worked out at the parish level, there are tools and principles that are helpful in most situations. One of the best is the *Catholic Faith Inventory* published by Paulist Press.[17] This questionnaire covers nine areas of Catholic life and practice. It was designed to assess a candidate's understanding and attitudes, in comparison with a national sample and a "preferred" Catholic position.

The 108 questionnaire items are intended to raise points for discussion within individual counseling relationships. However, the "preferred" responses can also be used as a tentative profile of Christian adulthood in the Catholic community, and therefore as goals for catechesis. For example, the following desired competences are typical of the nine areas represented: read the Bible regularly; pray and seek God's guidance before making important decisions; feel God's forgiving love; consider

51

the church's teachings when making a moral decision; be concerned about the problems of the poor; believe that Jesus Christ is fully human and fully divine; see some of the saints as models of the Christian life; feel a sense of belonging when worshiping with this Catholic community; participate in Mass every Sunday. Although many of the items are controversial, the parish RCIA team can easily use the list as a point of departure and reference for its own goal-defining process.

Whether planners start with church documents as a planning tool, or some prepared curriculum, certain basic principles should be kept in mind. First, the success of catechesis depends upon its context—a healthy parish. Church is not a static entity, but a dynamic way of being continually enacted through the interdependent ministries of word, care, and sacrament. These ministries thrive when they support one another and the parish's human and material resources are allocated wisely among them. In practical terms, this means that a parish that forgets the poor cannot teach its adults or children to recognize the Lord in the breaking of the bread. A parish that forgets how to confess sin cannot teach its people to make peace in their business and political affairs. These competences are intrinsically connected in the Christian tradition. Use them or lose them.

A second principle is related to the first. In Christianity, *knowing* always means *knowing who* and *knowing how*, as well as *knowing that*. The *that* is the component of Christianity able to be printed out upon a page, and since Gutenberg's revolution, this component has monopolized the limelight. Most people still expect catechists to read to them "the facts" the church teaches; even catechists themselves may tend to define their role in those terms. However, the ecclesial activities of sacrament and care require *who* and *how* knowledge as well. One must know *who* presents himself in the bread and in the needy little ones; one must know *how* to celebrate the intimacy of our relationship with him and with them.

Therefore what is to be imparted in sacramental catechesis is a capacity for recognition, and this gives us a third principle. Sacramental catechesis prepares people to recognize the

Risen Lord. To recognize is to identify something encountered in the present with something already known in the past. Therefore to recognize, one must both encounter and remember; and so we teach people to recognize by teaching them to encounter and to remember. Christianity includes a competence to *remember* in terms of the Scriptures and the doctrines of our tradition which explicate them. The point of those textual memories, however, is to familiarize us with who Jesus was, so that we will know him when we see him. For Christianity includes also a competence to *encounter* in terms of service—literal service as well as the liturgical variety. Within a program of Christian education for memory and service, then, the special focus of sacramental catechesis is to import the skills, sensitivities, attitudes, and desires needed for liturgical encounter with the Risen Lord.

The Teaching/Learning Interaction

Sacraments communicate aesthetically—that is, through image and symbol, as well as discursively. Moreover, they communicate with people who vary in age, temperament, gender, ability, race, culture, class, and political and sexual orientation. Because of this variance among people, different communities will appropriate the traditional liturgical symbols in many different ways. Local catechists are in the best position to devise the means that will work for their own people. Yet once again, some general principles can help them in this task.

Aesthetic Training

There is growing consensus in Catholic theology that sacraments communicate in much the same way as works of art.[18] Art is the interface of humanity with transcendence, and the innate human capacity for art can be developed by careful training. It follows that competence for sacramental celebration might be engendered in the same way art teachers help people engage with art.[19] But one must distinguish between art *appreciation* and art *participation*. Art "appreciation" is the concern of dilettantes bent on consuming the goods produced in the art industry. Sacraments, however, are not produced and consumed like commodities! On the other hand, when art participation is the goal, all become artists, in the sense that everyone the artwork touches gratefully receives the revelation that happens in it and opens out from it. The person who carves or stitches or paints feels that he or she is just as much a receiver of the emergent reality as are those who ponder, cherish, and preserve that which has been crafted. Through initiation into the ways of the art, people learn to celebrate and receive it.[20]

Aesthetic training, then, encourages "thinking from" artworks by "talking about" them as little as possible. One lectures about Van Gogh's biography only insofar as that brings the learner to a perspective of greater vulnerability to the reality bursting through Van Gogh's painting. By the same token, one lectures about early medieval penance manuals only insofar as that brings the learner to a perspective of greater vulnerability to the grace unfolding out of the sacramental celebration of reconciliation.

Learners must spend time with an artwork, waiting for it to open. One at a time is studied. A work of art that is there only in the learner's memory lacks the power to *work*, to be an event of creative disclosure. By the same token, catechesis does not take up *sacramenta in genere*, "sacraments in general," because there simply is no such thing as a generic sacrament. Sacramental catechesis happens in proximity to a particular sacramental celebration. It may take the form of preparation for a rite of initiation, reconciliation, or commitment. On the other hand, it may be mystagogy, reflection upon the enduring sacrament after the ritual has been experienced. The very efficacy of the sacrament depends upon catechesis and mystagogy. It is this teaching which draws us into the proximity of the sacrament and keeps us there.

If this rule has an exception, it occurs in connection with the basic liturgical requirement that we accept our own bodies and our creaturely need for sensuous symbolic communication, both of which develop very gradually. Sacramental catechesis begins when an infant learns to enjoy a cuddle, a flash of color, a sweet taste, a pungent smell, a smiling glance. Our earliest experience of making things contributes to our mature capacity to make ritual. To understand Eucharist, we must understand bread and wine: the work and resources that go into concocting them, what they mean to hungry people, their uses and abuses. To understand baptism, we must know what water does at the seashore, in the garden, in storms and floods, and at childbirth. In our society most of these elemental experiences have gone the way of shepherds and kings. As a remote preparation for all the sacraments, then, we should find ways to foster the capacity for playful enjoyment of simple things like baking, swimming, drinking, and eating, which often are perverted beyond recognition in our consumer society.

About People

Sacraments often mark life-stage transitions. Sacramental catechesis is adapted to the age and condition of the learners. Chronological age signals the level of cognitive and emotional development in young children, but is less closely correlated as girls and boys grow through their school years and into adulthood.[21]

The foundation of liturgical life is laid by participation in the assembly, from at least the point when the baptized child understands the sentence, "Jesus is here" (about 30 months of age). The reverent attitude of family and friends is the best lesson that something very special is going on. Before the first reception of the Eucharist (about age 7), before confirmation (in the early teens), and again before marriage (for couples who choose that way of life), the church provides a special intense period of preparation which parallels the catechumenate but is adapted to the level of understanding and competence for symbolic communication. This competence is epigenetic—that is, new skills build upon the skills and experiences of the previous level. One must be careful not to present too sophisticated an account of the symbols, but on the other hand, one must not inhibit gradual growth from a literal to a more critical and creative grasp of their meaning.[22]

55

Instruction also should take into account the various temperaments represented among the learners. People observe their surroundings and process the observed data in a variety of ways. Yet each person has a dominant mental process for receiving information. Catechesis, then, should be designed to offer something for every learning style. Some people need logically organized material such as that found in theology books, while others need to see that what they are learning is worthy of the gift of their hearts and souls. The former will benefit from a well-ordered syllabus, while the latter find the committed testimony of a mentor or sponsor a great help. Still other people need imagery from which to extrapolate patterns for planning their future; invite them to play with symbolic meanings in unconventional ways. And others need hands-on experience that shows the functional application of what they are learning; invite them to work as cup-bearers, greeters, or readers for the assembly, or in another liturgical ministry.[23]

North America includes a rich diversity of cultures, represented among immigrant and native peoples, among urban, rural, and suburban dwellers. Historically, the liturgy was an important means of enculturating the gospel. Now, however, liturgical experiences such as Christmas and weddings have become quite secularized. Yet Hispanic, German, Slavic, African-American, and Celtic customs and expressions often have a rich resonance with the aesthetic communication of the sacraments, and the cultural expressivity of Caribbean, Asian, and Pacific peoples and Native Americans should be integrated within liturgical preparation and experience.

Initiation, Reconciliation, Commitment

So far, we have noted several factors which shape sacramental catechesis—the aesthetic nature of liturgical communication and the age, temperament, and culture of the persons who celebrate the sacraments. In addition, the *res*, or intended effect of each sacrament, sets the agenda for the catechesis connected with it.

The sacraments of initiation lead persons into Christ and the church; therefore the catechesis of initiation should show them what life in Christ is like. For adults, the catechumenate is designed as a period of gradual conversion, often termed a journey, in the company of other seekers, including representatives of the parish community. It includes doctrinal and moral instruction as well as social events, common prayer, liturgical experiences, practical involvement in service, and one-on-one interaction with a personal sponsor. Usually there is a weekly group meeting with a dialogical format.

Teenagers preparing for confirmation and children preparing for first communion need the same sort of preparation, adapted to their own capacities. Above all, the individuals' freedom of choice must be respected. Parents receive the instruction for an infant's baptism, but it is well to borrow from the catechumenate where possible: for example, dialogical instruction, sponsoring by another couple, and emphasis on life as a journey of gradual conversion. New parents are instructed about their responsibility to provide continuing catechesis for the child and about the parish's resources to help them in that task. Conversely, parish experiences of preparing for initiation are one of the important sources contributing to the theology of Christian initiation itself.

The sacraments of reconciliation celebrate the oneness between God and humanity which Jesus accomplished, bringing this reality into confrontation with the particular life circumstances of an individual. Therefore the catechesis of reconciliation should model the joy we find in the recognition that God's love is greater than sin; it should pay less attention to petty human failings than to grace. Moral instruction belongs more properly to initiation; here we focus on the overwhelming goodness of God. It is important to help learners link the Paschal story to their own personal stories of hurt and hope.

For children approaching their first celebration of penance, catechesis builds upon family experiences of making up and forgiveness. For adolescents, we emphasize self-acceptance and decision. For adults, there often is need to heal habitual attitudes engendered by earlier pastoral practice.[24] Ritual experiences of reconciliation, with their communal dimension, give people the images and the competence to work for national and international peace. Conversely, these parish experiences are an important source for the theology of reconciliation.

The sacraments of commitment signal a mature decision to embrace a particular path of discipleship within the church community and in response to its needs.[25] For these sacraments persons need deep, practical knowledge of themselves. People become competent to celebrate these sacraments by living before God in Christ and by thus gradually coming to know themselves.[26] They must understand that their choice to love rests upon God's prior choice to love them. Formal programs of catechesis for commitment are designed to discern, support, and focus this process.

However, in today's Catholic Church, the catechesis of commitment is rather poorly done. Preparation for orders is absurdly long and introverted, while preparation for marriage is pitifully short and shallow. The seminary has become a postgraduate professional school, while marriage preparation has become couple counseling. Neither approach contains enough of the sacramental and the celebrational. Elements of the RCIA process could well be grafted into the catechesis of commitment: dialogical instruction, the sponsoring relationship, flexible timing, intermediate ritual celebrations, greater involvement with the parish community, and opportunities for service. Moreover, although continuing education and enrichment programs are common, mystagogy has scarcely been attempted in the sacraments of orders and matrimony. Therefore, parish experiences of preparing for sacramental commitment have so far contributed little to the theology of Christian discipleship.

Who Teaches Whom?

The dimensions of the liturgical revolution since the Second Vatican Council can perhaps best be appreciated in terms of increased staffing needs. Thirty years ago, in the postwar boom of the parochial school system, a far smaller proportion of Catholics was involved in formal teaching and learning than is the case today. For children, the two basic institutions of catechesis were the parish (diocesan, or private) school and, alternatively for those not enrolled in such schools, the Confraternity of Christian Doctrine (CCD) class on Sunday morning. For adults who could afford higher education, there were Catholic colleges. Adults seeking to enter the Catholic Church received brief private instruction from a priest; all other sacramental preparation was classroom based. Priests and vowed religious were the teachers of choice both for the schools and for the CCD classes, although many were lay volunteers.[27]

Today, sacramental catechesis has escaped from the classroom. Better professional preparation is available, but fewer of those who actually teach have had any training. An active parish develops a network of programs and planning teams connected with each sacrament. This involves many lay volunteers, and each person who participates in any capacity needs catechesis. For adult initiation (RCIA), this includes the pastoral staff, planning-team members, sponsors, catechists, candidates and catechumens, those who provide hospitality and support, and the worshiping assembly at large, especially during Lent. For first Eucharist and first penance, training must be provided for the children who approach each sacrament, their parents, siblings, friends and relatives, the catechists, and the worshiping assembly. In addition, there are training programs for readers, altar servers, and eucharistic ministers; those involved in infant baptism or teen confirmation; and those who assist couples approaching marriage. The weekly homily is the vehicle for ongoing mystagogy for all these sacraments and for remote preparation for Anointing of the Sick, but separate topical instruction is needed as well. Increasingly, the parish is also becoming the site for significant portions of preparation for ordination to the diaconate and the priesthood.

Who carries out all this programming? Structures are still evolving, but the general pattern is becoming clear. A core pastoral staff, consisting of priests and professionally trained

59

and salaried associates, has a twofold function: to call forth the teams and committees who will plan, conduct, and evaluate the catechesis, and to provide them with resources in the form of materials, training, feedback, and personal support as needed. In practice, a pastoral staff of four to six persons may "resource" a network of hundreds of volunteers.[28]

Where does the parish find all these volunteers? We saw above that the very nature of initiation, reconciliation, and commitment defines the character of sacramental catecheses. Now we can see that even the recruitment and training of volunteers is shaped in accordance with these sacramental experiences. Newly initiated Christians, those who have just enthusiastically taken on the responsibilities of church membership, are the best source of helpers for the next year's RCIA program.[29] Teenagers who have recently been confirmed should be invited to work with the next confirmation group, a logical follow-through for the completion of their initiation. New parents are catechized by parents of older children. Married couples sponsor engaged couples. The invitation to reconciliation is best extended by those who have known the pain of separation and the healing of reunion with the church.

Baptism itself is our commission to teach; however, one gradually grows into the role of catechist through increasingly responsible roles on a team. Teaching, is not the duty of any one member of the parish, whether priest or layperson. Rather, competence for sacramental catechesis resides in the ecclesial community as a whole and is diffused throughout the differing gifts of its members. Some are mentors, some sing, some listen, some sweep, some counsel, some question, some hug, some play, some type and photocopy, some bake and brew, some speak.

Materials

This rapidly developing situation has created a vacuum in the area of instructional media, into which a bewildering variety of electronic and print materials are pouring. Unlike many Protestant churches, Catholics have no official curriculum and rely instead upon the creative efforts of private publishing houses. From these firms, a number of excellent graded series are available for children and adolescents in Catholic day schools and weekly CCD classes. Understandably, most of these are adapted for Catholic "education" rather than sacramental catechesis. However, some materials have been developed specifically for the sacraments of Confirmation, First Eucharist, and First Penance.[30]

For catechesis of adults, the publishing situation is more fluid, and important questions about RCIA remain to be addressed: What kind of formal curriculum is best for adult intitiation? More basically, is it even appropriate to conceive of this journey of personal conversion in curricular terms? In practice, parishes tend to choose one of two alternatives. They may reduce the catechesis of initiation to a minicourse in theology and use materials designed as theological treatments of various topics. Or they may load the entire burden of instruction onto the liturgy and attempt to use the common lectionary as "the textbook of the catechumenate." The theological approach is too cognitive; the liturgical or biblical approach is not sufficiently systematic.[31] There is a great need for new printed materials, videotapes, and celebration aids designed specifically for use in adult sacramental catechesis. But there is an equally great need that these materials, the programs in which they are used, and the teachers who use them understand the catechetical tradition of the church.

Mutual Access

If sacraments give us access to Jesus as Risen Lord, they also give the Risen Lord Jesus intimate access to each of us. Sacraments are that component of the Christian traditioning process which can be most closely attuned to the individuality of the persons who stand in need of the saving touch of Jesus. The sacramental liturgy *adapts*.

Sacrament is the Risen Jesus reaching from eternity into the concrete circumstances of particular lives. His approach is conditioned by the human variables already mentioned: age,

61

temperament, gender, ability, race, culture, class, and political and sexual orientation. These dimensions constitute the range of human receptively to the sacramental touch of Jesus. Not only do they describe the particular ways we go to him; they also indicate the breadth and depth of the Lord who comes to us. A girl of seven brings the mind and heart of a child to her meeting with the eucharistic Jesus; therefore the One she meets, while fully the Risen Lord, is Lord and God precisely by being available to a little girl with childish cares and notions. Similarly, an older man who brings the frustrations and failures of a lifetime to the Rite of Reconciliation meets the one and only Risen Lord, but meets him as a Lord who desperately wishes to soothe and heal the very matters that have gone wrong over the years.

Examples are multiple, and in each case, the sacrament links what God did in Jesus with what God wants to do in a particular human life today. The limitations of Jesus' own race, age, and gender are overcome, since the Risen Lord identifies with people of every culture, language, and way of life. Moreover, the Risen Lord's sacramental access to all peoples is, at the same time, the access of various peoples to one another. Sacrament is the eschatological frontier, opened by and to the Risen Lord; the liturgy, in adapting to our cultural and historical particularities, lets us transcend them to meet one another in the Lord's new day.

Thus the parish experience with the living sacramental tradition opens up new theological perspectives upon risen life as the way Jesus Christ is available to every individual, and every individual, to Jesus Christ. The everyday steps in the process of sacramental catechesis not only emerge from our prior sacramental theology, but also lead into an ever more subtle pondering of the Paschal Mystery, now seen to embrace our own response as individuals and as a people of God. Catechesis moves forward toward its fulfillment the mystery of mutual availability between the Lord Jesus and his church.

CHAPTER 4

Feminist Theology and Education

Mary Elizabeth Mullino Moore

We stand in the third decade of an active and vocal feminist movement in the United States. We are inheritors of rich religious traditions, but we also hear cries of oppression within those same traditions. We seem to be faced with more questions than answers. Why?

Explosion of Questions

Perhaps this explosion of questions is due to an increasing awareness of the complexity of liberation movements and of religious traditions. Perhaps it is natural for an explosion to occur when we all bring our differences to the party and try to live together in one world. Perhaps it is to be expected as more women participate in theological dialogue and in the ministry of churches. And these participants are not alike. They are as colorful as a rainbow, and those from various religious traditions are beginning to interact and influence one another. What happens when Jews of the Orthodox, Conservative, Reform, and Reconstruction traditions join Roman Catholic, Protestant, and Orthodox Christians, who join Palestinian and North American Muslims, who join Buddhist sects from Japan and India and Unitarian Universalists from North America?

In such a mix, women often ask questions different from those men ask. Issues of God, creation, salvation, and ministry are expanded to include issues that have been in the background or have never even been considered. Communication theorists have demonstrated that women and men often speak different languages in different ways, with different values and assumptions.[1] Whether male-female differences are inherent or socially conditioned is immaterial. More to the point, we know that certain virtues and ideas traditionally have been associated with womanhood, and when these virtues and ideas are taken more seriously in theological discourse, the discourse changes.

Futhermore, women are not all the same, and they also bring *their* differences to the party. African-American women raise questions different from those of Korean or European-American women. Delores Williams, for example, pleads for the colorization of feminism, which has been dominated in the United States by white, middle-class, Christian women.[2] Orthodox Jewish women raise different questions from those of Reform Jewish women, and both ask questions different from those of Christian women. Witness, for example, the radical differences between Blu Greenberg and Susannah Heschel as to the relative degree of women's liberation. Blu Greenberg, an Orthodox Jew, argues that Judaism has most often been liberating for women; that when women participate in traditional observances, they stand in community with Jewish women over the centuries.[3] Susannah Heschel, on the other hand, sees the Jewish tradition as more problematic for women. Conflicts over interpretation are indicative of the contemporary confusion regarding the coincidence of tradition and feminism.[4] Even with these differing views, the issues raised by Jewish feminists are not exactly the same as those raised by Christian feminists, and Jewish women sometimes become concerned when Christian women read their own issues into the Jewish tradition.

When these colorful and varied communities of women begin to interact, not only are their own differences brought to the party, but new differences also surface. A binding fiber among Jews, Christians, and Muslims has been that we are all children of Abraham. But consciousness raised by women renews the memory that these religious communities were birthed by both Abraham and Sarah. And when African-

American women speak out, they sometimes plead that we also remember Hagar, the slave woman who was used and then cast out from the household of Abraham and Sarah.[5]

Feminist theology speaks in a chorus of voices, and those voices are not always melodious. They can be discordant in their sufferings and in their differences. On the other hand, women of different cultures and traditions affect one another and often share passions that motivate a sense of sisterhood even in the midst of discord.

Feminist Theology

Feminist theology is theological reflection in which the experience of women is assumed to be both the source and the measure of theological affirmations. The faith experience of women is an appropriate starting point for theological discourse, whether the focus is on women's experience in biblical texts, in historical events or in contemporary movements. At the same time, the effect of theological doctrines or ideas is tested by their effect on women. Are these doctrines and ideas liberating and humanizing, or do they perpetuate the devaluing of women and everything associated with women, such as children and the natural world? Although men often participate, most feminist theology is undertaken by women.

This is a perspectival approach, based on the assumption that all theological reflection is shaped by human experiences and assumptions, and that some persons' experiences and assumptions have been undervalued in the theological constructions we inherit. Therefore, feminist theology is an attempt to critique and reconstruct all of theology, to take into account women and the value of their experience. It is not intended to eliminate all other perspectives, but to contribute to the richness, criticalness, and wholeness of the theological enterprise.

Some African-American women have chosen to use the term

65

womanist theology to highlight the ideological differences between African-American feminist theology and the feminist theology framed largely by white, middle-class women in the United States and other Western nations.[6] *Womanist theology* will be used in this chapter to call to mind the differences among women who pursue theology. (The term will not be used continually, however, in the hope that this white woman will not coopt the term, thus compounding the injustices already done.)

What is happening in feminist and womanist theology, and how does that help to shape Christian religious education? This is a time when the foundations are shaking with new answers to old questions and new questions for old answers. The patriarchal biases in Christianity are becoming more visible as we reflect on our values, beliefs, and practices, and both women and men are responding.

Most responses to an early wave of the contemporary feminist movement in the United States were expressions of anger against the traditions, or of fear and protectiveness of treasured traditions. Those early responses gave birth sometimes to dialogue and transformation, sometimes to schism or apathy or more anger. The post-Christian movement was born, drawing women who could not see themselves within Christianity and could not foresee the possibility of reform in such a thoroughly misogynist tradition, one in which women were denied or, at best, distrusted. In more recent years, energies devoted to critiquing Christian traditions have been joined by new energies for reforming, reconstructing, and remythologizing the old traditions.

Since the questions we ask often limit the answers we seek, women in many religious traditions are beginning to raise new questions—questions that seldom had been asked or that had been resigned to the fringes. The asking of new questions promises to be frightening, even chaotic, but it also promises to be broadening and creative, liberating us to find new answers, and even more questions.

Re-forming Theological Questions

Here we will explore several questions that have been re-formed in feminist theology. In the next section we will deal with re-forming Christian religious education, in light of these and other theological issues. In both cases, these themes are overviews, as each by itself could result in a book. In fact, each already has resulted in more than one book.

Shifting Questions About God

There have been two very important questions in the Christian theological tradition: *Is God transcendent, or immanent, or both? How can God be both all powerful and all good?* Those basic questions about God's locus and activity are not eliminated in feminist and womanist theology, but they are less prominent than other questions: *Who is God? How does God relate to creation, including human creation?*

The person of God and the qualities of relationship seem more important than location and power. Women do not often ask whether God is up there or down here. They ask: How is God related to all that is? And many wonder whether God might better be called Goddess or Divine Spirit. In Jewish and Christian communities, the problem often emerges in very practical questions: What is God's name? How do we relate to God? These queries are very challenging because they speak to the heart of faith for theistic religions.

Biblically, the identity of our God has received much more attention than the question of whether God exists. Naming has always been important, even if answered with a commitment *not* to name or define God. The prominent name in the Hebrew Bible is Yahweh; in the New Testament, Father. Both are male-gender words, with male connotations. Both the Hebrew Bible and the Second Testament offer other names and images; some are female: Ruach, or Spirit (Gen. 1:2; Matt. 3:16); the image of a mother (Isa. 46:3-4; 66:13); Jesus' image of himself as a hen gathering her chicks (Luke 13:34).

67

Complicating matters still further are our problems of naming the Trinity and of relating to God as Father, Son, and Holy Spirit. Within Eastern Orthodox traditions, the changing of trinitarian language and imagery is especially problematic. The Trinity is important to Orthodox theology; further, the Trinity, as a community within God, becomes a model for human community. Deborah Belonick and other Orthodox women often cite the importance of this trinitarian community in representing the personal and communal nature of God and modeling more communal relationship for women and men.[7] By changing its language, we could even become destructive of the hope for more communal human relationships—that a hope resides in the doctrine of the Trinity.

In Western Christian churches, the Trinity has played various roles, and though trinitarian language usually has been prominent, the usage and formulation of the trinitarian image has been more fluid. For example, Julian of Norwich in fourth-century England described God as Maker, Protector, and Lover, and also as Father, Mother, and Lord.[8] She especially focused on the image of Jesus as Mother. Today many Protestant churches use the words Creator, Redeemer, Sustainer.

Paired with the question about God's identity is the problem of God's relation to creation—as Leader and Deliverer of the people, as Father, or as neither? We have theological choices.

One option rejects the image of God as Lord and Father altogether, and many feminists do, speaking instead of Goddess, Divine Spirit, or God within us. This theological choice could lead to a rejection of the God-images that have been primary in Christian tradition, and also to a rejection of God as Transcendent One, the creative and mysterious Power of the universe. The focus, then, might be more on the creative power immanent in the universe, particularly within women. This is a compelling view for many feminists, since ideas about God or Goddess can be drawn from the experiences of women. Such an approach respects women's experience as sacred and recognizes that the degree of oppression or liberation in our God-talk is very important.

Another theological choice could be to speak of God in many metaphors, as suggested by Sallie McFague in *Metaphorical Theology* and *Models of God*. Recognizing that no words can adequately express our experience of God, McFague warns against literalizing our language, thus conveying that our words define God.[9] As she builds on this idea in her later work, she expresses the view that our metaphors and models can be very important to our relationship with God and the world. Therefore she suggests models that can more adequately point us toward a holistic, just, and ecological vision of God in relationship to the world.[10] Rather than abandoning Christian imagery and the attendant concepts, she tests that imagery and those concepts by the way they function in the lives of women and in the creation as a whole. If we take this view seriously, we can speak of God as Spirit within all of nature, or we can speak of God as both Mother and Father, or as Grandfather or Grandmother. Such an approach can recognize the historical tradition as well as the female metaphors of God that reside within that tradition. But such an approach will also regard that tradition with a critical eye and an effort to remythologize the historical myths that have become dysfunctional.

At the very least, this discussion leads to some challenging conclusions. One can hardly say that God's identity and God's relationship toward creation are matters settled by the weight of historical tradition. The tradition itself never speaks with just one voice; we are challenged to listen to the many voices and to add our own voices. Christianity is a living and pluriform tradition. Further, we are challenged to judge the traditions of God by the effect they have on the creation, inspiring the care of life or the destruction of it. We are challenged also to allow the tradition and ourselves to be transformed as women and men theologize, at the same time respecting the mystery that lies beyond our words or experiences.

But even if God is beyond the limits of language, God is not beyond relationship with creation. Within feminist and

69

womanist theologies, the sense that God feels with the creation and exists within it is very strong. The divine is incarnate in all life; all of creation is viewed as sacred, and all of creation reveals God. In the words of Shug in Alice Walker's *Color Purple:*

> My first step from the old white man was trees. Then air. Then birds. Then other people. But one day when I was sitting quiet and feeling like a motherless child, which I was, it come to me: that feeling of being part of everything, not separate at all. I knew that if I cut a tree, my arm would bleed.[11]

Life is holy, and we can face it only with reverence and humility. This is a kind of transcendent immanence, in which the Spirit is understood to pervade everything, but nothing is believed to contain all of God.

Shifting Questions About Humanity

Questions about God, Goddess, or Divine Spirit are erupting alongside related questions about humanity. *Are people basically good or evil?* This question has yielded efforts to make sharp distinctions, to identify good with certain attributes and evil with others.

Such debates lead inevitably to value judgments regarding human characteristics, then to valuing some people over others. In the story of Mary and Martha, Mary is named as the one who chose the better part. The good is named very simply as quiet listening, whereas forthrightness and busy housework are bad. Since the church has emphasized this story more than stories about Martha's strong, bold character, Luke 10:38-42 serves to dishonor the woman and overshadow her testimony of faith (John 11:17-27), which is parallel to Peter's confession of faith (Matt. 16:16).[12]

In a similar vein, the character of Mary Magdalene has been flattened into a stereotype of sinful woman. Her loyalty and love are pushed to the background, and she becomes the

70

prototype of sin.[13] Such brief comments oversimplify the texts, but the issues are developed more fully by Elisabeth Moltmann-Wendel and others. The point is clear. The very simple, stereotypical answers to questions about good and evil yield a new question: *What do human liberation and wholeness mean?* This emerges especially when simplistic categories of "good" and "bad" deny liberation and wholeness to some.

The very phrasing of the new question challenges dichotomies, such as those between dominant and submissive, logical and intuitive, cognitive and affective, bold and gentle. The awareness of such dichotomies is often vivid, for women frequently feel pulled between these seeming opposites, faced with an either/or choice and knowing that one usually is valued more than the other.

One dichotomy that has been particularly problematic is that between "temptress" and "guardian of purity." These two images are represented in two major figures of the New Testament, Mary Magdalene (associated in the tradition with prostitution) and Mary the mother of Jesus. In feminist theology, one witnesses critiques of one-sided characterizations and the attempts to present more fully human, integrated characters. Rosemary Radford Ruether has described the problems of one-sided characterizations of the Virgin Mary, which reinforce the dichotomy between spirit and body. Ruether seeks to identify some of the liberating possibilities in a more full development of Mary's character, attending to the promises made to her and the choice she made to carry and bear this baby.[14] The efforts of Elisabeth Moltmann-Wendel, discussed earlier, exemplify the desire to recover the fullness of the women around Jesus, including Mary Magdalene. It was not Luke, but later interpreters, who connected this Mary with prostitution, and the power of such linkage converts her into a symbol of sin. Moltmann-Wendel asks, "What would our tradition look like if it had made Peter a converted pimp?"[15]

In the effort to ask new questions about human wholeness, women are unwrapping cultural stereotypes that have held women in bondage to submissiveness, intuition, affection, and gentleness; stereotypes that have held men in bondage to dominance, logic, cognition, and boldness. To undercut these stereotypes is to undercut many of the valuations placed on both women and men, so that the old question of human goodness reappears with a new casting. We no longer are so concerned with whether people are basically good or bad, but with how goodness is manifested in integrated human beings.

Other new questions arise: *What forces of goodness lie below the surface, pushing to preserve and enrich life?* This starting point does not contrast good and evil. The assumption here is that goodness is at work even in the midst of disaster, even if only in the sheer human capacity to survive. *Then how is the goodness of humanity manifested?* This sends us looking for goodness, rather than trying to prove whether it exists.

But what *is* goodness? What *is* full humanity? Is full humanity a certain set of qualities, or is it a fulfilling of creation, taking different forms in different individuals and communities? Feminist theologians often press such questions because they are aware that narrow definitions of goodness often have served to imprison our foremothers and sisters. As women recover their own stories and those of their mothers, they discover many ways to be human and to be woman. They discover goodness manifested in the determination of Asenie women in Ghana, Africa.[16] They see it manifested in a Cuban mother's words of advice to her daughter: "All we need to ask of God is to have health and strength to struggle. As long as we have what we need to struggle in life, we need ask for nothing else."[17]

And finally we face this question: *What is the impetus and standard of goodness in making ethical judgments?* As women press such questions, they discover that the ethical mandate may have less to do with a set of universal laws or principles, and more to do with respect for God in all of life. Our ethical mandate is to respect the world as the body of God and seek to preserve and support life in all its forms.[18]

Shifting Questions About Sin

The search for goodness leads to a sense of tragedy where goodness is not found, so the question of sin is raised: *What is the relationship between sin and sexuality; between sin and the will to power?* The answers to such questions have often put women in a harsh light, a situation where responsibility for human sin rests heavily on their shouldres. In much of the Christian tradition, celibacy has been seen as far superior to marriage. The association of sexuality with sin, and the association of women with the temptation to sexual misconduct, is a prevalent theme in the biblical witness—even more, in traditions of interpretation. In Revelation 14:4 we read praise of male virgins "who have not defiled themselves with women." These men are seen as "first fruits for God and the Lamb." In a different way, the association of sin with the will to power has burdened women, especially in those societies which teach women to be humble to the point of self-effacement and self-negation, and those in which women suffer from too little pride, rather than too much.[19]

Such questions about human sin in relation to sexuality and the will to power lead to answers in which sexuality and power are seen as destructive forces. *So how might we view sexuality and power as gifts of God, and how might those gifts be received and used to affirm life rather than to deny it?* Sin may lie in refusing to receive the gifts we are given, including the gifts of sexuality and power. Sin has less to do with specific acts of sexual disobedience and the seeking of power, than with missing the mark or not being what we were created to be. The view of sin as missing the mark is not new to the Christian tradition. To miss the mark is to destroy or deny life. We participate in sin as individuals and also as participants in social structures that destroy or deny life.

Shifting Questions About Salvation

In the face of sin and evil, the traditional question of salvation rises to prominence: *How does God save us and give us hope?* This question has led to answers in the form of God's salvation through Jesus Christ and God's salvific action in a fallen world. Since the fallenness of creation is often associated with the human sins discussed earlier, and since these views often have been used oppressively against women, feminist theologians often ask: *What vision of a more just and loving life can we look and move toward? What in creation do we experience as saving and hopeful?*

Both these questions focus on salvation within creation. One works to construct a more adequate vision of the future, with the idea that this will actually contribute to co-authoring a better future with God and with one another. One works toward listening and watching for the signs of God's redemptive work in the natural order. Both questions assume human participation in the redemptive work.

Nowhere is the issue of salvation more poignantly discussed than by Isabel Carter Heyward in *Redemption of God.* She describes her own search: "To what extent are we responsible for our own redemption in history?" Her overarching concern is the tendency in Christian theology to foster human loneliness—isolation from God, and even from our own humanity. God is seen as over and above the world, and we ourselves are called to rise above the world. She summarizes the problem: "In such a schema, 'redemption' is God's act of lifting us above ourselves, a process of divine deliverance from the human condition."[20]

Heyward offers a different view of God as the power of relationship itself; she speaks of redemption as a cooperative work between humanity and God. Our participation is our willingness to foster love and justice in the world. In Heyward's view, "We cooperate with each other and with God in a process of mutual redemption—that is, in the deliverance of both God and humanity from evil." Such a view requires the reimaging of God, of human beings, and of Jesus Christ. Christ is imaged not as a divine person sent from God, but as "a human being who knew and loved God." Heyward says she sees the power of justice and a right relation in Jesus, for he "can help us see the power, love the power, claim the power, use the power."[21]

The shift in Carter Heyward's view of redemption reflects a familiar move in feminist theology: The against-the-world view is replaced with a participation-in-the-world view—a view that is relational, incarnational, cooperative, and empowering. The movement of God within creation points to a new creation of justice and love. Further, if we have eyes to see God's Spirit in our midst, and if we have the will to work for justice and love, we can participate with God in the work of salvation.

Such a view of salvation suggests that Jesus Christ indeed incarnated God's own passions for love and justice, and thus inspires ours. Further, Jesus is with us in our humanity. One woman speaks of her relationship with Jesus: "We are getting *cachetadas* [slaps in the face] together and *aplastones* [crushings] together. He is like a partner or a brother, someone who is with me."[22]

Jesus Christ, as the most full incarnation of God, models a new humanity and opens new possibilities for our participation in God's redemption. In this view of salvation, however, Jesus Christ is not the *only* incarnation of God or the only avenue of God's grace. God's redemptive work is incarnate in all that is. God's presence in and around and under and over us is mediated through all of creation. Such abiding presence represents God's patient love and God's continuing work to guide and transform us and creation. God acts toward us without ceasing, but God cries out for us to respond, to participate in the redemption of the world.

Re-forming Educational Questions

The journey into feminist, or womanist, theology has hardly begun. Each insight cries out for more development as others cry out to be expressed. But this journey is one that has no end because it is the very locus of educational ministry. The questions already developed here suggest some important

75

aspects of Christian religious education that are shaped by feminist concerns, and others that relate directly to that practice will be identified.

Shifting Questions About Method

The discussion of re-forming theological questions already reveals a methodology, at least in broad strokes. Clearly, education is not simply a derivative of theology, but helps to shape theology and the questions theology must address. The practice of education and the expressions of theology continually interact and shape one another. A feminist-formed educational ministry would not simply focus on disseminating information, but would utilize methods of critique, reconstruction, and remythologizing. The traditions themselves are starting points, but they are not ending points because they are inherently dynamic. They also need continuous re-formation; too often they have been patriarchal and oppressive to women, to other oppressed peoples, and to the earth.

The educational methods would be not unlike the methods reflected in the above analysis of theological issues. The method of *critique* would include analyzing, with hermeneutical suspicion, dominant worldviews and doctrines, the cultures in which these worldviews were born, and how these worldviews have functioned in Christian history to liberate or to oppress. The method of *reconstruction* would include rethinking the traditions to re-form answers to old questions and re-form the questions themselves, in an effort to seek more adequate perspectives on God and the world. The method of *remythologizing* would include reimaging God and the world, as Sally McFague does, expressing metaphors and models of God judged to be redemptive rather than oppressive. When we begin to image God as Mother, Friend, or "power in relation," we are remythologizing. When we reimage Jesus Christ as a source of power or as a human among humans, we are remythologizing. When we reimage humanity as co-creator

76

with God and as care-giver in the creation, we are remythologizing. Reimaging gives the power to see and respond to the world differently.

These various methods suggest some concrete possibilities for action in educational ministry.[23] They are very similar to what Maria Harris metaphorically calls the steps of a dance in religious education—silence, remembering, ritual mourning, artistry, and birthing. She hopes for a pedagogy that is liberating and a teaching that is sacramental and a holy act.[24] Such a pedagogy requires various movements which build on one another. She suggests silence as the movement of listening, listening especially to the silences of women.

Listening opens the way to remembering—mythic, dangerous, communal, liturgical remembering. And remembering gives way to mourning. The very act of mourning prepares us for the artistry of creating together, birthing new fuller selves, more just communities. But teaching does not end here, because the dance continues, moving in and out of the steps. Harris concludes, "The rhythm of pedagogy must continue because none of us can be free until all are free."[25]

Shifting Questions About Content

Questions about content also rise out of feminist theological reflection: *What is the relative authority between Scripture texts and later interpretations? To what extent is Scripture or the historical tradition normative for Christians?* As women have struggled with the usual answers to those questions, new questions emerge: *To what extent are Scripture and historical traditions liberating? What are the various sources of authority?* In the way sin has been defined, we have seen how Scripture and tradition can be used in the oppression of women. The very realization that they can be used in this way raises questions regarding the absolute normativity of either. Perhaps other sources of authority should be taken seriously, such as the experience of women; the criteria used in making value judgments should be the criteria of liberation and humanization.

77

Within Christianity, this issue appeared early in the feminist theological discussions, and it continues to be important.[26] Some women see the Christian traditions as thoroughly patriarchal and beyond reform. Others see hope in seeking out the more liberating streams, or in separating biblical traditions from the later traditions, which often added layers of patriarchal interpretation. Still others urge that we understand our traditions within their contexts and seek to re-form them in relation to our present contexts.

The questions persist: *What sources will be taken as authoritative and therefore as appropriate content for religious education? How will these relate to women's growing consciousness of oppression in their experience?* These are not new issues. The tension between historical traditions and contemporary experience has long affected educational practice. Highlighted here, however, is the tension between *patriarchal* traditions and *women's present experience.* If historical tradition and contemporary experience are always interconnected, then the re-formation of one will always affect the other, and each needs to be considered in relation to the other.[27]

These new questions raise some challenges for Christian religious education. The first challenge is *to seek revelation through various sources,* including historical texts, the natural world, and the experience of contemporary peoples, including the oppressed and forgotten. This recognizes the possibility that God, or truth, may be revealed in many ways. The second challenge is *to seek patriarchal biases in the texts themselves.* And the third challenge is *to seek more inclusive interpretations of historical traditions by bringing new questions to the texts and correcting patriarchal biases in familiar interpretations.* These challenges place before the Christian educator the importance of posing questions and seeking truth. Teaching, from this perspective, has less to do with giving answers, and more to do with asking questions, diving deeply into the realities of God and the world.

Shifting Questions About Leadership

Questions abound in the contemporary world where nations are seeking new leadership patterns, and where churches are doing the same. Questions of leadership are usually tied to questions of ministry: *What is the historical form of the Christian community? What are the traditional orders and structures of leadership, of ministry?* Much effort has been made to understand and maintain those traditional forms and orders, but their adequacy is being questioned. Do they tend to be patriarchal? Do we need to re-form them? Hence, new questions emerge: *What is the mission of the church? How can that mission best be carried forward? What is the nature of leadership? What is the relationship between the leader and the people?* These questions do not displace the historical ones, but bring them into dialogue with future visions and with qualities important to the contemporary community.

In fact, women have been offering new visions for leadership in the Christian community. Rosemary Radford Ruether speaks of ministry as being centered in community, and she proposes that women have a special calling "to be witnesses against dehumanizing patterns of relationship in the church and society, and to raise up the Gospel vision of a new humanity in a new society."[28] Letty Russell has given considerable attention to a ministry of partnership.[29] In both visions, the mission of the church guides the shaping of ministry; we need ministries that will foster the spread of peace and justice. In both visions, persons are together in ministry, organized more as partners than as a hierarchy.

The first challenge for educational ministry is *to see the teaching ministry as a partner to all other forms of ministry in the church*. This suggests that teaching should not be isolated or designated to a few people who are asked to teach and are forgotten. The entire community should see itself as a teaching and learning community. The second challenge is *to seek inclusive participation in church leadership*—to seek, value, and

79

encourage the participation of women and men, of all ages, with varying gifts and abilities. The third challenge is *to make room for people with different leadership styles.* It is extremely important that the educational ministry respond to these two challenges; teaching is an important way to help people identify their gifts and discern their vocation, to equip them for full participation. One last challenge is *to reflect deeply on the meaning of ministry.* Even local churches and parishes need to engage in questions of the ordination of women, the orders of ministry, and the relationship between clergy and laity. If this is not done, the birthing of more just and participatory communities is less likely, and ministry will suffer.

The dreams expressed in this chapter are dreams born of pain and hope, of dangerous memories of oppression and inspiring memories of courageous women and life-giving communities. These dreams are intended to raise new questions for *your* old answers and to stir you to re-form your own visions for educational ministry. All the answers are not here, though these pages may offer some challenges and clues. What is here is an invitation to join the journey of seekers and artists who are trying to respond to the issues raised by women and other forgotten or oppressed peoples. The journey is not likely to lead to a comfortable ending place; we probably will learn, with Nelle Morton, that "the journey is home."[30] We *can* journey together, however, and we can teach and learn so that the world might be made new.

Part II—Church

Foreword

Is education redefined within the life of the Christian community? Does the church provide unique strategies and settings for education because it is the church? Moreover, how does the change that affects the church affect its education? Leonardo Boff, for example, has spoken of the transformation of the church in Latin America—a transformation so significant that it signals a major reformation of the church.[1] In addition, there is a shift from Western European and Northern American hegemony over the church. The fastest growing churches are in what once was termed the Third World. These churches, in particular, seek new strategies for education—strategies that speak at the intersection of tradition and culture.

Anthropologists have argued that religions tend to have common behavioral practices, that is, a *creed* or belief system, a *code* or set of moral practices for living, or a *cult* or set of practices of living and worship.[2] Each religion then has educational practices which emerge from and seek to communicate the creed, code, and cult within a community. In its education, each religion emphasizes certain of these practices. Education emerges as a people seek to communicate their deepest values and to replicate these values and practices in future generations. Education is a concern for the future of a people.

Peter McKenzie, in *The Christians*, has defined the unique set of experiences, concepts, and practices that make up Christianity.[3] To teach Christian faith, one clearly needs to be aware of how Christians

81

define the shape of sacred space and time, the content of sacred words and silence, and the nature of the sacred community. Education in Christianity is shaped by a particular community that is the church, and concomitantly, education shapes the community of faith.

The importance of church and its context to education and theology are examined in the essays by Charles Foster and Fumitaka Matsuoka. They seek to clarify how the church itself, as the primary form of Christian community, shapes the faith and its teaching. Both use the resources of theology and sociology of religion to analyze two different contexts within which the people have defined themselves and their theology. Foster addresses the majority form of church, the voluntary church, that emerged on the American frontier. He clarifies the limits of this approach to the church and advocates that Christian education engage self-reflectively in the quest for creating the church. Matsuoka examines the ethnic church out of his context as a Japanese citizen living in the United States. He illustrates how the church's education provides options for theology and faithfulness that can combat the culture's embedded racism. He describes the way communities engage the religious marginalization of minority persons.

CHAPTER 5

Education in the Quest for Church

Charles R. Foster

In his study of the dialogue of Old Testament scholarship and the discipline of education, Walter Brueggemann reminds us that "every community that wants to last beyond a single generation must concern itself with education."[1] At first glance his statement affirms the writing and work of Christian educators who, for decades, have diligently attended to the task of sustaining churches as communities of faith. With more reflection it reminds us that our educational theories and strategies mean little if we do not have a clear understanding of the community that is the object of our efforts.

Confusion, however, seems to dominate contemporary discussions of community—and therefore, of church. Martin Marty observes *a crisis of morale and mission* in mainline denominations. Wade Clark Roof and William McKinney note the growing *accommodation* of many evangelical and fundamentalist churches to the values and patterns of the dominant culture. Jeffrey Hadden points to a *gathering storm* in the churches, while Peter Berger writes of a sense of *homelessness* that dominates the consciousness of those who live into the end of the century. Robert Worley calls the typical congregation a *gathering of strangers*. Richard Sennett decries the *privatization* of contemporary public life. And Robert Bellah and his colleagues explore the dissipating moral impetus behind the *loss of commitment* in American society.[2]

On a more optimistic note, Avery Dulles observes many ecclesiological types in the church's approach to community.

83

He moves from the historic quest for a normative view of community to a pluralistic quest because he concluded that no one perspective can "do justice" to the variety in the mystery of "church." His proposal, however, is still an attempt to discern some kind of order in the midst of our diverse experiences of Christian community. Peter Hodgson, in contrast, is more intrigued by the newness of views of church in the writings and experience of community among Christians, ranging from feminist theologians to Latin American base communities. For Hodgson, the contemporary confusion over church may be more symptomatic of the possibility of living into a new paradigm, or worldview, which will inform whatever view of church may be emerging out of our quest for community.[3]

In the midst of the contemporary confusion, Christian educators no longer can assume the presence of a common view of community among church members. Neither can we continue to extrapolate educational implications from some widely accepted theological perspective, or from an operative ecclesiology in denominational practice, as we have tended to do in the past. Instead, if we are to engage in the business of "fashioning a people," as Maria Harris has imaged our collective task, we must participate fully in the contemporary quest for the church.[4]

Craig Dykstra took up this challenge for his inaugural address at Princeton Theological Seminary. Specifically he directed his attention to clarifying "what difference it makes that the church does Christian education." He concludes that the church engages in education because it is the community which knows that the "redemptive activity" of God is taking place and invites people into the processes of knowing and responding to that activity.[5]

The quest for church in this essay, however, has a different source. It is grounded in the recognition that any community draws upon a common set of images, metaphors, or principles which inform its visions, structures, and processes. Those images, metaphors, or principles lie behind the community's descriptions of itself. For those of us who identify with the church, they range from the covenantal confederacy of ancient Israel to the monarchical hierarchies of the Davidic kingdom and, later, the Constantinian empire. In North America the dominant principle that informs and transforms our language, doctrines, institutions, and social processes for community is voluntarism. Though rarely identified in discussions of community, its pervasiveness is duly noted by those who have observed our social experience, from Alexis de Toqueville to Robert Bellah.[6]

The story of the gradual dominance of voluntarism as the controlling principle for our expectations of community—even in institutions structured around different communal assumptions—cannot be told in these pages, but it is important to note that its triumph did not come easily. Robert O'Gorman and Fayette Veverka, for example, have traced the story of the creativity of Roman Catholic accommodation through its educational agencies to the commitment in the United States, to such voluntarist values as self-reliance, equality, and responsibility for the common good. In contrast, the story of the pain and possibilities experienced by cultural minority communities in negotiating their cultural assumptions for community with those for the dominant culture through the education of the church and the nation has only begun to be explored.[7]

This essay grows out of my growing concern that we may be experiencing the limits of voluntarism to give form to the way we live and work together. If that is the case the resulting quest for understanding church may not be resolved by reworking familiar ecclesiological categories. It may involve the search for a new ordering principle or principles to give meaning and purpose to inherited theories and theologies of human sociability and to inform the structures and processes of community polities. In our quest we are confronted with the necessity of entering into what Peter Hodgson has called the "thoroughly paradoxical, polar, dialectical, tensive reality" we know as church, to discern whatever "new paradigm" or paradigms may be emerging into consciousness.[8] There are few more effective ways to enter that reality than through the church's education.

Voluntarism in the Forming of Community

In voluntarism, the will, rather than the intellect, is viewed as the primary principle of human association. James Luther Adams, the prominent advocate of an associational view of history, similarly has asserted that "will or creativity is the decisive factor in human nature and that will is the ultimate constituent of reality."[9] From this perspective the impetus to the people's efforts to give order to their common lives is located in the capacity to *choose* with whom to associate, for what purpose, and for how long.

One prominent tenent of voluntarism is freedom of the individual. Another centers on the pluralism of options in life and nature. People have, in other words, not only the capacity but the necessity to choose. In an essay honoring Adams, Max Stackhouse observes that these tenents lead the voluntarist to conceive "of history and human experience in terms of conflict"; they entail struggle and contradiction as people weigh the merits of the options before them. They locate human fulfillment in the decisions and negotiations that effectively enhance the quality or meaning of experience. They shift the source of human tragedy from the inevitable suffering caused by acts of defiance against the harmony of a divinely established order (in more classical conceptions of social life) to the inability to choose among ambiguous alternatives or to negotiate successfully the consequences of whatever choices one makes.[10]

In the United States voluntarism has been significantly shaped by the covenantal theology of New England settlers and the republican polity of those who framed the founding documents of the nation. The authors of *Habits of the Heart* aptly point to John Winthrop, Puritan settler and early governor of Connecticut, and to Thomas Jefferson, writer of the Declaration of Independence and third president, as exemplary figures for these two traditions. In Winthrop's commitment to the biblical view that God initiated human community and that humanity is responsible for the common good of the community, we may discern one of the wellsprings

86

for the view of the role of the individual in society that has dominated North American voluntarism. In Jefferson's convictions that freedom and equality provided the foundation for any enlightened society we may locate the other source. Bellah and his colleagues have called the resulting commitment to individualism the nation's "first language."[11] Any other language for community—whether rooted in biblical monarchicalism, classical Roman Catholic ecclesiology, or Native American identification with the interdependent relationships of nature—has had to contend with this commitment to the primacy of the individual in the forming of communal relations.

Within this tradition the impetus to community belongs to independent, self-reliant, self-directed, free individuals. Communities formed through the mutual consent of such individuals gather together to work toward some common goal, join forces to accomplish some task, advocate some shared cause, or participate together in some activity. The resulting community of voluntarily consenting persons contrasts significantly with those based on an assumption of divine institution, a directive of external authority, or geographical proximity. The depth of that difference caught Richard Rodriguez by surprise when he first encountered, in the writings of the Puritans, their sense of sharing only "the experience of standing alone before God."[12] Voluntary community, in other words, is not distinguished by its continuity through time as much as by the mutuality experienced in meeting around some common concern, task, or mission. The emphasis upon community in "meeting" makes it possible for us to see how the voluntarist can so easily identify community with the vitality of mutual activity or with the subjectivity of intense shared experience.

Few communities work out of purely voluntary assumptions, even in a society where these are commonly assumed. Many Christians in North America continue to hold that Christian community results from God's initiative and is sustained by the responding faithfulness of individual community members to the relationship established in the action of

87

God. Other Christians live in communities with origins rooted in monarchical worldviews that precede the Reformation. Over time, even those in the most voluntary of ecclesial communities develop patterns of loyalty based upon kinship, tradition, precedent, and institutional structures designed to perpetuate the values and privileges of their originating members. And yet the pervasiveness of voluntarism in our society contributes to the fragility of all these communities. With amazing frequency, differences of belief or opinion, expectation, leadership style, program emphasis, or changes in the social or economic situation of the community can shatter community life, distort community purpose, and diminish community continuity. To counter the ease with which the voluntary community may be subverted or destroyed, its members have turned to such activities as the revival, the processes of goal setting and program planning, the granting of rewards and prizes, the use of advertising, and the hiring of consultants to motivate and sustain member interest and involvement.

The very efforts necessary to hold voluntary communities together reveal the limits of their continuing viability. At this point we encounter one of the intriguing paradoxes in the voluntarism that shapes North American expectations of community. Catherine Albanese, in her history of religion in the United States, points out that when it comes to telling the story of the nation's people, the stories of the many are woven into one. Martin Marty similarly describes the interrelationship of churches as a "communion of communions."[13]

This interdependence has given form to a variety of associations and networks that link similar voluntary agencies and communities. It has also contributed to the development of more complex patterns of cooperation, illustrated by the ecologies of agencies that dominated much of nineteenth- and early twentieth-century education. In this instance the patterns of interdependence moved beyond the linking of similar institutions, as in a council of churches, to a social strategy, or ecology, which encompassed the interdependence in ideology and function of schools (for public and religious instruction), churches, colleges, journals, tract societies, libraries, youth organizations, lecture societies, and so forth.[14]

In *Nation with the Soul of a Church*, Sidney Mead has observed that the nation functioned increasingly as the hospitable context for the diversity of its religious communities. That was possible, however, because the people (beginning primarily with the Protestant sector) increasingly identified the nation as the theological context for explicitly diverse Christian communities. To identify the elements in this emerging national ecclesiology, Mead quotes John Smyllie: (1) the nation served as "the primary agent of God's meaningful activity in history" and not the church; (2) the nation took the place of any other community as the source for both personal and corporate identity; (3) the nation assumed the responsibility to be a "community of righteousness" before all the other nations of the world. This theological rationale established a consensual context for national identity and mission which made it possible to disagree on particulars—whether they be based on doctrinal, political, economic, or social values—and agree on general values and ideas. It "set limits on the absolutistic tendencies inherent in every religious sect."[15] And it inhibited the potential for anarchy, rooted in the subjective choices of individuals, by appealing to the common good as a higher goal.

This American commitment to voluntarism "controls" our visions for church and for the education we employ to sustain and renew its communal life. The description of the individualism which distinctively shapes our expectations of voluntary community as the nation's "first language" is apt. As C. Ellis Nelson wrote several years ago, "Language is . . . a reflection of what people in a given culture have come to see and believe about the world in which they live." The implications for Nelson were clear. Language establishes a "perceptive system" so that children will see and hear what they are trained to see and hear. Through patterns of affirmation and negation, it produces in the next generation a conscience that affirms the continuity of the community's values. And it provides structures that develop in people a "self-consciousness," regarding their identities within particular families and primary societies, that will influence their attitudes toward all human relationships and activities.[16] In other words, the language of individualism integral to the voluntary impulse to community creates a particular stance for North Americans in appropriating and renewing certain ideals, values, and practices in the way we view the patterns for our common life. It casts a distinctive angle of vision which shades the way we view the meanings and expectations of the different languages for community found in other cultures and Christian traditions.

The recent assault upon the language of individualism, however, distorts our hearing of the view of community we have inherited. It shatters many of our expectations. And it alters our understanding of the relationship of the individual to the community. It is at this point that we begin to encounter the limits of voluntarism in the contemporary quest for community.

Encountering the Limits of Voluntarism

During the last forty years in North America the viability of voluntarism to order the common life of people has been diminished, if not subverted. This claim runs counter to the upbeat description of the "new voluntarism" that marks the essays in John D. Harmon's *Volunteerism in the Eighties.* Noting a "renaissance of interest in voluntarism in America," Stuart Langton, the author of the first essay, describes the emergence of a voluntary sector with the potential to balance and influence divisions of government and industry. He discovers in the new voluntarism three primary social functions: (1) to speak to conditions of injustice and depersonalization; (2) to supplement or replace many of the services currently being provided through the government; and (3) to model for the other sectors of society an experimental and innovative spirit.[17]

Langton's reading of the contemporary situation is more

sanguine than mine. My view is closer to that depicted in Roof and McKinney's discussion of the impact of what they also call the "new voluntarism" upon American religion. They point out that with the decline of the contextual consensus to provide a common bond, "choice means more than simply having an option among religious alternatives; it involves religion as an option itself." It means that people have the "opportunity to draw selectively off a variety of traditions in the pursuit of the self."[18] Langton apparently did not see the shift of attention to the quest for self-fulfillment as a primary impetus to contemporary voluntary communities. Instead he observes the increasing activism of volunteers. He affirms the strength of this "new voluntarism," albeit within the limits of its social "sector." He does not seem to recognize that this "re-location" of the voluntary community radically alters the place and function of the individual in society and constricts the social roles of churches to the voluntary sector.

The "new voluntarism" is based on changing perspectives on the meaning and function of the individual in society, involving an ideological shift in the way the language of individualism informs contemporary approaches to community. Roof and McKinney identify three implications for the church in this "new individualism."

1. It involves "the recovery of the experiential," in which salvation, for example, is identified with fulfillment, which can be found only "within the self." From this stance, community becomes an association of people who gather to fulfill personal needs, rather than to engage in outwardly directed activities such as the corporate praise of God or the service of the common good.[19]

2. It involves the "emancipation of the self" by eliminating those values and authorities which have ascribed identity to people and called for their loyalty in the past. This shift emphasizes the individual responsibility to find oneself or to create one's own identity. The effect upon the character of contemporary community was identified a number of years ago by William Irwin Thompson, who observed that in Los Angeles, people could move from community to community in

that paradigmatic city of the future, so that their living environment could reflect whatever life-style or value option dominated their current self-understanding or situation. More recently, George De Vos has explored the way certain groups of people alter their social status by redefining their ethnic heritage. In both quests the motivation is often redirected to enhance the sense of self, rather than to serve some common good.[20]

3. Roof and McKinney's third observation points to the tension that exists between individuals and institutions in the "new individualism." Similar observations led Robert Bellah and his colleagues to examine whether commitment is a continuing vital moral force in forming and sustaining the communal life of the nation. That question is relevant to those of us in the church. Contemporary patterns of individuals-in-community have strayed far from the Puritan notion that community begins in people's response to the initiative of God; from the biblical as well as republican notion that the focus of individual attention is upon the public good; and from the conviction that individual initiative is tempered by a commitment to corporate responsibility.

The evidence may be seen in an analysis of Langton's attributes of the "new voluntarism." He correctly identifies the presence of new and vigorous attention to issues of injustice and depersonalization in the advocacy of emerging voluntary groups. But that attention often concentrates upon single issues without an appreciation for the larger social picture. He appropriately describes the increasing efforts of volunteers who have been picking up the slack created by the drastic curtailment of social services during the Reagan administration. However, the possibility of voluntary agencies to handle these issues, in an era when the old ecologies and networks of community agencies have collapsed, is seriously challenged by the extent and complexity of the social policies, economic problems, and spiritual issues related to racism, poverty, corporate greed, homelessness, child abuse, environmental pollution, the care of infants with AIDS or drug addictions, the medical crises of the elderly poor, and the rise in crime and drug abuse; by the reality of diminishing resources to address these issues; and by the lack of communication across these "volunteer" social service agencies. The consequences are at least twofold. Any given act of volunteer service seems arbitrary, and the resulting reorganization of community resources only further isolates those who are impoverished, marginated, or oppressed.

Two dangers for our understanding of church may be found in this "new individualism." The first has to do with a significant shift in the way we understand the relationship of the individual to the community. No longer perceived by many as an agent of community, the individual increasingly approaches that community to meet personal needs and interests. This "socially unsituated" view of self makes it difficult to use traditional theological language in any meaningful way.[21]

Paul's view of the interdependece of community members is undermined, for example, by those who seek out others to fulfill personal needs, those preoccupied by the range of choices before them, or those whose participation is dominated by commitments to "single issues." Moreover, Paul's description of Christ as the head of the church is subverted by people's quest for communities with leaders whose autocratic perspectives provide them with a semblance of purpose and security. Marty's contemporary vision of a "communion of communions" is dissipated by the competition among churches for the attention of potential ecclesial consumers. Perhaps the choice by Arthur G. Powell and his colleagues of "shopping mall," as a metaphor for the contemporary high school, might be just as appropriate in describing the new "full service" congregations which increasingly dominate the religious landscape in many cities.[22]

A second danger may be found in the shifting relationships of congregations to the social context. Again this shift is due in part to the explosion in the diversity of social, economic, political, and religious options available to us. The old consensus has been shattered! Those on the margins of society (initially Catholics, Jews, eastern Europeans; then African

Americans; and more recently, other racial and cultural communities from South and Central America, Asia, and Africa) rightfully demand to participate in the vision and life-style of the nation. The presence of Buddhist, Hindu, and Moslem centers of worship symbolize a radical challenge to the ideological consensus that sustains voluntarism. The fact that the adherents of Transcendental Meditation now exceed Presbyterians, or that Hispanic-American Roman Catholics will soon outnumber those whose heritage may be traced to Ireland or Germany, illustrates the extent to which the influences of dominant groups on the contextual consensus is waning. Indeed, the conclusion of Roof and McKinney, Martin Marty, Parker Palmer, and others is that the old consensus exists only as a minority option. Christians in North America, in other words, now face not only options within the consensus that has sustained their understanding of church as community. We now live in a world in which the voluntary impulse toward community itself is an option.[23]

Education in the Quest for Church

Christianity embodies a distinctive call to community. This summons to relationship has provided both the origins for community and the impetus to its continuity. The church's education serves as a vehicle for its continuing faithfulness to the impulses of that call, in the midst of whatever historical circumstances challenge its future. The continuing liveliness of the church as a community depends significantly upon the effectiveness with which its education extends that call to community, into and through the next generation.

The educational task becomes especially vulnerable to changes in worldview which alter the way communities understand the impetus to the structures and processes that give shape and form to their convictions. That the Judaic and Christian communities have survived the transitions from the "languages" of covenantal confederacy through various forms of hierarchical monarchy to voluntary individualism may witness to the creativity and adaptivity of its education in the past.

A similar challenge now lies before us. In the midst of the contemporary critique and attack upon the adequacy of voluntarism to frame an ecclesial ideal and give structure and process to our understanding of church, the education of the church must continue. But it must continue in such a way as *to contribute to whatever new principle, model, or form will express and embody our longings for the power of the community celebrated by our forbears*. I would suggest two elements in any education focused upon the continuity and renewal of community that may illuminate and assist our contemporary quest for church. They are caught up in the words *participation* and *mediation*.

With insights from depth psychology, anthropology, social systems, and communications theories, we have begun to recognize that the act of participation contains many levels of meaning and experience.[24] Christian-education theorist C. Ellis Nelson was among the first to recognize the significance of this fact. He explored the integral connections between the socialization of persons and the transmission of the tradition which dominated the perceptive system of communities of faith.[25] Since his landmark study *Where Faith Begins*, Christian educators have increasingly focused their attention upon the role of education in "building God's people," "educating in the living Word," "traditioning" a community of faith, and fashioning a people.[26]

Integral to each of these metaphors is an awareness by its proponent of an educational process that emphasizes "the construction of a world, the formation of a system of values and symbols, of oughts and mays, of requirements and permissions, of power configurations." Implicitly, at least, they challenge traditional voluntarist notions of community built through the choices of self-reliant and autonomous individuals. Instead, as Dykstra has observed, this perspective emphasizes that "we come into faith by participating in the faith of the faith community, by knowing in its knowing and responding as a part of its response."[27] Through these

95

processes we are embedded in its identity and vocation, and we become its contemporary expression.

An education for participation in the quest for an emerging ecclesiology will attend to at least three actions. Walter Brueggemann points to the first: "the *binding* of the generations," in which the young are urged "toward a view of reality held by the older generation as definitional" for them.[28] The danger occurs, of course, when the older generation seeks to constrict youth to its view of reality. Perhaps that is why, for Brueggemann, the openness of story rather than the constrictions of catechism or law serves paradigmatically as the primal process for binding the generations.

In its concrete particularity, story avoids the tendency to make universal statements. In the open-endedness of story, it speaks to and through ever changing circumstances. Story evokes the imagination and invites the listener into its possibilities. Story consequently frames and mediates the experience of the listener. That which binds the generations is not a set of propositions or rules, but the commonality of engagement with, in, and by the story.[29] Story, of course, has many forms—narrative, ritual, dance, visual arts. But in all cases, story functions to gather people into a worldview—the mythos and ethos—of a community so that they might live out of that worldview in the extension of the story through their present experience.

Our dilemma is that to bind the generations, we must tell the story in a new time and place. The languages of monarchy and individualism through which the story has become familiar to us are increasingly inadequate for the contemporary communal quest. It is not the first time in our faith heritage that we have had to learn to sing a new song in a strange land or to adjust the ancient story for new circmstances. That educational challenge contributed to the renewal of community identity and vocation during the Exile, in the midst of the diaspora, after Constantine's conversion, following the Reformation and the Council of Trent, and is occurring now in Latin America, Asia, and Africa as local peoples reclaim the intent of stories long cloaked in the language of oppression and margination. The task confronts us as well.

A second educational action for participation in the identity and vocation of church gathers people in the historical reciprocity of appropriating and creating community tradition. The process, which Mary Elizabeth Mullino Moore has called *traditioning*, involves the efforts of the community in preserving the gift of its communal heritage initiated by God in the acts of creation and covenant.[30] It encompasses the efforts of the community to re-form its life in the quest to be faithful to the gift of its heritage, and thereby to incorporate the forms of church that emerge from the dialectic of its quest and its life.

Processes of traditioning embed people in the psychic reservoir of the community's history. They identify a person with a community. They mark a person as a member of the community. They establish the language through which community members order the events of their past and structure their anticipations of the future that is leaning in upon them.

The liveliness of the interplay between the preservation of a community's traditions and the community's appropriation of those traditions is evident in the rituals of the community. The liturgies of worship, the sacramental life of the church, the rituals of congregational fellowship and mission, engage community members in the corporate witness to the significance of its call to community. They evoke identification with that witness. Through ritual, community members suspend the claims of individual preference, knowledge, or approach to life. This pattern of suspension is evident whenever a Christian adherent to a post-Newtonian view of the universe consciously cites the creed of the apostles as the sign and testimony of personal faith—despite an awareness of its pre-Copernican worldview. The crucial activity is not so much comprehension as identification. Through ritual, the community celebrates and renews its corporate identity.

A third action in an education that may facilitate our quest to understand church can center on providing opportunities to

97

practice the life-style of the community.[31] This action is characteristic of the play of children but should be integral to the future steps of anyone who seeks to understand more deeply the experience and meaning of community. Children take on the attitudes and behaviors, the values, convictions, and worldview of significant adults in games of "pretend." The only pretension in their play, however, is the necessary transposition of child and adult roles. Their play is necessary to the continuity of the community, because through it, children begin to develop the competency to fulfill the roles and responsibilities that sustain and enliven the community. In a similar fashion, it is in the repetitive enactment of the actions of Christian community and the trying on of Christian attitudes and perspectives that we begin to discover their potential to give order and meaning to our daily living.

The task of practicing the life-style of Christian community extends into the deliberate instruction of persons in the knowledge, behaviors, and attitudes crucial to the continuity of the community. The act of prayer (public or private), the singing of hymns, the leadership of a committee, acts of compassion toward the hungry or dispossessed, may result from some spontaneous reaction to an event or situation. Their effective contribution to Christian community continuity, however, depends upon the disciplined practice of the perceptions and behaviors which reveal our relationship to the life and work of the Christ who modeled their practice.

The educational activities that contribute to member participation in the collective identity, memory, and vocation of a community both intensify member identification with the community and enhance the capacity of the community to apprehend imaginatively a viable future for itself. These educational activities, often identified with the processes of socialization and enculturation, are vulnerable in communities that do not project a clear identity. For this reason, the call for self-conscious ecclesial communities that stand over against the national consciousness in the work of John Westerhoff or Stanley Hauerwas should not surprise us.[32] They have grasped clearly the necessity for churches to engage in the self-conscious reformulation of their identities through successive generations.

Christian educators generally have been less attentive to the tasks of *reformulating and reconstructing* an understanding of community identity and vocation for the times in which we live. Communities that emphasize educational patterns directed toward the participation of persons in their own vision and life-style can become isolated from the emerging new worlds that will serve as contexts for future community life. The danger in an education for participation lies in its potential domestication of the community's vocation. It is at this point that *education as mediation functions as an important corrective.*

I first encountered the use of mediation as an educational concept in the writing of J. Stanley Glen. Teaching is, for Glen, a mediating activity. As such, it intervenes in the status quo of our knowing and doing. It brings into conscious view the disparity and incongruity betweeen the intent of the gospel and our appropriation of its heritage. The function of an education that mediates the gospel is predominantly hermen-eutical.[33] Its concern is to ensure the continuing relevance of the community's vision and values to new and emerging knowledge, understandings, and practices. It widens our horizons, that we might see beyond the limits of our experience. It insists upon discerning the innovations and discontinuities in our traditions, in the quest for faithfulness to the community's originating call into relationship and social purpose. It often requires us to embrace that which appears to be contrary, in the effort to impose some kind of order upon the confusion and chaos of our situation. It gathers the community into activities that bring ancient teachings and values up-to-date so that they might enliven and empower people in their contemporary situation. This is the contribu-tion of a Second Isaiah in the midst of Exile, of Thomas Aquinas after the "rediscovery" of the philosophy of Aristotle, of the Reformers in the midst of the ferment of the Renaissance, and those today who attempt to discern in our own heritage a new Word for our particular time and place.

The educational activities of mediation in Christian community involve not only our attention to listening for the gospel across the discontinuities of history; they include the community's interactions and negotiations with communities formed and guided by different visions, values, and life-styles. This work is highly political. It encompasses the historic Christian efforts to witness to the gospel, to embody the mission of Christ, and to live in redemptive relationship with all of creation. It involves prophetic discernment and wise judgment. It requires training to hear the voices and claims of the world, to distinguish among the principalities and powers which influence our decisions and actions, to speak and to act out the gospel within the idioms through which it can be heard and seen.

Perhaps there is no dimension in contemporary church life that is more confusing than that found in the efforts of Christians to be relevant to the social, economic, and political issues of our day. The tendency in church education to focus attention upon congregational life and problems of personal coping with life usually diminishes the gospel message and isolates congregations from the needs and forces that exist outside their walls. The relegation of the church to the voluntary sector of society diminishes the context for its mission. The preoccupation with the quest for self-fulfillment subverts its corporate witness. The encounter with the diversity of religious communities reveals the way churches all too often have distorted their witness and mission to enhance their cultural superiority. We are confronted with the necessity of finding new ways to describe the relationship of the church to the world.

Mediational education—whether concerned with the historical or the political relevance of the gospel—concentrates upon the development of skills that make it possible for the church to use the language of faith, appropriated through and heightened by participation in the knowing, believing, and doing of the church. The ability to interpret Scripture; to speak of the gospel (whether to people living out of a worldview that predates Newton or one that postdates

Einstein); to negotiate through the varieties of values and structures to be found in the pluralism of communities that dominates the modern landscape; to witness to the power of the gospel without the pretensions of cultural, social, or theological superiority—all this requires practice in skills appropriate to the task. A mediating education, in other words, ensures that all the people of a community have the opportunity to develop the interpretive and political skills to receive and respond to the gospel, in and through the structures and processes of modern life. This educational action completes the processes of traditioning, which, as Mary Elizabeth Mullino Moore has pointed out, occur in the encounter of the continuities and changes in the relationship of the church community and its worldly context. It moves beyond education to ground the community in its heritage—the task of constructing the community's future.

In the quest for an emerging ecclesiology, the resources for imagining and discerning its possibilities are to be found in the depth and vitality of an education for participation in Christian community. The resources to articulate and construct the community's future are located in an education to develop competency in the skills to mediate its gospel heritage for our ever changing circumstances. No community can survive if the memory of its originating and animating events do not have the power to evoke possibilities for its future. The witness of a community to its heritage is not credible if it is unable to articulate and act upon its core meanings and values at the juncture of its historical and social situation. These two tasks establish the agenda for the education of Christian communities in our current quest to understand church. They create, as well, an environment for the experience of Christian community which tests and refines whatever understanding of church is emerging from our contemporary consciousness.

CHAPTER 6

The Church in a Racial-minority Situation

Fumitaka Matsuoka

The World Council of Churches' International Consultation on Racism and Racial Justice speaks for racial-minority churches in the United States today:

> We have come upon clues and answers [as] colleagues in Christ refusing to become resigned to racism . . . striving to recover land lost to colonial powers and principalities . . . striving to recover trust betrayed in broken treaty after broken treaty . . . striving to remain steadfast in rejecting racism by individuals and institutions . . . colleagues who have called out of us the consciousness that we are connected by our pain as well as by the promise of a reign of love and justice . . . the conviction that we are called to break the silence that keeps our church and cultures captive to the evil of racism.[1]

Experiences of pain and promise are the locus of faith formation for the people of racial-minority churches. The pain of racism and the "promise of a reign of love and justice" speak of our lives. The place of the holy—the place where the divine dwells and is given to the members of the community—is the place where the promise of a reign of love and justice is present and acknowledged. The Christian church embodies this promise in the midst of our ongoing experiences of racism and marginality. The promise is expressed through the trustworthiness of the faith community, the courage the community provides its members in order to live in the midst of an often hostile society, and the willingness of the community to advocate for justice.

Christian education, then, is to attend to the ways these

102

expressions are continually affirmed, strengthened, and handed to succeeding generations. Christian education in a racial-minority church is appropriately stated as a formative experience, whereby the church and its members endeavor to articulate, in light of Christian faith, the issues and meanings that arise out of our own state of marginality.

To be sure, there are profound differences among various racial-minority groups and their churches in their perceptions and articulations of these issues, and in their responses. But a thread of mutual intelligibility and interdependence exists across racial and ethnic boundaries because we are connected by our pain, as well as by the promise. We have a common conviction that people of color need "to break the silence that keeps our churches and cultures captive to the evil of racism; and . . . we need to coalesce in continuing our combat against racism."[2] Racism is too powerful to be challenged singularly. It needs to be faced by linking our efforts into a corporate and comprehensive whole. Moreover, the thread of mutual interdependence and intelligibility is necessary in order for each person and group of color to become aware of who we truly are. Self-understanding is not possible until we recognize our dependence upon the rest of humanity.

The experiences of pain and promise in the fringe existence of racial-minority people gathered as faith community sets the context of Christian education for our churches. Christian education serves as an enculturating function for people of color in their respective communities. Asian/Pacific Islanders, African Americans, Hispanics, and Native Americans often are quite conscious of the communities in which our enculturation takes place. Ethnicity, as Max Weber accurately defines, is really a belief system—not a physical reality—and thus needs to be learned.[3] People of color learn certain expressions, language, and manners which provide us with a particular perspective on life and form each of us into a particular person within a community united by our consciousness of race, ethnicity, and culture. Our awareness of the community to which we belong is quite pronounced because of our fringe existence relative to a dominant group in the society. We are conscious of living under the domination of a "host of lords" who attempt to manage and manipulate our lives. Through the process of enculturation and socialization within our own communities, people of color acquire a particular outlook on life and are able to sustain it within the wider society. The community of faith is indeed the place for such a powerful enculturation for Christians of a racial minority, rooted in the faith tradition that is rearticulated in light of our own uniqueness. Christian education for the churches of racial minorities thus serves a formative function to give our people the skills, insights, words, stories, and rituals we need to live this faith in a society that is often hostile.

Dynamics of Race and Ethnicity in a Racial-minority Church

The reality of American experience is dynamically multiracial. From the first encounters between the English and Native Americans at Jamestown to today's infusion of Hispanics and Asians, the interplay between peoples of differing national origins, religions, and races has shaped the character of our national life. Moreover, the experience of one racial group has had direct consequences for others. In the angrily stated comment of Winthrop Jordan, one sees this reality:

> [It would be] impossible to see clearly what Americans thought of Negroes without ascertaining their almost invariably contrary thoughts concerning Indians: in the settlement of this country the red and black peoples served white men as aids to navigation by which they would find their safe positions as they ventured into America.[4]

The socialization process across racial lines, the social introduction to an aggregate of the people who make up society, is an introduction to a rule-governed milieu of dynamic and most likely asymmetrical societal organization and relationship, and its communication and practices are likewise asymmetrical in nature.

104

The interplay among racial groups, and between them and the dominant Anglo group, has produced certain dynamics that have profoundly impacted the nature of the church in a racial-minority situation. In order to explore this topic we need to focus our attention on a particular racial group. The group chosen here for this task is the Asian-American church, particularly the Chinese-, Japanese-, and Korean-American churches.

The history of Asian-American churches is replete with rich experiences of pain and promise. Some specific issues include the nature of cross-cultural and cross-perspectival contact, patterns of immigration, forces of assimilation and enculturation, and the impact of racism. These issues have left deep imprints upon the character of our churches. Particularly significant are Asian Americans' struggles with the oppressive forces of an ever-present racism, struggles with a tenuous state of changing ethnic identities, and experiences of intercultural and racial liminality. These experiences and forces have shaped the nature of Asian-American churches and also have led the churches to express the meaning of Christian faith in their light.

The Christian church has served as an advocate for justice and equality for Asian Americans in the face of tenacious racism. The story of God's redemptive acts, deliverance, and liberation speak deeply to our own struggles, providing us with hope in the promise of God's reign.

The church is also the place where we collectively search for a freedom and courage to live in the face of our shifting ethnic identities. It is the place where we receive "courage to be" in the midst of ambiguity and instability of what it means to be Asian American. It is the place where we hear the stories of the biblical past, letting the evocative and symbolic power of these stories reshape our understanding and identity.

The church is the place where we share our "in-between" state of life with one another and accept it as a legitimate state of being. The church is a trustworthy oasis in a world that does not understand the peculiarity of our liminal existence. It is the place that captures our yearning to break down the walls of hostility that divide the world. The Christian church is truly the locus of the holy, the place where the promise of God's reign of justice and love dwells.

Racism and Oppression

Racism is, has been, and will continue to be a core value and practice in American culture and life. Racism has been incorrectly diagnosed in a manner which suggests that society is gradually eradicating it. Because of this inaccurate understanding of the nature and inner logic of racism, it is continually perpetuated in both the individual and the institutional life of this society. It is impossible to talk about the life of any racially ethnic people without taking into account this reality. For the racially and ethnically oppressed, racism is real, permanent, and unavoidable. It cannot be dislodged from the psyche by any maneuver. It is an ever-present reality.

What is centrally involved in racism is a difference in perspective toward life. For people of color, the reality of racism informs all activities of life. *It is the fundamental problem from which other issues are perceived.* Unless a basic change in the patterns of human interrelationships takes place, life for people of color cannot be altered. In this sense, racism sets the basic tone of their perspective toward life.

Racism and oppression are subcategories of a culture designed to enhance the well-being and survival of certain members of a society at the expense of other members of that society. An understanding of a society's economic, social, and political context is extremely important in beginning to understand the causes of oppression. A recent rise in anti-Asian violence is but the overt form of deeper problems—for example, the economic disparities that continue, despite the higher than average median family income of Asian Americans.

106

In reality, Asian Americans suffer from a lower per-capita income, underemployment, restriction of occupations, and oppressive conditions for Asian women workers. Asian Americans also suffer from stereotypes in the media and the poor quality of life in our communities. All this belies the image of Asian Americans as the "model minority"—an image that has been propagated in numerous media. Most of these argue that Asians have succeeded and suggest why this is so—because we draw on our cultural values and work hard.

Despite evidence to the contrary, the model-minority myth persists. It seems to be based on the perception that Asian Americans no longer need the public policies that benefit deprived minorities, since they are financially successful; that Asian-American success validates the widely held assumption that the United States is a land of opportunity; and that Asian Americans are indeed responsible for their own failure in this land of opportunity.[5]

The model-minority myth thus functions to preserve the existing system. Furthermore, it shifts the responsibility for failure to Asian Americans, instead of acknowledging the systemic nature of oppression and racism. This results in institutional racism. It is not merely the fact that a particular individual or institution is racist. Rather, the very society in which we live is structured in such a way that people of color are always at the bottom of the societal ladder and the dominant racial group is at the top. This society is structured and formed in such a way that, intended or not, racism persists as a cultural hegemony.

Asian Americans are a people with "pathos"—stories of the deep pain and suffering of racism. Their story is the story of violence, massacre, and internment. It is the story of discriminatory legislation with regard to immigration and migration, taxation, land ownership, and miscegenation. It is the story of violation of basic human and civil rights. It is the story of stereotypes—inscrutable, exotic, lecherous, immoral, as juxtaposed to quiet, enduring, diligent. The Christian church is no less culpable in perpetuating such a myth:

107

> We are deeply pained. The response of the Churches has been deafening silence. Ecumenical bodies have failed to share power and instead model hierarchical, racially exclusive structures rather than structures that point toward the beloved community. There was a day when Church leaders were identified by their stand on issues of racial justice—where are they now![6]

And yet the Christian church is also the place of vision for the promised humanity. It was not necessary for history to happen as it did, nor does it need to continue to happen. The most penetrating way to understand racism is to grasp its absolutizing of prior historical development:

> For our communities' sake the question has to be asked too, for so often there seems to be no broader and deeper goal. Is much of what we are involved in really an attempt to gain access to the system, to get our piece of the 'pie'? In our attempts to overcome racism are we really just seeking to climb up the ladder of an unjust social order? Or do we have an alternative goal? Do our communities have alternate visions?[7]

Several years ago group of Asian-American Christian leaders responded to this challenge through the development of church school curriculum. They chose the Book of Judges to develop, as the basis of the curriculum, a theological piece based explicitly on an Asian-American perspective. This particular text was chosen to help Asian-American Christians understand the immigrant experience and give them theological insight into issues such as assimilation and marginality.[8]

"In those days there was no king in Israel; every man did what was right in his own eyes" (Judg. 21:25 RSV). The meaning of this appears obvious. Anarchy ruled the day and there was turmoil in the land. Each person was on his or her own and there was no social cohesiveness. But even such a conventional reading of the event is still an interpretive statement. The perspective for this particular interpretation was shaped by the Deutronomic reform initiated by Josiah and was part of a call for reform and repentance under an imperial order.

108

These Asian-American pastors went beyond such a conventional reading and interpretation of the passage. They were interested in the stories—of Deborah, Gideon, Jephthah, Samson—themselves. They found that these stories were about people who rebelled against an unjust social order. In the city-state setting of 1200 B.C.E., the masses of people were oppressed. Peasants in a feudal society were exploited. At that particular time, the possibility of revolt was present for a number of reasons. Thus a Hebrew coalition, or community of people, was formed and revolted against the unjust social order in which they lived. They were unsuccessful; nevertheless, they had challenged the prevailing order.

In this light, these pastors saw how this verse could change in meaning: "In those days there were no kings in Israel; every man did what was right in his own eyes." And they said to themselves, "Thank God some people were willing to rebel against an unjust order. People were acting on the basis of their consciences."[9]

The important point for consideration was the equal attention these pastors gave to their Asian-American experiences, in addition to the various Bible study resources they used. They spent an inordinate amount of time and effort discussing where they were today in this society, their own experiences, what was happening in their communities, and how various issues were being interpreted. It was only then that they found themselves reformulating their original questions—from "What does it mean to be in a foreign land; what does it mean to emigrate?" to "What does it mean to come together as a people?" or "Does God take sides?"

What does all this mean for Asian Americans as we move from an Exodus experience to that of a Judge engaged in trying to reshape our world? So rather than issues of assimilation or the question of psychosocial identity, those Asian-American pastors were led to consider the question for social location.

Unveiled here is the historical component which deeply informed the very patterns of injustice and oppression. If the historical issues are not rectified, the patterns will continually reduplicate themselves, for in the received tradition of this society resides the unfolding assumption that freedom is a gift won by the dominant cultural and racial group—one it will bestow only on those it welcomes.

Such a reading of reality is profoundly theological in character. Central to the question of the future of Asian Americans is the question of faith being witnessed in history for Christians. Here the question of racism is inseparably linked to biblical metaphors and images of love, justice, peace, and compassion. The gospel that transcends cultural and historical variations is thus signified in terms of the particular history of Asian Americans. Their faith formation derives to a significant degree from their experience of the pain of racism and their trust in the vision of the promised humanity of the gospel. Asian-American Christians' experience of Christ within our faith community is precisely the setting in which racism is understood in its true nature. Such an experience is also the setting in which an alternate vision of human community is sought, in place of yet another system which would perpetuate the "climbing up the ladder of an unjust social order." "Reestablishing community in situations of suffering" is the substance of faith formation for Asian-American Christians.[10]

"Holy Insecurity" Amid a Thrust Toward Assimilation

We look for security in this life but seldom find it. We are driven to look for meaning regarding our own situation. If we don't find meaning in our present condition, we look for an alternative which has promise of short term satisfaction. Once we begin to look to this relationship to the Ultimate Power, and rearrange our personal and social relationship to that power, we discover tremendous possibilities open to us. We are introduced to real freedom.[11]

The place of Asian-American churches in the denominational and ecumenical scene reflects the very struggle that Asian Americans as a whole are undergoing in North America in our attempt to claim our own identity and integrity, in a society whose very cohesiveness depends upon an assimilation of diverse groups into a particular idea of homogeneity, a worldview developed by a particular group that has assumed the dominant role. We come to realize that courage and freedom to live in the midst of the "Holy Insecurity" is the faith response to the question of our true identity.

The slogan *E Pluribus Unum*—From Many, One—adopted during the mass immigration into the United States in the late nineteenth and early twentieth centuries, intensified patriotic feeling and made a quasi-religion of citizenship. Its underlying assumption was that immigrants would one day constitute a single people, united not only politically but, in a deeper sense, by the ideals and worldview in existence in this nation.

This assumption is reflected in the founding of Asian-American churches on the West Coast. Chinese churches were established to meet the needs of the new immigrants who were culturally, socially, and linguistically isolated from the rest of society. The Presbyterian Board of Foreign Missions began its first mission in 1852, primarily to attend to the sick who came from China aboard "old and rotten ships" with "bad insufficient food given to them on ship board." No sooner had the worship services begun, however, than the church opened "a night school, with which was connected lectures on astronomy, geography, chemistry and other sciences, illustrated by proper apparatus or a magic lantern."[12] A gradual process of assimilation into Anglo-American culture had begun. Missions sponsored by other denominations followed—the Baptist church in Sacramento in 1854, the Episcopal Church in San Francisco between 1855 and 1856, and the Methodist Episcopal Church in San Francisco in 1868. All this was carried out by missionaries who had been in China. The fear of divisiveness, turmoil, and repression was equated by the Protestant churches during that time of Chinese cultural and social isolation from the predominant worldview of Anglo-American society.

Americanization of Asian immigrants was a two-tier

111

process—first political and then cultural. In many cases the people were willing and often eager to comply with this process. Chinese, and particularly Japanese, were susceptible to the cultural change, since the majority of them had chosen to come here. They had uprooted themselves from their native lands. They were often acquiescent, ready to make themselves over, and this was especially true in the area of language. Hard-core ethnicity seldom survived a second generation.

But experiences of Asian-American churches in the last hundred years have revealed that the power of assimilation is woven into the very fabric of this society, that Asian Americans remain marginalized, despite our attempts for empowerment in the spheres of education, economy, and politics. Both externally and internally, we are caught in a web of assimilation and enculturation that will not let us go.

The crisis is deepened by the fact that a greater American identity is problematic; there is no common shared history or religion in which Asian Americans can participate, with the exception perhaps of patriotism or the "civil religion" which is itself tenuous in its ability to unite people in this pluralistic society. Furthermore, Asian Americans are increasingly a product of bicultural, multicultural, and ancestry groups, and the very definition of our ethnicity is changing due to generational differences and the rising rate of interracial marriages.

To compound the complexity of the subject, the arrival of new immigrants from such places as Hong Kong, Korea, Laos, the Philippines, and Vietnam is adding Asian-American groups that did not exist here previously. Some find their identity in national ancestry associations, others in a more inclusive group of Asian Americans, and yet others in bicultural or multicultural relationships and backgrounds. This phenomenon is reflected in a variety of Asian and Asian-American churches that have emerged in recent years. An authentic Asian-American collective identity is much more fragile today than in the past; thus ethnicity among Asians and Asian Americans is a fluid and dynamic matter.

How, then, is the Asian-American search for an identity understood in light of Christian faith? It has, first of all, to do with one's capacity to live in the midst of an ambiguous and fluid state of life. A search for identity, as reflected in the Asian-American communities of faith, has more to do with what it means to live a life that defies definition, rather than with who they are socially, psychologically, or even ethnically. The question of identity is, in fact, a quest for freedom to live in the midst of such ambiguity and instability.

> We, Asians, as a whole, have worked hard in the United States. We've done so in the hopes of achieving a reasonable level of security. We've also discovered that diligence and hard work strike a harmonious chord with the best of the American spirit of industry and achievement.
>
> It is no small truism to say that the sojourner/stranger wants to be acceptable and secure in the land of which he [sic] is a part. The American notion of success and happiness has within it a passion to get rid of suffering. However, as we would avoid suffering and pain, we discover that these are an integral part of life. The anguish of our living becomes more painful when we feel that our struggles and our suffering in life, the very existence which we endure, is meaningless. . . .
>
> It seems . . . that Jesus helps us to realize that God, who is the Creator and Sustainer of life, touches individual lives and leaves a stamp of significance and meaning on us so that we are able to live our life with courage.[13]

Sojourners in Asian-American and Biblical History is a study material conceived in the notion that Asian-American perspectives on Christian faith would prove significant in discerning what it means for Asian Americans to be Christian in today's world. The section titled "Remembering Our Significant History" focuses on this question of identity as a quest for courage and freedom to live in the midst of ambiguity. Such freedom and courage come from an understanding that the experiences of a particular Christian people, Asian Americans, are important for all Christian people.[14]

The lesson begins with the activity "Remembering," in which participants recall one or two persons who personally

113

experienced the process of immigration and who have had a significant influence upon the participants' lives. The activity includes remembering what it was about those persons that impressed the participants most—their characteristics, capacities, capabilities, values. Then the participants are guided to study the historical circumstances that surrounded these persons: Did they contend with anti-Asian sentiment, discriminating legislation, evacuation and detention?

When a scriptural passage, Deuteronomy 26:5-11, is introduced, the objective is not merely to find a commonality between Asian sojourners and Israelite sojourners but, more important, to "live positively as sojourners. . . . Feelings of discomfort or uneasiness in the present society and feelings of not belonging can be channeled towards working for God's purposes, instead of society."[15]

The lesson concludes the participants, individually or together, writing a Haiku poem or prayer to express gratitude for the assurance that God is a God who delivers the people from hostility and the bondage of fear. One such poem reads, "To me, God's love is as a steady rock on sand, Hallowed out for me."

To embrace the ambiguity and instability of ethnic identity is to receive the gift of courage to live in the midst of "Holy Insecurity," the basic incompatibility between the quest for an ethnic identity and the universalism of society, without being bound by its oppressive power. Such a challenge is still a powerful force for the faith formation of Asian-American Christians.

Intercultural and Interracial Liminality, and the Christian Faith

No ground that provides a norm for communication across cultural or ethnic boundaries is independent of the communicative encounter itself. Because of our deep cultural and linguistic roots in the heritage of Asian civilization, Asian Americans are particularly aware of the peculiar state of

114

liminality we encounter again and again in our attempt to communicate. We talk about feeling not quite part of United States society. Liminality is an experience of an in-between state of life, a state where we say, "I'm American," while the people around us are saying, "You are Asian." It is a state in-between thresholds of life, a state that invites both danger and opportunities.

Liminality is experienced by Asian Americans both internally and externally. An inner liminality is the juxtaposition of two or more separate worlds in a person's life. In a racial-minority situation, we learn to function in a certain way within our own ethnic groups, but these worlds cannot be easily translated into the world of the dominant group. Conversely, the world of the dominant group has its own language, culture, and tradition which cannot be readily translated. One lives in the middle, faced with a multiplicity of layers within oneself.

Outer liminality is experienced in encounters between people from different worldviews, cultures, or ethnic groupings. In such an encounter, the domination of one group over another is inevitable and results in various forms of social relationships. Yet one must find a way to relate with others without violating personhood and dignity.

In order for communication to take place between Asian Americans and those outside our own groups, we strive for a mutually constructed ground of experience and understanding, or a sphere of tenuous common sense, which often breaks down, yet needs to be patched up and constantly reexamined. This is so because the community in which Asian Americans find our immediate identity—our family or church, for example—does not necessarily provide readily communicable and transferable values and tools in order to function outside in the wider society. At the same time, our experiences in the wider society, particularly our acquisition of public school and higher education, with its implied worldviews and values, are not necessarily congruent with what formed us in our own ethnic and cultural communities. Asian Americans live within, but at the margins of, at the limen of, our own cultural and linguistic worlds.

Therefore, we Asian Americans find ourselves in a state of liminality, the state where one needs a certain liminal common thread of life, no matter how fragile and tenuous. We have come to acknowledge that however significant our own ethnic and cultural values, we cannot exist independent of the cultural traditions and social interpretation of the wider society, which can provide an arena for either faith or human relationships. Our values and standards need to be placed within a communicative encounter, since they do not possess their own intrinsic power.

The church can be a place where such a fragile but common thread is built and lived out among people with differences. But such a task requires experience of the community's trustworthiness. Chinese- and Korean-American Christians, in particular, are experiencing that challenge to build a liminal thread of commonality. Chinese and Korean groups are composed of people with different time-frames of values and life-styles: a few surviving older immigrants; their American-ized children; continuing waves of new immigrants, including the American-educated; the Chinese- and Korean-educated; and the undereducated and their children, both American-born and immigrants.

Faced with such a human mosaic, Chinese- and Korean-American churches highlight Christian education programs that emphasize reinforcement of young adults and exploration of their needs. Admittedly, liminality is a difficult issue to tackle. An outreach ministry in New York City's Chinatown, CMCC, offers a dynamic center for children, youth, and adults, for the purpose of building a common thread of liminality.[16] In its efforts to join the generations and minister to the Chinese-American community, CMCC is a bustling center of church and community activity. It serves some five to six hundred children, youths, and adults each week in a variety of programs.

Strengthening the family by improving communication is one of the goals toward which CMCC constantly works.

More than one hundred people, ages thirteen to twenty-one, are enrolled in the youth programs. A significant mark of the program planning is the belief that the young people themselves must play an active role in the organization. They must realize that their ideas and talents are essential to the quality and quantity of the programs. The center is a trustworthy place for Chinese-American youth to build a fragile but necessary thread of liminality. Ming Guy Quock, president of the CMCC board, sought to embody Christ's love. Her question was Jesus' question: "Who is my neighbor?" She answered:

> Our neighbors were youngsters, who needed to know the rich heritage and language of their ancestors; they were working parents, who were desperate for a place to send their preschool children; they were new immigrants, young and old, whose inability to speak English was holding them back from achieving their dreams in a new land; and they were teenagers, who had no place to go and nothing to do and who yearned for a way to channel their creative energies.[17]

The CMCC is a place where the generations of Chinese Americans can build a bridge toward one another.

In the midst of Asian Americans' often painful and frustrating experiences of liminality, certain observations and concerns have emerged:

1. Education in this society too often uncritically bears the marks of a socially and culturally dominant group and, to this extent, is not open to the challenges of the cultural and ethnic diversity unmistakenly present. Unless we are aware of the limitations of our own social and cultural location, no liminal world of encounter is possible. Such a world is a shared world, a world that tolerates as proper neither privileged position nor absolute perspective. It is a world that interrupts both certainty and comfort, that goes beyond our awareness of cultural and social differences and creates crucial space in which webs of values and significance are shared.

2. There is a need to create opportunities for asking and hearing questions apart from the preestablished ways operative in this society. It is the existential reality of the dominant groups of North America—the psychic distortion, the general malaise, the breakdown in cultural and moral norms—that makes such asking and hearing difficult, particularly in the ordering of langauge and a norm that revolves around the categories of internal/external differentiation, identity, and preservation. It is this tendency toward detachment from that which is different—toward self-preservation—that makes such asking and hearing problematic.

3. The experience of liminality drives one to strive toward the building of a visible unity in a broken world. To break down the wall of hostility in the increasingly diverse and pluralistic society of North America, it is crucial to foster the building of a fragile yet shared world of liminality. Asian Americans are aware of the traditions formed in the acts of violence that demand the repression of certain themes. And those submerged themes will continue to stalk the tradition. A liminal world requires respect for the emergence of previously repressed themes. One needs to listen to those voices—not because of mere intellectual curiosity, but because to do so means to reaffirm the increasingly liminal nature of human living in today's world, to strive toward a more humane world of interrelatedness among diverse groups of people.

Quest for Peoplehood: A Religious Angst and Faith Quest

It is no accident that in their faith communities, Asian Americans faith view their history as that of sojourners.

> Though arriving at the end of our first century and celebrating it, we still are seekers. . . . But we are not alone, nor helpless. Our fathers crossed over the Pacific for a new life in this land; they were immigrants, away from their homes. They found what the life of sojourners was like, and yet, wherever they

118

were, they were not away from the Lord's field. They met him, and built their churches.[18]

The majority of early Asian immigrants had no intention of becoming permanent residents. Some came to accumulate enough wealth to remedy impoverished home conditions; some came seeking training and skills to take home; still others came as refugees from threatening political situations and planned to return home, once conditions improved. Those Asians maintained a strong primary identification with their homelands. This, along with the obvious cultural and physical differences between Asians and Anglo Americans, was a factor in the creation of ethnic/cultural enclaves. Moreover, forces of racism played a strong hand in generating and maintaining alienation from mainstream American society, thus reinforcing ethnic identity.

These situations have changed somewhat today. More and more Asian Americans have been assimilated and enculturated into the mainstream of society. There are now second, third, fourth, and succeeding generations of Asians, and for them the possibilities of association seem unlimited. Yet in reality, they still choose one from among those many and tend to live, for the most part, within their own group, continuing to experience separation and displacement.

A composite picture will show that Asian-American churches have held two contradictory postures in regard to their own role in society. On the one hand, they have played a critical role in building and sustaining community for their own people. In the church, people found a place to gather, a place to see familiar faces, and a place to partake of a familiar culture. Many church programs were American in form, but indigenized in content. To be sure, churches also functioned to transmute culture. Asian activities were blended with those of the West, and some traditions were given Christian meaning. Then too, churches provided or secured needed social services. It can truthfully be said that all areas of community need, at one time or another, were addressed by the church.

119

On the other hand, churches, as carriers of a particular American religious and cultural tradition, often served to set that tradition against the Asian communities. The style of organization and operation of these churches, informed by social and cultural values of the dominant group, often became confounded with their religious values. To become Christian, to a certain extent, was to become American. And to be American was to be Christian. In this interplay it was assumed that civilization was best reflected in a Christian America, and churches then were viewed by Asian Americans as being a major route and catalyst toward assimilation. But assimilation really meant accommodation and enculturation into the values of the dominant cultural group.

Questions of ethnic identity and peoplehood have arisen out of the profound angst of these experiences. Should ethnicity be a primary factor for identity in this society? Can Asian Americans ignore ethnicity, if in fact that is possible, in order to claim their peoplehood? If this is not possible, what provides their primary identity? What is the relationship between the particularity of being—for instance, Chinese—and the commonality of being Asian American or being a member of this society? How should they reconcile their individual rights to identity with a sense of collective peoplehood? What does it mean to be a community of people? What, in fact, is the glue that holds people together in the midst of the ever-present racism?

The Asian-American search for a response to these questions and others is gradually being transformed from a sociocultural into a *religious and spiritual quest*. It is no longer adequate to talk about their peoplehood only in terms of ethnicity and cultural, social, and historical belonging. Rather, the primary issues of ethnicity are profoundly religious and spiritual in character. Neither is the quest for peoplehood any longer a narcissistic quest. It is highly relational and communal in nature. Thus the quest properly belongs to religious communities, and Asian-American churches thus function as an arena for such a quest.

In this light, Christian education in Asian-American churches is defined as the formative experience of its members, both individually and collectively, in understanding and articulating questions and issues that arise out of our state of marginality in this society, in light of our faith in Christ Jesus.

The setting of Christian education is the dynamic and yet tenuous state of Asian Americans in this society, as lived and reflected in our churches. The context is the juxtaposed struggle with the pain of fringe existence, on the one hand, and trust in the promised humanity of the gospel, on the other. This juxtaposition is expressed in experiences of liminality, a changing state of identities, and the oppressive forces of racism. A crucial task of Christian education for our Asian-American churches is to attend to the way the marks of our faith communities—trustworthiness in search of a common thread of liminality, courage and freedom to live in the midst of the Holy Insecurity, and advocacy for justice in the face of racism—are lived out in faithfulness.

Part III—Person

Foreword

The late nineteenth-century revolution in the understanding of the human being effected a revolution in the understanding of education. Education was no longer conceived as a process of imprinting content, whether cultural or biblical, into an "empty" mind. The person was seen as actively and mutually participating in his or her own learning, in relationship to personal abilities and development. The person was a "developing individual." As such, images of nurture and growth tended to replace those of tradition and content, both in the society and in the church.

In focusing on the person, the church, in particular, became much more sensitive to biblical images of human beings as children of God and members of the household of faith. Though freeing educators to honor the human being and to discover more mutual forms of education that interact with individual development and culture, the focus on the person also tended to imprison church education and theology in developmental psychology. Educators no longer can talk about education without attention to the interaction of tradition, person, and culture; yet because of developmental psychology, several theological definitions of human beings have been ignored.

The issue remains: How is the person to be defined? The theological tradition is filled with attempts to understand humanness, some of which reflect ancient anthropologies. The psychological tradition, in turn, must itself be criticized for the populations it ignored in forming its definitions. Most early studies reflected a middle-class, Western, male bias, and many also ignored the religious dimension.

The task for the church is to discover a theological approach to humanness which creatively and faithfully interacts with the insights of contemporary social and human sciences. Susanne Johnson and Romney Moseley, both trained within the traditions of theology and human sciences, demonstrate the possibilities and limits of these conversations. Johnson expands the contemporary psychological definition of the individual with the insights of Christian spirituality. Moseley begins within the conversation on faith development and probes the assumptions which shape the research. Both suggest a reinterpretation of the person and of education in light of the image of Jesus Christ.

CHAPTER 7

Education in the Image of God

Susanne Johnson

At a "Conference on the Professions" I attended, the theme was "mid-career burnout" in the traditional professions. As we listened to one another's stories, the phenomenon called burnout seemed pervasive, and yet elusive.

From those who live in the very midst of abundance and achievement, we heard a chorus of discontent. Its verses were many: boredom, stress, emptiness, exhaustion, loneliness, dissatisfaction.

What accounts for this? Why is it that so many people today are apt to feel that way, though they live in a good environment, surrounded by success and status? Why would a person whose ambitions and needs are satisfied, who has a good home, a loving spouse and family, a good job, and professional recognition, feel so bad without knowing exactly why? As Walker Percy asks, "Why is the good life which [humans] have achieved in the twentieth century so bad that only news of world catastrophes, assassinations, plane crashes, mass murders, can divert one from the sadness of ordinary mornings?"[1] What is going on? How can we account for the sadness of ordinary mornings?

A prominent attorney described some factors in his profession that seem to contribute to burnout. One becomes valued in that profession, he allowed, only by achieving results, winning cases, earning stupendous fees. If one is to fulfill the dream of someday becoming a partner in a law firm, one must incessantly produce clients, dollars, results.

Someone asked the attorney his thought about the primary

motive today within the legal profession: Is it concern for profit, or for justice? "Profit," he said, adding, "Off the record!"

When everything in life is subordinate to profit, to the "bread" it can earn us, says Dorothee Soelle, then death—by bread alone—lays hold of us in the very midst of life. This is what the Bible fears when it speaks of death: There are worse things than our final departure to the grave. One is the slow, strangling death that surely comes to all who try to live by bread alone. For when we live by bread alone, we die by bread alone. Ordinary mornings, *of course*, become sad. Certainly, we still buy, we sell, we produce, we consume, we work hard, we come and we go, but we do not really *live*. Deep down we are still very hungry and very needy. Not that we immediately notice it, however. Modern culture is engineered to cover up such death.

The alienation the Bible calls death is taught and learned, says Soelle—learned in the workplace, in society, in culture. Deeply embedded within our culture are socially celebrated, socially mediated, and mutually reinforced patterns of death and destruction—for instance, competitiveness, or achievement addiction, or workaholism.

Consumerism is another prime example. Our culture leaves the impression that life is just one big matter of buying and selling. Everything is turned into a purchasable commodity. Absentmindedly, at the same time very self-absorbed, "We push our shopping carts up one aisle and down the other while death and alienation have run of the place."[2] The world for us is nothing but a factory and a supermarket, designed to produce and to consume bread alone, Soelle suggests. Death and alienation are built into the systems and structures of everyday life.

Spiritual existence is a way to transcend, resist, and reform the structures of death. To believe in God is to end our alliance with death.[3] Christian spirituality is an option for life as Jesus taught it; the search for spirituality today can be read as a cry against death and a bid for life. Yet the extent to which our

125

spirituality helps us overcome death is the extent to which we truly understand this thing called spirituality, and ourselves as spiritual beings. Spirituality, too, is taught and learned. But by whom, and where, and how?

Fortunately, Christian churches and seminaries in North America today are struggling to replace spirituality into their self-understanding and daily life. Gustavo Gutierrez recasts an Old Testament image to warn us that if we are to appropriate an authentic spirituality, we must drink from our own well (Prov. 5:15). Spirituality can continue to exist, he suggests, only because (and when!) it sends believers back to their own decisive sources.[4]

In attempting to understand ourselves as spiritual beings, we naturally draw from sources most readily available to us. Spiritual seekers today perhaps have an overabundance of resources from which to choose—classical and contemporary, Eastern and Western, psychological and theological. Partly because the church allowed its own ministry of spiritual guidance (*seelsorge*) to lapse, many Christian believers unfortunately have turned to an uncritical ecclecticism, wed with only tag ends of Christianity.[5]

Drinking from Other Wells

Modern psychology, rather than the Judeo-Christian tradition, is the primary well from which contemporary Americans, including churchgoers, draw in their search for spirituality. Modern psychologies have leapt out of their empirical, scientific base. No longer are they used simply as tools to investigate this or that piece of data. Instead, they now function as quasi-religious visions of who and what we are to become as mature adults.

Taken together, modern psychologies form a basic fund of meanings, myths, and metaphors called psychoculture, to which Americans turn for practical life guidance.[6] Daniel Yankelovich defines psychoculture as a web of meanings popularly held in common by Americans, which focus almost exclusively on inner psychological needs and processes.[7]

126

Don Browning suggests that in the modern psychologies, we tacitly ask ourselves questions about who we should be and what we should do with our lives. We wonder about the kind of world we live in, its ultimate context, and what it is all coming to. Based on the world we see, we ask what we ought to do and be within such a world.[8] These are basic questions about *human becoming*.

As we begin to consider what it means to call ourselves spiritual beings, we need to become aware of how psychoculture already has shaped our self-understanding. What do self-actualization psychologies recommend concerning spirituality? Do they adequately describe the human vocation? What sort of people do they suggest we ought to become?

According to David Norton's analysis, the vision for human becoming implicit within the modern humanistic psychologies, is that of eudaimonism.[9] Within the ancient Greek philosophy of the human person, at birth every individual is perfectible according to an inner *daimon*, or true self. The Greek aphorism "know thyself" is an imperative to discover not one's actual, empirical self but rather an ideal, "real" self, hidden somewhere within. The *daimon* is the self we may become through introspection and self-discipline.

This philosophy is called *ethical egoism*.[10] It does not necessarily mean that one is selfish, but that one assumes that the moral imperative is to fully realize one's potential or supposed *daimon*. Ethically, we *ought* to focus on self-development. We self-actualize by going after what philosophers call nonmoral goods such as self-knowledge, positive attitudes, spontaneity, self-esteem. This philosophy forms the heart of the human potential movement.

In exploring the way this theory implicitly influences our spirituality, there are four areas of concern:

First, within the coinage of psychoculture we seem to associate the drive toward self-actualization with the image of God, imago Dei, in human beings.[11] But is the imago Dei itself really such an individualistic metaphor? In a Christian perspective, does the imago Dei imply an unending escalator

127

to self-actualization and fulfilled potential? Do not the romantic, "blossom" theories of personality development ignore the reality of human sin and self-deception as profound hindrances to Christian growth and change?

Second, on the basis of eudaimonism, we reduce our various commitments, including marriage, religion, politics, and work, to simply means for self-actualization. This implicitly treats society as but a network of arrangements to meet individual self-interests—that is, utilitarian individualism.

Third, much of the contemporary literature subtly collapses God into the inner human psyche. Scott Peck, for instance, suggests outright that "our unconscious is God."[12] Is not Christianity, however, the good news that something decisive has been given to us from outside ourselves?

Fourth, within eudaimonism, to build up the community, everybody must seek his or her own self-actualization first. The extent to which all people achieve it is then the extent to which we arrive at a healthy community. Without lapsing into self-abnegation, in self-giving love, do we not sometimes make costly choices for the sake of another, freely relinquishing the opportunity to realize some of our own given potentials?

In sum, through psychoculture, modern Americans are apprenticed in an ahistorical, atomistic, autonomous model of human becoming.[13] Spirituality is constructed as a psychological issue alone, focused on inner processes and needs, as if today's people clearly know their deepest needs. This brand of spirituality assumes the sufficiency and primacy of the inner life, apart from any recognizable tradition or historical community. We are led to believe that spiritual guidance can be purchased in the marketplace, in the form of psychotherapy. We are told that life energy is mainly to be devoted to our own self-enhancement. The impression is given that freedom lies in self-knowledge, in a minute understanding of our own inner machinery. Dangled before us is an extremely voluntaristic view of the church, as though it is simply an arrangement for the individual spiritual quest. Spiritual disciplines are packaged and sold as technologies for self-discovery and self-actualization. This is the well from which many Americans draw their spiritual self-understanding.

Drinking from Our Own Wells

When we have a genuine spirituality, we are possessed by a Story true to the character of reality. Further, we are rooted in a community borne by that Story. As the church, we tell the Story of God's work through Israel and in Jesus Christ because we believe "on good authority" that it is a truthful account of human existence. Christian Story counters the distorted self-understandings imposed upon us by culture. When we draw from it, we are given a radically new way of experiencing ourselves and the world.

The biblical story portrays us as spiritual beings, but nowhere is spirituality defined for us. We are only told stories of God and shown who and what people become when they undergo God's reality in their lives.

In the Beginning . . .

"God formed a human creature of dust from the ground, and breathed into the creature's nostrils the breath of life; and the human creature became a living being." (Gen. 2:7 ILL, Year A)

We are created beings. According to the Story, we are beings animated by the breath or Spirit of God. The Old Testament portrays the human being as a living *nephesh* (Gen. 2:7), an animated whole person. The Hebrew *nephesh*, equivalent to the Greek psyche (cf. Matt. 16:26; Mark 8:36), may mean *breath*, but also may be rendered simply as *person* or *self*. We are persons created in the image and likeness of our Creator, the imago Dei of our Creator (Gen. 1:27), and in that, we image a creative, free, whole person.

We are rooted in bodily, historical existence. Whereas Greek philosophy taught a body-soul dualism in which material existence is evil and mortal, the soul good and immortal, in

129

Hebrew thought there is no dichotomy. For the Hebrew, the soul is an alive body. We are bodies, we have bodies, and that is good. Thus when the apostle Paul referred to those who live "in the flesh," he was not denigrating material existence, the body or sexuality. He was referring to human life as it refuses and resists the Spirit of God. To live "in the flesh" is to live on as if God does not exist. To live "in the Spirit" is to posture our whole lives in the presence of the Everlasting.

We are given a share in who God is and what God does! The imago Dei affirm our share, corporately and individually, in God's triune reality. We are grounded in it, we share in it, we belong to it, we participate in it. As spiritual beings, we are endowed with the self-transcendent capacity to recognize and participate in God's creative and redemptive work. Theological symbols for this activity include the Kingdom of God, the Realm of God, the Household of God, the New Creation, the New Humanity.

We exist in relationship to all that God creates and loves because we are created in the image of a *triune* God. From the outset, the church has used the symbol of the Trinity to show us how God's own self—three Persons in one—is expressed in terms of community and relatedness. The Trinity can be seen as a connected, inclusive, relational metaphor. Through it, we see the possibility of relating to others expressly for their well-being. When God breathed life into us, God breathed us into community and connectedness. The imago Dei, therefore, is a communal, relational metaphor, not an individualistic one. Because they participate in the imago Dei, all other human beings are seen as our neighbors, our fellow creatures, our fellow sufferers.

After the Fall . . .

Whereas we were created for community with one another and our Creator, that is not what we experience. We do not always, or even very often, live for one another and for God. Our fundamental sin, according to Scripture, is the delusion that we can prosper without God (cf. Rom. 1:28; Rev. 3:17). We forget that we are God's own creatures. Rather than receiving our daily bread from God, we attempt to secure it by means of things in our environment (i.e., idolatry). Acquiring, owning, and consuming become much more important to us than being, and relating, and loving.

When we live as though we must (or can) generate our own self-worth and security, we begin to regard others as potential threats to it. Or we simply use people as objects in order to get what we want. Yet when we treat others as enemies, or threats, or objects, we inevitably become manipulative, mistrustful, deceptive, competitive, callous, calculating. Is this not what it means to live "in the flesh" (Gal. 5:19-21)?

This condition of human existence is what the biblical story means when it uses the symbol of the Fall, whose wages really are death. Death is what happens within us, says Soelle, "when we look upon others not as gift, blessing, or stimulus but as threat, danger, competition."[14]

When we live by bread alone, we forfeit the one thing upon which our lives most fully depend—the giving and receiving of unconditional love.[15] Each of us longs for ascriptive, not achieved, worth; this is one of the deepest aspects of our spiritual hunger. We yearn to be loved simply for who we are, with all our fears, failures, and faults. We do not want to earn, achieve, or purchase our sense of self-value.

The New Covenant

Jesus organized resistance against death by bread alone, says Soelle. We see his conquest of death in the resurrection, and also in the stories connected with his life.[16] God in Jesus Christ, and in the Spirit, sides with life against death. Death, in all its ugly faces, is being undone by God (I Cor. 15:24-26).

God is on the side of life! It is God through Christ who delivers us from entombment in competitiveness, hostility, prejudice, self-absorption, indifference, deceit, and despair. Only God's infinite love can free us from our self-captivity, free us for our fellow creatures. God's grace redeems our mutual

131

failings of one another. It is God alone who slices through our patterns of self-destruction and death.

Through Christ, therefore, God frees us from the need to secure our own significance, especially against physical death.[17] We believe that our significance, our self-value, and our everlasting home rest in God alone. Our lives are secured *by* and *in* the eternal presence of God. Whether we live or die, we belong to God (Rom. 14:8). It is only in our acceptance of death that we truly are freed to live. To become a Christian is to pass from the fear of death into life. First we die, then we are born![18]

Our Story is about fall, bondage, slavery, oppression, exile, alienation, and estrangement, the symbols of disrupted community and disrupted relationships. They signal the death of spiritual existence.

But our Story is also about exodus, promised land, covenant, advent, resurrection, and new life, about community forfeited and redeemed. It is about death and rebirth.

Formed, Not Developed!

"Do not be conformed to this world but be transformed by the renewal of your mind, that you may prove what is the will of God." (Rom. 12:2*a*)

A Christian is one who lives under the promise of redeemed existence. This life includes real changes in the individual believer as well as in human community. The process of Christian change and growth involves a creative tension between God's objective actions on our behalf and the subjective impact, or effect, of those actions upon us. The Reformers used the language of justification and sanctification for this dialectic.

For several decades religious education has relied—over-relied?—upon developmental psychology as a way to articulate the doctrine of sanctification and its corresponding effects upon the individual throughout the human life cycle. In addition to the humanistic theories, educators have used Erik

132

Erikson's eight psychosocial stages to understand the human journey to wholeness and maturity. Of increasing influence during the past decade has been the structural-developmental theory of faith articulated by James Fowler, in which faith develops through a series of six successive stages. Each stage represents an increasingly complex and differentiated way of structuring the world, following a preset, invariant, hierarchical pattern. Fowler contends that a faith stage is a formal category—that is, free of any particular content. Unfortunately, we have become preoccupied with *how* faith structures work to the neglect of *what* is being structured.

Tertullian was right—Christians are made, not born. But they do not simply develop in a linear fashion. Christian spiritual formation is much messier than that; it is full of detours and deserts, regression and progression, dark nights and surprising rebirths. Christian formation is not best mapped by structurally invariant, linear, and hierarchical stages. Rather, it has to do with how, over a lifetime, the *total self* acquires its basic identity, decisive content, and dominant orientation under the impact of the Christian Story.

Christian educators talk about personality growth and change as "ages and stages." A more fruitful way to understand the human being in terms of sanctification is through formation of *character*. Fundamentally, our character is our self-identity. It is the content of who we are as unique persons.

Speaking of character is a way to talk about the paradoxical, persistent sense of sameness, even in the very midst of radical change, growth, and eventual decline. A basic sense of self perdures throughout the many ways we recount "ages and stages," and that self essentially is our character. For instance, D. Campbell Wyckoff notices this in reflecting on his own life:

> When I was a child, I knew myself more as a self than as what they were describing as a child. When I was an adolescent, the same thing applied—I knew myself more as a self than as what they were describing as an adolescent. . . . My experience is that it is the same self—grown, expanded, enriched, altered in some respects, and subject to decline—but essentially the same.[19]

133

To have our character formed distinctly as a Christian believer, Stanley Hauwerwas notes, is basically no different from having our character formed as a nonbeliever. The difference does not lie in the dynamics, the structures, or the processes of formation. It lies, rather, in the consequent *shape* of our formation, in the actual orientation we acquire because of the particular content that qualifies us. *Character* refers to the way our self-agency is qualified by holding certain intentions, convictions, and beliefs rather than others. According to Hauerwas, what we believe, think, and feel does not make *some* difference in what we do and who we are—it makes *all* the difference.[20] What we believe about the world is decisive in determining who we are and what we do with ourselves within it.

To acquire Christian character is to intend to see the world, and oneself, and all others, as redeemed and as *being* redeemed by God's work through Israel and in Jesus Christ. It is to see the world in terms of God's inbreaking Realm. We "see" this by having our attention and our discernment trained by the faith community.

Spiritual formation is the formation of Christian character. It is the lifelong process of conforming our lives (our characters) to the Story that Christ lived and continues to live among us. Spiritual formation is seen biblically as being changed into the truly human form revealed in Jesus Christ.

The Christian spiritual life becomes a matter, then, of working out, with the guidance of the faith community, the implications of our primary loyalty to the Realm of God. Spiritual discipline is partly a matter of bringing every aspect of our character into harmony with this basic orientation. Spiritual maturity rests in having brought, or at least in attempting to bring, everything we believe, do, or do not do, under the dominion of our primary loyalty to God's Realm in Jesus Christ.[21]

This dominant orientation toward seeing the world as redeemed in Christ is constantly at stake. We are vulnerable, inconsistent, self-deceptive, and easily manipulated by cultural dictates. Daily, we must make decisions that repudiate the old form of existence and opt instead for the new. This requires ongoing confession and repentance. It also requires that we learn to receive that which we cannot generate for ourselves. Only when rooted in the infinite love and freedom of God are we able to forgive instead of retaliate, love rather than ignore, hope rather than despair, trust in the face of the tragic, treat the enemy as fellow sufferer and the stranger as neighbor. Daily renewal of spent inner resources was part of Paul's understanding of spiritual formation. We must learn to depend upon more than bread alone.

The growth that is implied here cuts across a plane different from the linear hierarchy of structural stages. The language that speaks of *deepening* our character is more adequate to our experience than that of *developing* the ego through invariant stages. Formation will involve a lifelong dynamic of centering, decentering, and recentering ourselves in Christ, so that it is not I, but Christ who dwells at the center of self.

Sanctification, therefore, can be seen as the lifelong formation and transformation of character. To be sanctified is to learn how, more faithfully, more wholeheartedly, more deliberately, to live the Story that Christ lived among us. To this, there is no final stage.

The Context of Spiritual Formation

Burnout is one way secular society refers to its experience of death by bread alone. In the conference mentioned, the professionals eventually turned to the clergy and asked if burnout is a reality in the church as well. Yes, if we want to call it that.

When we are involved in the church, we are caught up together in the same mutually reinforced and socially celebrated patterns of death and self-destruction that lay hold on the wider culture—achievement addiction and competition, racism, sexism, clericalism, classism, and the like. The church, like the rest of the world, has lived and continues to live unredemptively, half-heartedly, sinfully.[22] It too knows the experience of alienation and self-destruction.

135

Yet transformation still happens here! For what is also real and true is that we, as the faith community, are caught up together into profound and powerful patterns of transformation and redemption.

The church is a form of existence where the patterns of self-destruction are being modified and their destructive effects on us transformed.[23] Life in the church is an experience—no matter how limited or partial—of redeemed existence. The church, like the individual believer, is both redeemed and *being* redeemed.

As Edward Farley points out, the Christian faith heralded the appearance in human history of a new form of corporate existence called the ecclesia. *Ecclesia* is actually the recovery of the truly human, interdependent existence for which we were created.[24]

Therefore, it is not only the *context* of spiritual formation; it is the very *shape* of Christian spiritual existence. The ecclesia is called to reflect redeemed existence. Hence, redemption is the renewal of human community as well as the renewal of individual hope, faith, and freedom. The faith community is the decisive environment in which our very existence is altered *toward* redemption.

Participation in the faith community, therefore, is itself a primary, if not *the* primary, means of grace. The ecclesia is built up by all the other means of grace we practice, such as the sacraments of baptism and Eucharist, searching of the Scriptures, prayer, meditation, confession, repentance, works of mercy, and other spiritual disciplines.

As we can see, it is impossible to speak of "the person in spirituality" without also speaking of "the person in community." Christian spirituality is born in the company of God's people. While grace, forgiveness, and agape for one another are radicalized in the church, the decisive thing about the faith community is its startling redefinition of the status of the stranger.[25] The spiritual freedom that is ours is not simply for others already in the church. It is freedom for *all* others.

Christian Education and Christian Formation

Spiritual formation is not something we do in the church apart from, or in addition to, Christian education. In its essence, Christian education implies Christian spiritual formation. Christian education is ministry that helps persons form their self-awareness as beings created in the image of God. We catch people up into who God is and what God does. Such participation is not individualistic or private. It is communal. To become a Christian is to become a member.

It is the church that calls our attention to God's Realm. Yet the church does not exhaust that Realm, does not take it over, and sometimes does not even completely comprehend it!

If in the church we come within sight of the Realm of God and are built into it, then Christian education is ministry that helps the church learn how, more deliberately, more deeply, more appropriately, to initiate believers into the mystery of that Realm. Through initiation into the realm of God, and through ongoing attention to its reality, Christian character is decisively shaped, formed, and deepened over a lifetime.

Christian education consists of three intentional, interrelated, and lifelong processes by which the church itself, as well as the faith of individual Christians, is built up and built into the creative and redemptive activity of God in all creation. (If this does not happen, the church is simply a social gathering, no different from any other sociological entity.) The three organically related processes are worship, praxis, and instruction. Together, they create a rich, multifaceted ecology of spiritual care and Christian formation.

Worship emphasizes the office of spiritual direction, the priestly office of the church. Through worship and reflection on worship, we help believers assimilate the church's liturgy and thereby posture themselves in worship of God as a pervasive style of life. Through the gestures of worship, we engage in certain concrete, communal, personal, and difficult practices necessary for becoming Christian. Traditionally,

137

these were called the means of grace; today, the spiritual disciplines. They lend us the skills we need to make the Christian Story our own story. They help us negotiate all its surprising twists and turns, its how-tos and what-nexts. Through the disciplines, we posture our bodies and our souls rightly to hear, to tell, to do, and to become the Story together.

Praxis emphasizes the prophetic office of the church. It refers to our total complex of action (including reflection on action), along with, and on behalf of, the dispossessed, the needy, the powerless. Praxis means we actively seek to place ourselves in the company of strangers. Moreover, we address ourselves not only to people, but also to the systems and structures of death, whatever and wherever they may be. It is only when we are in the company of those whose needs are so plainly visible that our own need for more than bread alone is exposed. Through the dynamics of praxis, we teach believers how to read, resist, and reform the powers and principalities (Eph. 6:12) in the dominant culture. These are the forces that dehumanize us and deny our status as creatures in the image of God.

Instruction emphasizes the teaching office of the church. Through instruction, Christian education helps the church retell, rehearse, and reinterpret the Christian Story so that believers may become ever more faithfully conformed to the reality it renders. Instruction is, therefore, more than simple transmission. Through the dynamic, intentional process of teaching and learning that instruction entails, we help the church critically reflect upon and faithfully revise itself. We help it investigage and inquire into what it means to call itself the family of God, the body of Christ, the household of faith, the new covenant.

When seen, therefore, as including worship, praxis, and instruction, the spiritual life will be the heart of Christian educational ministry. Understood as the way we posture ourselves in God's creative and redemptive work in the world, the disciplined spiritual life becomes a dangerous and daring exercise of hope for the New Creation.

Christian education, therefore, is ministry that helps the

church immerse believers in the many forms of spiritual discipline, reflect upon their meaning, and integrate them into their lives as skills or aspects of Christian character. In this respect, Christian education helps believers to:

- *pray*, talking with God about the anguish and delights of our world, with, for, and in the church, and even when alone;
- *meditate*, connecting ourselves with all persons who center their lives in God;
- practice *solitude*, *silence* and *simplicity*, creating the space, inward and outward, where we may wait for God to speak and also listen to one another's hearts;
- *confess*, acknowledging how utterly helpless we are to *make* ourselves acceptable to God, learning instead to allow God's gifts of grace and mercy to work on us;
- *repent*, refusing to create ingrown enclaves that pose as church, to protect male privilege and deny female power; to render invisible the poor and people of color;
- *proclaim* the good news of the Eternal One who leads us out of entombment in hostility, indifference, and self-despair, into the promised land of hope for a fully reconciled creation;
- *praise* God, posturing in heartfelt gratitude for all that God is and does;
- celebrate the *Eucharist*, opening ourselves to more inclusive company around the Table;
- *fast*, remembering those who have no bread;
- *search the Scriptures*, training ourselves in God's Story and learning to look where God's love is looking;
- remember our *baptism*, celebrating our inheritance as daughters and sons of Sarah and Abraham, sisters and brothers of Christ (Mark 3:33-35);
- engage in *service*, learning to identify those who are hungry, not only for food, but for love and care; with the naked, not of clothing only, but of compassion; with the homeless, who lack not only shelter, but others who care; with those in prison, not only in jails, but entombed in

139

self-despair; with the thirsty, not simply for water, but for human justice; with the sick, not in body alone, but the faint-hearted; with those who are strangers, not just to friendship, but power to shape their own existence.[26]

As Aristotle noted, we become builders by building. By the same token, we become Christians by taking up the habits and practices ingredient to the Christian life. Christian education is that dimension of ministry which initiates believers into these practices, the spiritual disciplines. Through them, we dispose ourselves to certain heartfelt affections, virtues, capacities, and competencies which together comprise Christian character.

Spiritual disciplines build up not only the individual believer, but a liberating, inclusive, just church, a church that is fully alive to God's redemptive work in the world. Only in this kind of church can Christian education itself become fully alive.

An Environment for Education

"Lord, teach us to pray" (Luke 11:1b). Spirituality is taught and learned. It is taught and learned in the company of people born by the Christian Story and reborn by water and the Spirit. If a student is ever to learn how to pray, to repent, to serve God in the world, it will depend upon being introduced to people who already know, in at least a rudimentary way, how to go about such things, and who are willing to guide others. Those are the persons we call out from the faith community as teachers.

"Choose this day whom you will serve" (Joshua 24:15). All teachers called out by the church will guide students into the service of one god or another.[27] The question is, which one? Every teaching environment implicitly reflects the god we have chosen to follow. The god we worship determines the kind of community we become, the character we encourage, the classroom politics we practice, the values we cherish, the vision we follow.

140

Some education tacitly models a tyrannical god who lords it over others, who is unmovable and unapproachable and demands blind obeisance. In this environment, students accept the domination and power of the teacher until it is their own turn to exercise power and control. They simply sit passively, memorizing the information doled out, expecting nothing new.

The God of the Christian Scriptures wills our fullest participation in the creative and redemptive process. Does our teaching environment, then, imply a God who invites all creatures into co-creativity, partnership, and participation?

The God who parts the Red Sea is also the One who stoops to wash dirty feet. "For I have given you an example, that you also should do as I have done to you" (John 13:15). In this model, the power and authority of the teacher are based on service, humility, mutuality, compassion, companionship.

To teach, in terms of Christian education, is to invite the learner to share a journey into the Realm of the Everlasting God, as both seek to live out their entire existence there. It is to see and treat the learner as a mutual pilgrim in the journey of redemption and transformation.

To be called out as teacher, one must already have begun to be formed and informed by the Story. Teachers are those who, simply by virtue of having been at it a bit longer, are more familiar with the surprising twists and turns, the detours and deserts of the journey. They have learned how to find or cut pathways of participation and to be a compassionate companion along the Way. Teachers must know their own spiritual hunger and their own need for more than bread alone. Only as teachers consciously run the false gods out of the room, can the students' deepest, most authentic spiritual hungers be exposed and allowed to help shape the teaching/learning environment.

Fundamentally, it is the matrix of the interpersonal that mediates God's transformation and redemption of human existence. At the heart of Christian teaching is the *presence* of one human being with another. Being present with another can take many forms. It means to notice and value the

141

presence of another, but most of all, it means to be *with* another, to claim another's joys and sorrows as our own (Rom. 12:15). It means we lay ourselves open to what others are going through, and go through it with them (Heb. 13:3). It means to care, to be there, to be vulnerable, to be compassionate.

Our presence with one another can take cues from someone like Mother Teresa.[28] She sits there in Calcutta, holding the hand of a man dying with leprosy, as though she were in it *with* him (Heb. 13:3), when she could be in North America, raising funds. She models faithfulness to God's Realm, not effectiveness as measured by cultural standards. This is not to suggest that we should be sloppy and unsophisticated in our Christian witness or that we should withdraw into privatistic pietism. It is to say that we cannot rightly see what God's justice requires of us until we enter the ways the human heart is formed in God's own image. Some of those ways may appear foolish to the world; the service of humble presence is one of those ways.

An environment attuned to God's creative, redemptive, hovering Spirit is shaped by mutuality, humility, and presence between teachers and learners. This kind of teaching environment is not a static thing. It is a moving, fluid, dynamic reality. It emerges, unfolds, veers off course or fades away, needing to be recovered and reformulated. There are times when tyrannical and self-interested gods sit in the classroom. There are times when the teacher does not know an answer and is tempted to bluff; times when the teacher is threatened by a student who challenges an interpretation; times when the teacher uses power to silence students rather than hear them; times when the teacher stages a soliloquy rather than creating a dialogue. In an environment of mutuality and equality, the teacher must choose and rechoose to be an honest, vulnerable, compassionate companion at every step along the Way.

An Ecology for Education

The church both *does* Christian education and *is*, by its very nature, a rich ecology of spiritual guidance and formation. The three dynamic, organically related processes of worship, praxis, and instruction provide the basic settings in Christian education.

Worship as Setting

"Assemble the people, men, women, and little ones, and the sojourner within your towns, that you may hear and learn to fear the Lord your God . . . and that their children, who have not known it, may hear." (Deut. 31:9-13a)

Christian spiritual existence acquires its basic motivation and pattern in the liturgy of the congregation, where we first learn to pray, to meditate, to confess, to repent, to praise and proclaim, to search the Scriptures, to view the stranger as neighbor, to care about others. Christian formation begins as we invite children and other uninitiated persons to worship with us. Participation precedes understanding! First we take part; then we begin to understand.

Worship touches us at deep levels because of its prereflective, experiential, symbolic nature. But because it is an uncritical incorporation of persons into the Story, we need to provide occasions for critical reflection together upon our experiences in worship.

Recently I visited a friend's congregation. I was greeted at the door, given my bulletin, and ushered to a pew by two young girls, no more than third-graders. Now there's a congregation that cares about children! As the service progressed, children served as acolytes; youths helped collect the morning offering; lay people helped lead the liturgy. Everybody was involved. If we could think of worship as a family gathering, rather than as a slick performance, we might move toward broader lay participation. This is essential for spiritual renewal in the congregation.

Instruction as Setting

Many of us Christians, says Roberta Bondi, long to be what we call ourselves; however, we cannot see how to do it.[29] Many

143

persons who have taken on the name Christian have never learned the Story that determines the meaning of the name they bear, nor have they been taught the skills and spiritual disciplines needed to negotiate that Story in their daily existence. This is a primary instructional task.

Christianity is not only a message; it is a particular Story, with particular characters, events, times, and places. The Story is expressed in Scripture and tradition, but also in doctrines, holy artifacts, rituals, creeds, practices of piety, and by many other means.

Instruction is a process of immersing believers in the Story, but the Story is transformative only insofar as believers are helped to rework, retell, and reinterpret their own life stories in light of it. The Story does not just sit there inertly. It qualifies us to feel, to believe, to act in new ways. In order to allow its power to act on us, we need to ask not only, "What past does this recall?" but also, "What future does this open up for us?" Only as we get inside the Story can our own experience contribute to its ongoingness and its faithful, critical revision (i.e., the traditioning process).

Instructional settings can be enriched by paying closer attention to the multiple forms in which the Story comes to us—as parables, poetry, prayers, liturgies, laments, symbols, songs, stories. We can read the Story and we can also dance it, sculpt it, sing it, paint it, role play it, mime it!

Attention to the Story probably will mean that the Bible is at center stage, but the Story includes the church's experience from many times, places, and circumstances. Through investigation, inquiry, and interpretation, we can learn from both the church's faithful *and* its unfaithful responses to the yearnings and needs of people.

Praxis as Setting

"He judged the cause of the poor and needy. . . . Is not this to know me? says the Lord." (Jer. 22:16)

Praxis is our attempt at faithful obedience to the God who identifies with the hungry, homeless, sick, poor, enfeebled, imprisoned, naked, despised. As the church, we are called to *actively* search out strangers, not just stumble across them in a doorway (Matt. 25:31-46). The Lord requires those who would be spiritual to take up the cause of justice.[30]

Often we have the power to protect and shield ourselves from the conditions of suffering to which fellow human beings are condemned. Justice means refusing to do this, however. Christianty demands that we be present with others, that we seek justice for them and practice equality with them. We are not born equal, says Craig Dykstra: "Justice makes us equal."[31]

The best settings for praxis may sometimes be away from the church building. Whereas the church begins with its existing settings, we cannot assume that education is limited to or by such pregivens. Christian education must get out of the church building and into the places where people live and work. The church must search out hidden pockets of need, isolation, loneliness, and hunger within the world, as well as in its own midst.

There are appropriate ways to help all age levels be present with persons who are different and those who are in need. Children could visit a nursing home and get to know an older person, or "adopt" a grandparent. Adolescents can help serve the hungry in soup kitchens and food pantries.

Since character is shaped by and results from our sustained attention to certain things, Christian education will carefully choose experiences, settings, and resources which sensitize believers to their own spiritual hungers and expose them to the needs in the world around them. The character of a congregation is tested by how well it includes persons with infirmaties, retardation, or handicapping conditions—those whose presence might be embarrassing in some way. When we are with them, we are in the presence of Christ.

CHAPTER 8

Education and Human Development in the Likeness of Christ

Romney Moseley

The belief that God, theos, became human, anthropos, in the person of Jesus the Christ is fundamental to Christian theological anthropology. Inspired by this belief, Christians seek to be formed and transformed according to the norms of selfhood set forth in the life and teachings of Jesus Christ. One such norm is the kenosis, or self-emptying, of Christ. This image of God, incarnate in the Christ who triumphed in weakness, ruptures our contemporary fascination with images of a God who became incarnate to empower humans to triumph over adversity and enjoy unlimited success. Such a triumphal image contrasts sharply with the paradoxes and ambiguities of power and powerlessness, fulfillment and emptiness embodied in a kenotic theological anthropology.

The task at hand is to interpret human development in light of this kenotic theological anthropology anchored in the suffering of Christ. It calls for a constant attentiveness to the victims of the inhumanity that human beings inflict upon one another and therefore engenders a "hermeneutics of suspicion" regarding theories of human development which reinforce elitism and progress at the expense of victims of cultural domination and oppression. That God in Christ would suffer for the sake of humanity pushes us to look critically at what it means to be a developing human being and to ask whether theories of human development illumine the nature of the humanity we bring into our relation with Christ and with one another. These are not the usual concerns of developmental psychology.

In recent years Christian educators have relied heavily upon developmental theories for their interpretation of the religious formation of persons and to formulate pedagogical strategies and curriculum. Perhaps the attractiveness of developmental theories lies in the notion of *development* as a root metaphor for the entire trajectory of human existence. With this come neatly ordered stages with a clearly identifiable endpoint. In contrast, theological anthropology is permeated by ambiguity and paradox. Each stage of development is an occasion for discerning the images of God represented by the human. Furthermore, the endpoint of becoming human has an eschatological proviso which relativizes all final stages of development.

It is not surprising, therefore, that Christian educators would be criticized for confusing the goals of the Christian formation of persons with those of psychological theories of human development. One of the strongest voices of dissent against the psychologizing of education is Gabriel Moran:

> If *human development* is a legitimate term at all, it does not belong exclusively to psychologists. Instead of the psychologist peering into the individual psyche to uncover the laws of development, we have today a complex interdisciplinary task of tracking a movement whose laws depend in part on what is outside the organism.[1]

Moran's appeal for a broad-based interdisciplinary approach resonates with Kieran Egan's critique of the limited educational applications of Jean Piaget's claim—that knowledge is *constructed* in the interaction between the genetically given cognitive propensities of the individual, and the data derived from the environment and logically ordered along hierarchical and invariant stages.[2] This constructivist view has been adopted by Lawrence Kohlberg and his associates in their differentiation between cognitive *structures* and *content* issues such as religion and faith.[3]

They also maintain a somewhat arrogant distinction between "hard" and "soft" stages. These latter include Erik Erikson's psychosocial stages of identity formation and James Fowler's stages of faith development, both of which incorpo-

147

rate powerful religious elements. Left to the seekers of "hard" stages, human development would be mapped as a trajectory of stages, with appropriate statistical correlations. Their preoccupation with the empirical validity of stages and their condescension toward religious dimensions provoke my interest in widening the horizons of human development beyond its psychological dimensions.

One of my fundamental assumptions is that the divine-human relationship is a significant dimension of human experience. Thus any theory of human develement that considers this relationship irrelevant is contrary to the interests and objectives of Christian religious education. My concern, therefore, is to examine the images of the divine-human relationship operative in theories of human development.

Theology and Faith Development

Fowler's theory of faith development stands out as one of the most significant contributions to the discourse on theological perspectives on Christian education.[4] This theory occupies a rather ambiguous position since it relies heavily on Piaget, while culling from Erikson's psychosocial theory a sensitivity to the formation of the self, particularly in its religious dimensions. Furthermore, this theory owes its theological foundations to H. Richard Niebuhr's interpretation of faith as a fiduciary relationship to a radically monotheistic center of value and power.[5] Piaget's dualism of structure and content is appropriated as a conceptual tool, by which to separate the psychological operations of meaning-making from their religious content. Thus Fowler defines faith as a process through which persons apprehend their relatedness to a transcendent center or centers of meaning and value. This definition brackets considerations of the object of faith— God—and the contents of faith—images, symbols, and rituals. In so doing, he injects the constructivists' interest in empirical structures into a domain intrinsically permeated by mystery and the metaphysical.

This encroachment of the constructivist hermeneutic of

148

structures and stages into the religious realm has serious implications for theological anthropology. On the one hand, there is an overriding concern to identify structurally ordered patterns in the evolution of the divine-human relationship. While Fowler does not specify the transcendent center of value as the Judeo-Christian God, it is evident that, following H. Richard Niebuhr, all other centers of value—henotheistic or polytheistic—do not sustain an ethic of living in a covenantal relationship with God the Creator, Redeemer, and Judge. Identifying developmental stages in the evolution of this relationship might satisfy the empirical concerns of constructivism, thereby providing educators with a grid for organizing the divine-human relationship on the basis of an individual's cognitive developmental propensities.

On the other hand, cognitive/affective structures and stages tell us very little about the divine-human relationship. A stage of faith is but part of a larger picture, a whole that is not attained even at the last stage. Knowing one's stage of faith is certainly not a prerequisite for growing into a deeper and more meaningful relationship with God. Neither does this information lay the groundwork for a logically planned trajectory of spiritual formation, one that will eventuate in a higher stage of enlightenment, satori, nirvana, beautification, salvation, or the like. Fowler himself acknowledges that the task of differentiating the "structuring power of the *contents* of faith" from the structure of faith becomes increasingly ambiguous as faith development progresses.[6] The structure of a stage of faith is defined empirically on the basis of seven "aspects": form of logic, moral judgment, bounds of awareness, social perspective-taking, world coherence, locus of authority, and symbolic functioning—which together form a coherent whole.

Once adolescence has been reached and the final stage of Piaget's cognitive development (formal operational thinking) has been attained, the focus of the stages of faith shifts toward the formation of persons-in-relation-to the transcendent. As Stuart McLean notes, there is a change from the organic root metaphor of *structure*, which dominates the organization and

149

description of faith development in the years from childhood through late adolescence, to a *covenantal* metaphor, which illumines the transformation of the self in a community of faith.[7] One of the reasons for this shift in focus is the fact that Piaget's genetic psychology is of limited usefulness to a theory primarily concerned with the shaping of persons in relation to the transcendent.

Fowler attempts to get around these limitations, at the same time affirming his allegiance to constructivist empiricism, by maintaining a dual system of cognitive operations—a "logic of rational certainty" and a "logic of conviction."[8] The former is consistent with Piaget; the latter testifies to the mystery of the human capacity for self-transcendence. These two forms of knowing underscore the need for a mutually critical conversation between developmental theories and theological anthropology. To simply apply developmental theory to strategies of Christian education without engaging issues of theological anthropology is not only myopic but dangerous, insofar as it contributes to the heightening of psychological empiricism over theological anthropology.

One way to address this problem is to undertake a careful examination of the function of metaphors in both developmental psychology and theology. In developmental psychology, structures and stages are inferred from observable patterns in the organization of physical reality—for example, concepts of volume, number, time, and so on. Herein lies a dilemma for the theory of faith development. On the one hand, the theory embraces the empiricist position that a stage is a precise and unambiguous concept. On the other hand, a stage is regarded as a product of our capacity to imaginatively compose "some kind of order, unity and coherence in the force fields of our lives."[9]

In other words, a stage is a *paradigm*—that is, "it shows forth a pattern, a coherent nexus of relations, in a simple and straightforward manner." As such, each stage functions "heuristically by revealing the constitutive patterns in more complex aspects of our experience that might otherwise remain recalcitrant, incoherent, or bewildering."[10] Accordingly, Fowler refers to faith as the "structuring of meaning." In short, he proposes that there are "constitutive patterns" in our complex and ambiguous relation to the transcendent and that these patterns are organized as a sequence of developmental stages, from birth through adulthood. The problem is that the term *structure* is ascribed to these constitutive patterns. This locks us into a rigid constructivist empiricism and obscures the metaphoric character of structures and stages.[11]

In the final analysis, Fowler joins Wilfred Cantwell Smith in demythologizing faith. Consequently, we fail to hear the language of the "structuring of meaning" as religious language, metaphorical speech through which images of God are disclosed. This is unfortunate, since the theory of faith development defines the person as being formed and transformed in a triadic relationship of trust and loyalty between self, world, and God. The self is acting and being acted on by the world, interpreting and being interpreted, constructing and being constructed, and called to respond to the sovereignty of God, Redeemer, Creator, and Judge. It is only in the last stage of "universalizing faith" that we are given a clear vision of the human vocation to live covenantally with God and with God's creation. This "ontology of communion" is lost in the organic metaphor of structural stages.[12]

Education and the Religious Imagination

Undoubtedly, Christian religious educators are dedicated to the task of drawing out and cultivating the paradigms by which persons imaginatively shape their relation to God. The discipline of Christian education is not served by those who are merely content with devising strategies for moving persons through plateaus of moral, faith, or spiritual development, which are, in effect, narrowly construed stages of cognitive development whose cross-cultural validity should not be taken for granted.

Furthermore, I assume that Christian religious educators are very concerned with the ethical and theological implica-

151

tions of developmental theories. Developmental psychology maintains certain assumptions about what persons ought to become. These are spelled out in various concepts of maturity and integration: Erikson's final stage of Integrity vs. Despair; Jane Loevinger's Integrated Stage; Kohlberg's Principled Morality; and Fowler's Universalizing Faith.[13] Each theory uses language that expresses a commitment to a specific paradigm of the whole, though the latter is not always expressed in religious language. It would be unrealistic to expect social scientists to indicate the images of the whole that are operative in their theories of human development, but it is the responsibility of Christian educators who use these theories to discern what those images are.

Fortunately, Erikson is not adverse to disclosing his images of the whole. He makes it clear that the healthy personality depends upon the intergenerational transmission of the experience of the "numinous" from the earliest stage of identity formation: "Whosoever says that he [or she] has religion must derive a faith from it which is transmitted to infants in the form of basic trust; whosoever claims that he does not need religion must derive such basic faith from elsewhere."[14]

In a more recent volume, Erikson continues the same theme. He reminds us that the course of healthy identity formation is shaped by "the lifelong power of the first mutual recognition of the newborn and the *primal* (maternal) *other* and its eventual transfer to the *ultimate other* who will 'lift up His countenance upon you and give you peace.' "[15]

Christian religious educators should make explicit this imaginative capacity that guides and shapes human development, a crucial component of which is the belief that the human is created in the image of God and that the exemplar of this incarnation is Jesus Christ. This theological anthropology is a necessary corrective to scientific positivism.

The main problem for religious educators who employ developmental theories in their work is that of preserving the tension between the imaginative capacities of the person and the empirical concerns of developmental psychology. This

152

tension is dramatized in the struggle between metaphors and concepts. Metaphors have an "underlying analogical" grammar; they are used to refer indirectly to something else. As an example of metaphoric speech, a stage of faith is an analogy of a person's commitment to a particular paradigm—that is, to "a normative model of 'what the world is like,' " sometimes "embodied in a canon of scripture and expressed in the life of a religious community."[16]

Armed with a coherent theological anthropology and metaphoric speech, Christian educators can attempt to engage in a mutually critical conversation between developmental psychology and theological anthropology. This conversation may be centered on the conviction that faith is "a form of the imagination." Here Fowler and Green are in agreement. "Imagination is thus the organ of faith: neither its ground, nor its goal or perfection, but rather a penultimate means of grace in a world whose final redemption remains the object of hope."[17]

Through catechesis, Christian education nurtures the religious imagination. In a world of competing and conflicting religious paradigms, pluralism is most desirable—not simply based on persons at different stages of development, but pluralism that accommodates persons at different levels of commitment to different religious paradigms. The proposal that stages should be understood metaphorically is a starting point in this direction.

Paradoxes and Wholes

Driven by the desire to establish empirically validated stages of moral reasoning, Kohlberg regarded the question, Why should persons be moral? as a "metaphorical stage seven."[18] He considered this a metaethical question that did not fit the strict logic of structural stages of moral reasoning. In other words, this question has to do with the justification of moral action. I would say that it is the centerpiece of the moral *imagination*. In typical Kantian fashion, Kohlberg subjugated moral imagination and religious imagination to moral

153

reasoning. Religion and faith are ascribed legitimacy only insofar as they conform to the logic of structuralism. Similarly, the formation of the moral self, such as described by Erikson, is considered secondary to moral reasoning. Accordingly, Kohlberg and his associates have exerted considerable effort to establish institutions intended to facilitate movement to the highest stage of moral reasoning.

Fowler is less ambitious, though individuals and churches have been attracted to the possibility of expediting their development to the highest stage of faith. Their goal certainly is not the formation of a religiously pluralistic society. Encouraged by the lure of individualism, they envision stages of faith as steps in the ladder of privatized religiosity, rather than as windows for widening the horizons of moral and religious transformation, not only of individuals but of communities of faith. What should matter, however, is not the movement of persons through a grid of stages, but the ability of communities of faith to live with the paradoxes and differences that emanate from the religious imagination.

This issue of differences is sharpened by Carol Gilligan's analysis of differences in the psychological development of women and men. Gilligan argues that an ethic of care and responsibility is a dominant paradigm for women, in contrast to the ethic of rights and rules that characterizes the moral development of men. Gilligan is not merely clearing a space for pluralism in the moral arena; she is radically changing the paradigms used to validate developmental theories. Citing Piaget, she notes that the highest stage of development is indeed the zenith maturity; hence, "a change in the definition of maturity does not simply alter the description of the highest stage but recasts the understanding of development, changing the entire account."[19]

Gilligan's attempt to recast developmental psychology by heightening the ethic of care and responsibility in human development discloses the futility of relying on cognitive structures as categories of logic that integrate reason and affect into a "structured whole." Similarly, Fowler tries to avoid worshiping exclusively at the neo-Kantian altar of

154

structuralism by adopting a neo-Hegelian idealist view of the Whole as a "commonwealth of being," interpreted theologically as the "kingdom of God."[20]

In a world fragmented by suffering and meaninglessness, the disclosure of a transcendent Whole is a paradoxical affirmation and the heart of Christian theological anthropology. We live with the paradoxes of brokenness and wholeness, guilt and forgiveness, sin and salvation, the fundamental elements of what Garrett Green calls our *"faithful imagination*—living in conformity to the vision rendered by the Word of God in the Bible."[21]

We should be hard pressed to find theories of human development compatible with the paradoxical elements of Christian theological anthropology. For one thing, developmental theories are closed systems of stages, with a clearly defined end point or *telos*. In contrast, Christian theological anthropology asserts that the person, though created in the image of God, is in the process of becoming what God intended in creation. The reality of sin undercuts any notion of completion and finality in human development. Here again, a stage must be interpreted metaphorically as "is and is not."[22]

Developmental theories are not only closed, they are also steeped in progressivism and optimism. The affinity between faith-development theory and Niebuhr's optimistic reading of creation is well established. Radical monotheistic faith supports values of trust and loyalty not found in henotheistic and polytheisitic faith. In short, Niebuhr lays the theological foundations for leading persons into deepening convenantal relationships with one another and with God, but he does not dwell on the negative dialectic, which pushes against the covenantal ethic. It is the covenantal self, formed and transformed in social solidarity with other selves under the sovereignty of God, that is important.

How then do we form persons into a covenantally grounded community of faith? Is it enough to identify the constitutive patterns or structures operative in the grasping of a transcendent Whole? And, since it is impractical to separate structures from their existential context, what ethos is necessary for the formation of covenantal selfhood? These are difficult questions, but they need to be raised if we are to maintain a mutually critical conversation between theological anthropology and developmental psychology.

Dialectical Psychology and Human Development

Dialectical psychology focuses its attention upon the linkage of persons to their historical context. Klaus Riegel criticizes Piaget's lack of attention to a dialectic beyond the complementary cognitive processes of assimilation and accommodation.[23] In contrast, Riegel extends the concept of development beyond its strictly biological roots as a process of adaptation to the environment and emphasizes constant change over adaptation—specifically, the changing relationship between the changing individual and the changing world. Thus stages of development, especially a final stage, are not identified. Development is viewed as an ongoing process.

Fowler incorporates Riegel's dialectical psychology into his theory of faith development in order to demarcate structural changes in adulthood beyond Piaget's last stage, formal operational logic. Dialectical thinking in Fowler's fifth stage, Conjunctive Faith, facilitates the apprehension of paradox.[24] It is interesting to note that concomitant with this departure from Piagetian constructivism, an explicit covenantal theological anthropology emerges. The dynamics of transformation shift from development to the process of becoming selves before God.

Dialectical psychologists emphasize continuity in the midst of discontinuity, in a number of different arenas of life. The most that can be expected of any person is a synchronization, or balancing, of the self/world relationship. Synchrony is a gathering together of psychological and environmental resources to respond to the crises, contradictions, discontinuities, and doubts in one or more arenas of existence. It does not resolve all these arenas of conflict and is always temporary. It does not carry the connotations of a stage. Its historical medium is the dialectic of the temporary and the eternal.

Life is characterized both by the experience of continuities and discontinuities and by that of numerous progressions—biological, psychological, cultural, sociological. Therefore the "structuring of meaning," faith, also involves a multiplicity of continuities and discontinuities. This is not to affirm chaos and confusion as the essence of dialectic. Rather, it is to suggest that whatever is affirmed as a stable system of coherence or a stage is met by conflict in another arena of existence. The paradox of power and powerlessness remains intact. And so those who are identified as actualizers of "mature faith" at stage six do not escape "immaturity" in some arenas of life. A dialectical psychological view of the life-span is an ethical posture against self-deception. The individual is inextricably connected to a complex of changing relationships and sociopolitical contexts. Attention is directed toward that which does not fit or cohere, that which is left out of the balancing act. These are the painful, tragic, negative experiences, the difficult issues of evil, sin, and alienation. As far as the dialectical psychologists are concerned, transformation is authentic only when one is willing to connect imaginatively the psychological demands of personal transformation to those of the historical and political context in which one lives.

Toward a Kenotic Theological Anthropology

In recent years, the church has been challenged from a number of different geographical centers by the cries of the oppressed. These voices call for changes in theological discourse to accommodate experiences of injustice and oppression of women and nonwhites from the so-called third world. These voices rail against the partialization of the imago Dei by those who are bent on preserving an intransigent patriarchy and a sexist and racist fragmentation of the human community. There are also those countless souls broken by economic and political oppression. An experience common to

157

all these is the history of humanity as the history of suffering. Faced with this reality, Niebuhr advocates a theological anthropology that affirms the inclusiveness of God's creation.

The United States has been indelibly stained by the blood of those who have died for the cause of an inclusive and just society. Guided by this vision of wholeness, the martyrs of human rights held up to the world the terrible contradictions that define the person in American society. But fulfillment of the majority race is still the dominant metaphor of citizenship and selfhood. In a culture that thrives on superficial expressions of community and Christian solidarity which avoid fundamental issues of injustice and oppression, a theological anthropology that emulates triumph over suffering and collapses the tension of paradox will be found rather attractive, as will developmental theories that offer an idealized vision of human fulfillment.

The irony is that this culture will never escape the painful paradoxes that permeate its testimonies of freedom, equality, and receptivity to the poor and oppressed. It cannot escape the pain of God. Developmental theories which reinforce progressivism at the expense of human suffering need to be challenged by a kenotic theological anthropology which reaffirms the pain of God in the person of Jesus Christ. The incarnation is not a speculative unity of God and humanity. On the contrary, to paraphrase Kierkegaard, it is an offense to reason. It is, in the strictest sense, an absolute paradox. It is a synthesis of the temporal and the eternal which is inherently paradoxical and therefore offensive to reason's principle of contradiction as an inviolate rule of logic.

This paradox of the God-man who died on a cross as a common criminal is a part of the Christian faith that has enough staying power to effect the religious transformation of persons and the world. It is a negative dialectic that recapitulates the dangerous memory of Christ's paradoxical exaltation and humiliation. At a time when so much of our human and natural resources is geared toward the technological conquest of the world, it is not fashionable to speak of the paradox of power and powerlessness in the kenosis of Jesus

158

Christ. We would rather be saturated by images that emulate the power and blessings of God; yet we are also faced with the powerlessness of the crucified God. This paradox of Christ's self-exaltation and self-humiliation is poetically expressed by Paul in his letter to the Philippians:

> Have this mind among yourselves, which is yours in Christ Jesus, who, though he was in the form of God did not count equality with God a thing to be grasped, but emptied himself, taking the form of a servant, being born in the likeness of men. And being found in human form he humbled himself and became obedient unto death on a cross. (Phil. 2:5-9)

The kenosis, or self-emptying, of Christ is a root metaphor of Christian theological anthropology that is especially useful to educators whose business is the empowering of persons through the teaching offices of the church. The centrality of this metaphor is beautifully expressed by Maggie Ross: "If God's love were other than kenotic, there would be no Christ, God would have no wounds, and we would have no grounds for faith in transfiguring love."[25]

Admittedly, it is difficult to find evidence of a kenotic theological anthropology in our modern culture of progressivist theories of human development and rampant religious triumphalism. On the one hand, the task of becoming a Christian is easily framed as a psychological or psychosocial journey. On the other hand, this adventure is packaged by religious triumphalists as a formula for moving expeditiously through the myriad centers of power in Christendom. Caught between these two worlds, one might be considered blasphemous, even unpatriotic, to call for the retrieval of a kenotic theological anthropology. And yet, above everything else, Christian religious education pivots upon our "capacity for suffering-with" and "discerning and enabling others' growth into God."[26] There are no easy formulas for living out this vocation.

> We are all vulnerable in a culture where greed perpetuates the illusion of ever-more narrowly focused control, where unen-

lightened self-interest promotes the grandiose delusion of omnipotence to be achieved by means of technology that fails. This dissipated vision can lead only to tyranny. We mistake confusion for paradox.[27]

A kenotic theological anthropology deconstructs constructivism and interrupts progressivism by introducing into our consciousness the need for discerning and tolerating the religious paradox that authenticates our quest to become selves before God. Here, Kierkegaard reminds us that we are edified by the thought that before God we are always in the wrong.[28] In this paradox of sin and forgiveness lies the experience of grace, without which we cannot undertake the arduous demands of suffering, meaninglessness, and despair, nor can we imagine eternal blessedness.

A kenotic theological anthropology is also a stark reminder that human development is unfinished and imperfect. Any final stage that promises an "ontology of communion" or some all-encompassing Whole must be understood eschatologically. As an eschatological statement, the already-but-not-yet Whole cannot be defined simply as the highest stage of achievement or the fulfillment of competencies. Rather, it is a radical paradox of fulfillment and emptiness. Hence, it is inappropriate to identify any person, living or dead, as an actualization of the highest stage of faith, especially when such a person has not been subjected to the same methods of empirical analysis used to validate the progression of structural stages.

Implications for Christian Religious Education

In this pragmatically and teleologically oriented culture, it is very tempting to settle for coherent wholes, structures, and stages. The pragmatic impulse is to focus on something that works, something that produces a coherent system of relations. There is little tolerance for paradox. Paradox is always to be overcome. The root metaphor of selfhood is the integrated self.

In light of the fact that pragmatism has had a decisive influence on the history of Christian education in America, the retrieval of paradox becomes all the more pressing.

In employing structural-developmental theory as a hermeneutic for mapping the transformation of persons, Christian religious educators need to weigh the empirical validity of stages against the imaginative capacities of persons to maintain the inevitable paradoxes of constancy and change, attachment and loss, borne throughout the life history. It is regrettable that in the interest of identifying stages as "structured wholes," these paradoxes might be diagnosed as evidences of psychological dysfunctioning.

Second, while the structuralist view of structure and content is intended to prevent the atomistic organization of experience into random associations (geneticism without structuralism), and the structuring of experience without a developmental trajectory (structuralism without genesis), this dualism encourages educators to ignore the critical political and social institutional structures which relegate a growing mass of humanity to a permanent class of poor, uneducated, and "truly disadvantaged."[29] So-called third-world people are acutely aware of this form of developmentalism. The importance to Christian religious education of a kenotic theological anthropology lies in its attention to those who, by all standards of development, are the powerless and the weak, those whose empowerment does not fit into neat categories of growth and development.

Christian religious educators therefore are challenged to devise curriculum that are consistent with the intellectual capacities of persons and, at the same time, evoke the imaginative character of the gospel. In other words, the changing historical context of the religious imagination is illumined by developmental theory, but this needs to be brought into a mutually critical conversation with the norms of human conduct and maturity revealed in the Bible. It seems to me that such conversation provides a basis for a practical theology of Christian religious education by articulating a theory/praxis relationship which sets forth the theoretical foundations of the psychological

161

formation and transformation of persons, and an emancipatory *praxis* which embodies the values necessary for human becoming—freedom, love, and justice. Both the theoretical assumptions and the emancipatory praxis should inform the methodology and goals of Christian religious education. A kenotic theological anthropology casts the divine-human relationship in terms of the paradox of God's self-emptying and our empowerment to become what God intends us to be. The self imagines its freedom to change and to grow only in relation to the One who gave freely of himself on the cross.

Finally, a kenotic theological anthropology injects into the conversation elements of humility before God and surrender to the transforming power of God that are absent in theories of human development. The ancient experience of waiting patiently for the Lord, which permeated the religious imagination of the psalmists, prophets, and pilgrims, is lost in a world where discernment and contemplation are pushed aside by the need to evaluate persons on the basis of stages of development, where religious pluralism has been replaced by religious privatism; kenosis, by triumphalism.

Somehow, a stage-based curriculum which posits a clearly defined psychological end point needs to be informed by a theological anthropology which acknowledges that "whatever is, *is* only in relationship to God, both in its existence and the possible transformation of that existence toward fuller realization."[30] Specific suggestions for such a curriculum are beyond the scope of this essay. Suffice it to say that psychological and theological hermeneutical tasks should not be confused: One relies on the precision of empirical data; the other, on an eschatological proviso that refuses to subsume to the priorities of empirical science the vision of human becoming revealed through the life, death, and resurrection of Jesus Christ.

Part IV—Mission:
The Church in the World

Foreword

In his classic study *Christ and Culture,* H. Richard Niebuhr described five approaches used by the church to relate to the cultures within which it found itself over the centuries.[1] Niebuhr himself argued for an approach whereby the church was actively engaged in the transformation of culture. In each of his five models, strategies for education also were apparent. For example, in Christ against culture, education was a means of shoring up the wall between the church community and the world. Whether through formal instruction or community socialization, education provided a rationale for the contrast between the church and the world, offered understandings about the way of salvation provided by the church, and defined the way of life expected by the church.

Central to any approach to education is this question: How does the church seek to respond, engage, and shape the world? The church cannot ignore the world; such attempts merely allow the world to continue its own agenda, which, in turn, shapes the living environment for both those in the church and those in the culture.

The church's education, in recent years, has increasingly denied its responsibility to the world. In some cases church leaders have argued that mission and education are two distinct functions. In others, the church has chosen a domestic task—nurturing the household of faith—and thereby ignoring the world. In the voluntary form of church, education has been so focused on membership growth and retention that questions about the way the public has

163

educated those within the church and the way the church should shape the public often are ignored.[2] The reality is that the context within which the church finds itself profoundly shapes the environment for education.

Strategies to understand the church's mission in this context are offered in the following essays. Each is written from a distinct perspective. Choan-Seng Song considers the emerging global dialogue among religions, calling for Christians to redefine religious education in terms that honor pluralism and create linkages among religions. David Merritt's work is focused through his experience as moderator of the Education Working Group of the World Council of Churches. He advances the approach to education for mission called ecumenical learning, arguing for a global education—an approach grounded in religious diversity, in the context and issues of global living.

CHAPTER 9

Christian Education in a World of Religious Pluralism

Choan-Seng Song

The word *pluralism* is much in vogue today. It expresses the social and political realities of the world in which we live. It points to the economic structures of human community. It is indicative of a variety of ideologies that shape people's outlook on life and world. Pluralism has been recognized as an important factor in international political and economic orders, and it has begun to affect the way people treat one another across the boundaries of race, sex, or nationality. The world always has been pluralistic, but it is only now that we have come to terms with it and have attempted to adjust our lives, both private and public. That adjustment is not without pain and agony, but the richness pluralism brings far surpasses the cost. Above all, we have come to realize that we have so much to learn from one another. At last the days of looking at the sky from the bottom of a well, as the Chinese expression puts it, are over.

Christians as members of human community also have adjusted themselves to this world of pluralism. There is, indeed, no choice. But if they have adjusted well to the world of social, political, ideological, and cultural pluralism, they have not, on the whole, come to terms with the world of religious pluralism. If this is true with Christians in the West, it is also the case with most Christians in other parts of the world. In Africa and Asia, religions other than Christianity have had a much longer history; they are dominant social, political, and cultural forces which have shaped the life of the people and the history of the nations.

How can we Christians, then, be engaged in "Christian nurture" in a society nurtured by other religions? How do we understand our faith—not in isolation, but taking into account other religious faiths? What is the primary content of Christian education in a religiously pluralistic situation? How should it enable Christians to develop positive attitudes toward people of other religions? Questions such as these have not been faced, much less answered, by most teachers and leaders in Christian education. But these are real and urgent questions for Christian religious educators, not only in the third world but also in the West, where the presence of Islam or Buddhism, for example, is as real as the presence of Christiantiy. My attempt here is to explore the implications of such questions.

To set the stage of our discussion, let us share a story from a Christian community in India.

> It was Diwali time in India. As dusk began to settle over the village of Dipri in Uttar Pradesh, Victor Pakraj, a Christian pastor from Madras, trudged along the street to his home. His troubled mood was not lightened by the lights 'twinkling merrily from the little clay lamps that decorated most of the homes he passed. In fact, they were part of his problem! He was trying to find an answer for the question Dhuwarak Prasad had asked him the night before. Dhuwarak's voice had been respectful as always, but his eyes held almost a pleading look when he asked, "Why can't we light our house with beautiful little lamps and decorate our rooms at Diwali? Or, if we can't do it at our Hindu festival, could we do it at Christmas time?" . . .
>
> As Diwali approached, the villagers began to decorate their homes and prepare the many lamps they would place around them. They thatched their huts with new grass and bought new clothing to celebrate the festival, but this year, it was a depressing time for the Prasad family. Their own home was dark and undecorated. . . .
>
> Victor Pakraj knew very well how important it was for new converts to make a clean break with Hinduism. If they did not really understand the difference, the Christian community might be absorbed back under the umbrella of Hinduism.

Then its distinctiveness and its evangelical witness would be lost.

On the other hand, Mr. Pakraj also knew that he must help the Prasad family find a way to restore the joy of their salvation. He wondered just how he could do that.[1]

This story is open-ended. Mr. Pakraj wondered just what he could say to twelve-year-old Dhuwarak Prasad. But Christian teachers in India have been wondering about such things ever since Christianity was introduced, and so have Christian pastors and leaders in other countries of Asia.

It Begins with Stories

Christian nurture begins very early in the Christian church. In a church that practices infant baptism, it begins soon after the child is born. The parents, godparents, and members of the congregation solemnly vow to bring up the child in the faith. The whole people of God gathered in the church is engaged in Christian education. Although the debate continues as to whether an infant should be initiated into the faith while it has neither the awareness nor the understanding of what is being done on its behalf, the vow the congregation makes has become a formality rather than a reality.

Formal Christian education begins in Sunday school. In spite of the fact that awareness on the part of some theologians of the importance of stories in Christian theology is a relatively recent phenomenon, storytelling is the time-honored method of Sunday school teaching in most churches in the USA and in Asia and, I am sure, also in other parts of the world. Quite unintentionally, the churches have grasped something fundamental to humanity—that human beings are story-making, story-telling, story-listening beings.

"In the beginning," one could paraphrase the opening verse of John's Gospel, "were stories." Human beings are "story" beings because God is the maker of stories, according to a fascinating Jewish story:

167

When the great Rabbi Israel
Baal Shem-Tov saw misfortune
threatening the Jews it was
his custom to go into a certain
part of the forest to meditate.
There he would light a fire,
say a special prayer, and the
miracle would be accomplished
and the misfortune averted.

Later, when his disciple, the
celebrated Magid of Mezritch,
had occasion, for the same
reason, to intercede with heaven,
he would go to the same
place in the forest and say:
"Master of the Universe, listen!
I do not know how to light the fire,
but I am still able to say the prayer."
and again the miracle would
be accomplished.

Still later, Rabbi Moshe-Leib
of Sasov, in order to save his
people once more, would go into
the forest and say: "I do not know
how to light the fire, I do not
know the prayer, but I know the
place and this must be sufficient."
It was sufficient and the
miracle was accomplished.

Then it fell to Rabbi Israel
of Rizhyn to overcome misfortune.
Sitting in his armchair, his head
in his hands, he spoke to God:
"I am unable to light the fire
and I do not know the prayer;
I cannot even find the place
in the forest. All I can do
is to tell the story, and
this must be sufficient."
And it was sufficient.

> God made [human beings] because
> God loves stories.[2]

God loves stories! And God made human beings to tell stories! That is why creation stories are found not only in our Old Testament but in the scriptures of other religions. Is this not the reason many tribes and peoples have their own stories of the flood? What is history, if not stories—not merely human stories, but stories of God with humanity? What is life, if not stories—stories of human suffering and hope, in which we have glimpses of God's suffering and hope? In religious ceremonies, people tell the stories of their gods with singing, dancing, and drumming.

If God loves stories, we human beings also love stories. As a matter of fact, we cannot do without stories. When stories cease, we will cease to exist, because there will be no more stories to tell. But then God might also cease to be, because the God who loves stories would have lost the very thing God loves. In traditional theology this vital nature of stories is not appreciated. One seldom finds stories in theological textbooks and they have disappeared from theology classrooms. Christian theologians have relinquished the God-given ability to tell stories; the art has been relegated to novelists, artists, or professional storytellers. But storytelling has not left the church entirely. That God-given ability enlivens Sunday school teaching, evangelistic rallies, and sermons by imaginative preachers.

Separation of Theology and Education

We come up, however, with a problem here, and a grave one at that. Since theology has lost interest, considering it beneath its dignity to deal with stories, a divorce has taken place between theology and education. At least this has been the situation in most churches in Asia. Christian education has had either a marginal status within theological curriculum, or separate existence, with a polite but indifferent nod from other disciplines.

And this has resulted in some strange things. To be engaged in theology, it is assumed, is not quite the same as being engaged in education. The task of theology is to explore the origin, development, and formulation of the content of the Christian faith. As to education, the main concern is focused on theories of education, psychology of learning, application of educational skills. This division of labor between theology and education proves detrimental to the growth of Christian people and the Christian church. The result is bad theology and bad education. Is it because of this division that when we speak of theological education, Christian education usually is absent from our reflection and discussion? The fact, however, is that we cannot talk about Christian education without talking about theological education; or about theological education, without Christian education.

The separation has resulted in another serious matter—wrong storytelling. It is bad enough that stories have left theology. Even worse is the way storytelling is done in most churches. On the whole, those stories have not gone beyond the inculcation of "Christian" moral values, almost totally ignoring the social/political and religious/cultural settings of the stories. Stories are used chiefly as means to illustrate the "truth" of the Christian faith. Biblical stories are told to show how God rewards "good" people with good things and "bad" people with bad things. Stories not related to the Bible—particularly those from outside the Christian church—are cited to prove that people who do not believe in Jesus are not really capable of goodness and truth, and therefore are not accepted by God. The integrity of stories, biblical or not, has been breached; theological insights that cry out from stories escape the Christian churches and theologians.

It is true to say that most churches in Asia, and those in the West also, have not found the theological confidence to take seriously the religious and cultural pluralism in which they live. They are not able to heal the alienation which Christian nurture has created in the minds of believers in their early youth—alienation from their own culture and society.

For churches and Christians in this world of pluralism, the time is long overdue for theology and education to overcome the division that has existed. They should join forces and construct education that is theologically informed and theology that is educationally viable in this world of many cultures and religions.

Victory of Good over Evil

In recent years Christians and theologians both in the East and in the West have put enormous emphasis on salvation as liberation from the social, political, and economic forces that oppress people, exploit them, and impoverish them. Christian churches also have been forcefully reminded that they must be liberated from the forces that immobilize them to the status quo. The tide of liberation has engulfed both the oppressive governments and the complacent churches, and there is no turning back.

But Christians and churches have yet to be liberated from their Christian centrism and set free for the world of religious and cultural pluralism. To the question of twelve-year-old Dhuwarak Prasad, "Why can't we light our house with beautiful lamps and decorate our rooms at Diwali?" we must learn to be able to say, "Yes, you can!" This is a very big step for most Christians. How can they be helped to take that step? What could be the new foundation that will enable both Christian education and theological education to address the world of pluralism creatively? These are the basic questions for Christian education and theological education.

In answering these questions, we should be aware that doctrines alienate, while stories unite. In churches and theological schools, we have been taught, and we teach others, to deal with the Christian faith and the faiths of other people with a set of doctrines and propositions. There is, for example, a belief that there is no salvation outside the Christian church. There is also a firm belief that Christians are the chosen people of God, that those outside the church are heading for eternal

171

punishment. Education conducted in churches and theological schools has been based, implicitly or explicitly, on such propositions. There is little wonder that this has been alienating in the world of religious pluralism. It has deeply affected the way Christians look at the life and world outside their own church. It has distorted our relationships with our neighbors. It has done injustice to the stories used in religious instruction.

This is the burden Mr. Pakraj, the pastor in our story, has inherited. He finds no way out of it. What is worse, he does not seem aware that the heart of his problem is this doctrinal burden, this faith proposition, this working hypothesis of his faith. It is something that cannot be negotiated, an absolute that must be the basis of his judgment and decision. Confronted with the celebration of Diwali, a Hindu festival, he cannot go beyond the question posed to him by the boy. The answer must be yes or no. This is a big dilemma. And this pastor, like most Christians and pastors, is inclined to answer in the negative.

But there is something more to Diwali than just lighting beautiful little lamps and decorating one's room. Diwali is a story of the victory of the god Siva over the evil god Narakhaasura. Siva is considered by its followers to be a merciful god, despite its fearsome characteristics. The festival of Diwali has to do with the victory of good over evil. It is the celebration of the triumph of cosmic forces in a struggle against the power of destruction. More important, that victory affects human life. How much people need such celebrations in the harsh realities of life! It is the celebration of life, an affirmation of life, a renewal of life! It gives hope and strength to the people for the year to come.

Is Diwali entirely foreign to the Christian faith? Is it totally alien to the Christian church? Is this story of victory of good over evil, whether of cosmic magnitude, social dimension, or personal realm, utterly unacceptable? Is this not a familiar theme in Christianity? Our creation story in Genesis is a story of God the Creator over the power of chaos and darkness. The

172

story of the Exodus is the story of the triumph of the enslaved Hebrews over their slavemasters. The prophets do not tire of exhorting people to do good and forsake evil. Above all, the cross of Jesus is the supreme symbol of God's victory over the power of evil. Is it not this victory, this triumph, that we Christians pray God to bring about in the world and in our life? Do we not commit ourselves to it through what we say and do?

The more we realize the heart of the story of Diwali, the more we are forced to recognize the deep human struggle we as Christians also share. Hindus and Christians, we are all part of that struggle. It is entirely beside the point to ask whether that struggle conforms with Christian tenets, whether that celebration of a victory of good over evil is doctrinally valid. These are metaphysical questions, remote from the life of people. Jesus himself had little taste for them. His controversies with his opponents revolved precisely around such questions. Once he was asked whether it is allowed to heal someone on the Sabbath. Jesus responded with a counter question: "Suppose you had one sheep, which fell into a ditch on the Sabbath; is there one of you who would not catch hold of it and lift it out?" (Matt. 12:11). The answer is obvious. In Christian education and theological education, we have taught more like Jesus' opponents than like Jesus. Is it, then, not true that doctrines alienate and stories unite?

The Parable of the Arrow

I am reminded of the parable of the arrow in Buddhist scriptures:

> It is as if a man had been wounded by an arrow thickly smeared with poison, and his friends, companions, relatives, and kinsmen were to get a surgeon to heal him, and he were to say, "I will not have this arrow pulled out, until I know by what man I was wounded, whether he is of the warrior caste, or a brahmin, or the agricultural, or the lowest caste." Or if he were to say, "I will not have this arrow pulled out until I know of what name or

family the man is . . . or whether he is tall, or short, or of middle height . . . or whether he is black, or dark, or yellowish . . . or whether he comes from such and such a village, or town, or city . . . whether the bow with which I was wounded was a chāpa or a kondanda . . . whether the bow-string was of swallow-wort, or bamboo-fibre, or sinew, or hemp . . . whether the shaft was from a wild or cultivated plant . . . ." That man would die . . . without knowing all this.[3]

Jesus, who healed the man with a withered arm on the Sabbath, could have told that parable himself. If we Christians are humble enough, we cannot fail to be impressed by Buddha's teaching. What we find in that Buddhist parable is not just pragmatism. It has to do with the life and death of a human being. Where the arrow comes from, what it is made of, how it is shot, are purely academic questions that do more harm than good. But it is with such academic questions that we Christians are preoccupied. We are taught, from our Sunday school days, to ask such questions, and the result is that we miss the substance of the matter, fail to grasp the heart of a story, and perpetuate our distorted perceptions of the way other people live and believe. That is why Pastor Pakraj is preoccupied with the boy's question and completely loses sight of the meaning of Diwali—victory of good over evil.

There must be a fundamental reorientation in our Christian and theological education. We must learn how to penetrate stories to allow them to disclose their "ultimate concerns." We can leave the questions of where the arrow comes from and what it is made of to polemics and theorists. We must deal with a life in a critical condition, a soul in perplexity, a spirit in agony—in short, a human being in search of the meaning and purpose of life, in pursuit of hope and vision in this life and in the life to come. When stories are approached in this way, they yield secrets hidden deeply in human hearts and in human community. With these secrets disclosed, we can set out to reconstruct the Christian faith and redesign our educational programs, both in churches and in seminaries.

In this way, our Christian horizon expands. Our theological perimeters are extended. This can be an enriching experience. We will no longer fancy ourselves to be the center of the world. We are called to be in solidarity with men, women, and children who strive for justice and peace. We will be together with them in search of God's purpose for humanity. We will learn from one another to discover the richness of God's creation. And we will assist one another in mobilizing the spiritual forces against the demonic powers of destruction.

One cannot fail to realize the enormous implications for Christian and theological education. As Christian educators and theological educators, we need to cultivate an artistic sensitivity to penetrate the external world we can see, smell, and touch, and enter the inner world of things and people. We need to acquire the ability of a creative writer to resonate with the genuine hopes and longings in human hearts, and in the heart of this make-believe world. Above all, we must develop a capacity of the spirit to transcend the limitations imposed upon us by our Christian traditions, so that we are able to enter the spiritual world of people of other faiths and religions.

A Clean Break with Hinduism?

Thus a clean break with Hinduism, the concern that preoccupies Mr. Pakraj, is no longer a legitimate concern. It is, in fact, a wrong concern. It deprives Christians of being in touch with the spirituality nurtured by celebration of the victory of good over evil, the conquest of despair, the strengthening of hope for the future. To make a clean break with Hinduism and other religions only forces us back into the "Christian" world that no longer exists, although both Christian education and theological education have been designed and carried out to make Christians do just that.

Statistics show the religious reality of the world in which we live:

175

All Christians together, in 1966, were only 30.9% of the population of the world, after 2,000 years of missionary labors! And now another shock: in the near future, because of demographic explosion, the proportion will not improve but will worsen in favor of the non-Christian majority. Assuming present trends continue, experts predict that if Christians were 34% of the world population in 1900 and 31% in 1955, they could be only 16% in 2000.[4]

To make a clean break with Hinduism in such a world? We Christians, whether in India or elsewhere, will be left behind. To make a clean break with Buddhism? We will be taken less and less seriously by our Buddhist neighbors who make up the majority of people in East Asia. To make a clean break with Islam? We would only alienate ourselves from our Muslim fellow human beings in Indonesia and the Arab world.

To make a clean break with other religions is no longer a viable option for Christians. Demographically, it is impossible. Socially and politically, it is an illusion. Religiously, it is sheer arrogance. But theologically, is it a valid position? If it is, then these other external factors do not really matter. The truth is not necessarily on the side of the majority. But to make a clean break with other religions theologically, in my view, is not a viable position either. God, for one thing, is not the God of Christians alone. God is the God of all humanity. This is what we Christians profess. How can we, then, exclude God from working among other people in different ways, even in ways not compatible with what we believe and the way we live as Christians? God, not we Christians, presides over the complex world of peoples and their religions. This is at once a sober and a liberating thought. Christian education and theological education must be redesigned in relation to this world of religious pluralism.

Restoring the Joy of Salvation

If Mr. Pakraj had followed our reflection based on his story, would he now know what to say to that twelve-year-old boy? Let's hope so.

An episode connected with the destruction of the cities of Sodom and Gomorrah is found in Genesis 18. As the story goes, when Abraham was told about God's intention to destroy the sinful cities, he pleaded with God to spare them if some good people could be found: "Suppose there are fifty good people in the city; wilt thou really sweep it away, and not pardon the place because of the fifty good people?" This was God's reply: "If I find in the city of Sodom fifty good people, I will pardon the whole place for their sake." In this way Abraham's plea and God's reply continue until the number of good people is progressively reduced to ten, and Abraham enters his final plea: "Suppose ten can be found there?" Instead of becoming angry, God answered, "For the sake of the ten I will not destroy it."

This story is suggestive for us in more ways than one. It calls for a fundamental shift in the orientation of Christian nurture in relation to the world around us. Instead of looking for failures, shortcomings, or incompatibilities in other religions, we should explore the happenings that contribute to the reform of a nation and the betterment of a society. Instead of judging all people outside the Christian church as sinners, we should be able to resonate with the longings and despairs deep in their hearts and identify ourselves with those who dedicate their lives in the struggle to bring hope and meaning into their community.

We must learn to listen to the stories of all people. This will inevitably force us to reconstruct our Christian education and theological education on a foundation laid by God the Creator, not by the Christian church as the sole possessor of God's truth. That foundation is built with the realization that God is disclosed not only in the history of Israel and Christianity, but also in the histories of other nations and peoples. That foundation is built by acknowledging that God's saving activity is to be encountered in the lives of people of other religions, as well as in the lives of Christians. This is big leap of faith, which we must take if we are to reconstruct Christian and theological education in the midst of a world of cultural

177

and religious pluralism—a world, after all, created by our God.

I cannot but wonder whether there are other ways to restore the joy of salvation to Christians than the way indicated here. The joy of salvation made possible by excluding ourselves from the world around us is a selfish joy. The joy of salvation gained by denying God's saving activity in other people is a false joy. And the joy of salvation derived from not allowing a celebration of the victory of good over evil is a depressing joy, the kind experienced by Dhuwarak Prasad and his family. And of course, a depressing joy is not a joy at all.

We then return to the question with which we set out to explore Christian education and theological education in the world of religious pluralism: Can a Christian celebrate Diwali? The answer must be Yes. Christians can celebrate it because it is a celebration of the victory of good over evil, because it is an annual renewal of life and community, and because it strengthens people's faith in the ultimate goodness of God's creation and gives them power to live with the adversities and hardships of the present. Would not Christians' celebration of Diwali be also a witness to God, the God of all humanity? Would it not be a testimony to what we Christians hold to be central in our faith, that God loved the world so much that God gave God's only Son? It is on this biblical faith that Christian education and theological education in the world of religious pluralism must be reconstructed, enabling us as Christians and ministers to find the joy of salvation, and work to expand and enrich that joy in the world.

CHAPTER 10

Ecumenical Learning in a Global Perspective

David Merritt

A New Context

As we approach the end of the twentieth century, we live in a different world from that of any other generation. For the first time in the long history of the human race, a global perspective is required for responsible everyday thinking and living.

Television brings into our homes vivid scenes of life in other countries. When unusual tragedy strikes in a distant part of the world, agonized faces and shattered lives appear on screens in our living rooms, and international organizations mobilize relief from across the planet.

Large migration programs in some parts of the world, including the United States, Canada, the United Kingdom, and Australia, have diversified cultures within those countries, resulting not only in an enrichment of the culture, but in increased tensions, and uncertainties of the unfamiliar.

Concern for the preservation of an environment that will sustain life has made us conscious that the human family is more interconnected than we had thought. What happens in the forests of Brazil affects the air we breathe on the other side of the world. An explosion in a nuclear reactor at Chernobyl leaves a trail of destructive fall-out across a large part of the planet. Dumped chemicals seep through the soil and contaminate the drinking water of distant communities. The list could go on. A global perspective has become part of our thinking and everyday life in the late twentieth century.

The knowledge that cultural, racial, and religious differences are characteristic of humankind has never been so widespread—even if the understanding of those differences

179

and positive attitudes toward them are less common. The growth of the ecumenical movement has increased the awareness of many Christians in regard to both the common aspects of Christian experience and the diversity of those practices in churches across the races and cultures of the world.

When we think of our physical environment, we know we must find ways to live with more recognition of interrelationships, or future generations will not be able to live at all. When we think of the transmission of cultural values, we know that the context for that transmission has changed. "Our" values, including our faith and religious traditions, no longer can be seen neatly on their own. Everyone knows there are alternatives, that choice is essential and that the potential for conflict is great.

New Issues for Christian Education

All this has powerful implications for the educational task of communities in general, and of community agencies with strong values in particular. For the churches, new issues are raised for Christian education.

It is remarkable how little attention churches have given to these aspects of Christian education in their basic learning programs. When theology is primarily about past ways of formulating beliefs and, in turn, dominates the content of Christian education, that education responds slowly to new issues that arise from the relation of the church to the contemporary world. And when Christian education focuses primarily on either methodological questions or the transmission of traditional values of a local or national community of faith, the result is the same.[1]

The challenge for those involved in Christian education is not so much the development of a new definition of goals as it is the inclusion of a new pervasive dimension to the educational task. In our day, church education requires a global perspective for the understanding of *church*. And

180

education for living as Christians requires a global perspective for the understanding of persons as part of the one worldwide human family.

While the issues raised affect adults as well as children, there is special poignancy to the questions about the destiny of the next generation. Are our children being educated to be members of the worldwide church of Jesus Christ? Are our children growing up to know themselves as part of one worldwide human family?

Few of today's churches could confidently answer both questions in the affirmative. At best, we are beginning a process of transformation in the understanding of our educational task. However, as global issues increase, it is difficult to escape the conviction that our difficulty in answering such questions necessarily involves some distortion of the Christian gospel and some failure to equip people for discipleship in the contemporary world.

In recent years we have begun to identify the implications for life and education in the baptismal declaration that a baptized person is declared a member of the Holy Catholic Church. There has been strong stimulus to activity to assist churches in reflecting on ways the community of faith expresses its values and beliefs in its life together—in words and actions, including ritual. It is important in the coming decade that equivalent energy be devoted to the implications of the global dimensions of that baptismal declaration. While liturgical words refer to the worldwide church, follow-up action frequently has been about absorption into the preoccupations and understandings of one part of the world church, which is, at best, vaguely aware of other parts of the church; at worst, hostile to anything that differs from "our tradition."

Tradition vs. Traditions

The Word became flesh under particular cultural conditions, in the Palestinian world of the first century. The church's mission involves the expression of that gospel in

181

terms appropriate to new cultures. Indeed, the missionary task of the church requires that people in as many cultures as possible hear about and respond to the Christian gospel. The message is for all the world (Matt. 28); in this way, the universal nature of the gospel is declared.

A World Council of Churches conference on faith and order distinguished between *Tradition* and *traditions*. *Tradition* is "the gospel itself, transmitted from generation to generation in and by the church, Christ himself present in the life of the church"; *traditions* are the ways this one Tradition has been variously understood and transmitted in different Christian confessions and different cultural situations.[2]

To hear appreciatively the expression of the gospel in the varying terms of different cultures strengthens our awareness of the universal nature of the gospel and of the relation to God we have in common with the people of other cultures. In a curious but powerful way, the diversity of Christian traditions is an invitation to recognize and celebrate the worldwide dimensions of the faith and the church. The gospel is about the nature of the church *and* the nature of the world.

Our Understanding of Church

In recent educational theory widely used among Christian churches in the West, considerable attention has been given to the concept of the church as a community of faith which provides the context in which the educational process takes place. The community of faith provides both the motivation to explore meanings and the words and action that are the focus of that exploration.[3] However, with very few exceptions, the concept of community of faith has been interpreted in local terms as *congregation* or, less frequently, in confessional terms, as *denomination*. Relatively little attention has been given to the communion of saints or to the worldwide church of Jesus Christ. Of those denominations or individuals that have affirmed an ecumenical perspective, it clearly has not been easy to identify a body of knowledge about the practical educational implications of such an affirmation.

There has been a recognition of the importance of the message the church expresses in its life. Thomas Groome, for example, stated that "only by embodying within itself the truth of its own message can the Church be a credible sign of the Kingdom in the midst of the world." Groome went on to speak about the importance of "loving service to the whole human family."[4] However, what are the implications of that conviction in this new situation of global awareness at the end of the twentieth century? How is it possible for the Christian church to be a credible sign of the Kingdom, when one of the most visible characteristics of churches is their unrelated fragmentation, and when few churches are known for their public approval of the diversity of traditions? How is it possible, in a world of diverse peoples, to be a credible sign of the Kingdom if there is no affirmation of all other peoples as part of the one human family?

Gabriel Moran recognized the new situation that confronts the churches in our "obviously pluralistic world":

> What can a child or an adult make of exhortations to follow "the way" when it is evident that there are many ways? At the same time, it is obvious that those other people are not stupid, insincere, or irreligious. . . . No religious group can relinquish its claim to "the way," and yet increasingly each group has to live with other people who are just as certain that they know "the way."[5]

The church's biblical and theological traditions commit it to a worldwide understanding of the church. The churches' popular thinking and customary practices accustom them to more local and partial assumptions. The new situation of increasing global awareness confronts churches with the need to reaffirm the church's essential worldwide dimension and to discover the educational implications of that fundamental understanding of the nature of the church.

183

Experiences in the World Council of Churches

The impetus for the contemporary ecumenical movement came from two dramatically different experiences during the Second World War. On the one hand, the almost overwhelming destruction in Europe and the dimensions of the task involved in recreating a better social order required much more than the churches separately could possibly undertake. The size of the problem was a challenge to discover new worldwide dimensions for Christian thought and action. On the other hand, many Christians found that the things that had divided them during peacetime were of little significance compared to the deep convictions and awareness of spiritual resources that linked them together in the face of hardship and suffering. The experiences of shared faith and humanity under the conditions of war were a challenge to carry into peacetime a vision of the unity of the church and the interrelatedness of all human beings.

The World Council of Churches has provided a unique meeting place for the diverse traditions that make up the worldwide Christian church and the enormous range of cultures and races that make up the worldwide human family. The Council has focused on two broad objectives: the discovery and expression of the unity that is God's gift to the church, and the implications of the Christian faith for mission and service.

A Changing Perception of Education

From its formation in 1948, the World Council recognized the educational implications of its two objectives. In 1968 the Educational Working Group at Upsalla stated the task: "To stir up and equip all of God's people for ecumenical understanding, active engagement in renewing the life of the churches, and participation in God's work in a changing world."[6] The sources from which the reshaped understanding of education has come are varied.

The international composition of commissions, committees, and consultations has encouraged a sharing of insights from educational experiences across the world. The present Working Group consists of twenty-six people from twenty-two nations, and the staff of the subunit on education has cooperated with regional and national councils of churches in education projects around the world. In the 1960s a series of regional curriculum consultations stimulated new developments in churches, and these activities frequently were carried through as cooperative projects, moving beyond the objectives of any one church.

The experience of people cooperating across traditional boundaries of culture, race, and tradition, especially in times of desperate human need, has again and again produced changes in understanding of the church, and in the attitudes toward people from churches different from their own. Emphasis on "joint action for mission," while primarily for the purpose of achieving tangible results from cooperation in specific services, also produced significant educational outcome as people reflected on their experiences of cooperation, their discoveries of what they had in common, and the removal of the barriers of prejudice and misunderstanding.

Particular experiences in Bible study have added to general experiences of cross-cultural and interdenominational meeting. The pioneering work of Hans-Ruedi Weber, who for a quarter of a century served as staff for biblical studies in the education subunit, introduced people to increased richness and depth in study of the Bible. In many countries people have discovered that traditional assumptions about meaning are enlarged by the perceptions of people from other cultures and traditions, who see and hear a different message in the biblical text.[7]

Against such a background, in recent years an exploration of the practical implications of ecumenical learning has become a major focus of the education subunit. Global consultations on ecumenical learning were held in 1982 and 1986.

Another major program, Justice, Peace, and Integrity of Creation, contains important educational components closely linked to the concerns of ecumenical learning. New ways of understanding the connection between faith and responsible living on planet Earth as part of the human family are high priorities for the contemporary mission of the churches. These new understandings present challenges for a revitalization of education to deal with such major issues.

Equally substantial changes in theological education have been pointed to by the work of the Program on Theological Education. In recent years its dominant theme has been Theology by the People. Implications have been identified both for the theological vocation of the whole people of God, and for the kind of ministerial formation that would train ministers as enablers of the theological task of the whole church. "The proper place of theological work is the local church or congregation. It is done by the people, who may of course include professionals as they gather in community."[8]

Ecumenical Learning

From many sources, therefore, has come a strong conviction that the educational task of the churches requires new dimensions—particularly, global dimensions. The concept of "ecumenical learning" is neither self-explanatory nor clear. The phrase, like most expressions taken up in international dialogue and subject to translation in a number of languages, is helpful to some and confusing for others.

It is clear that the concept is not simply about understanding attempts to reunite churches or about the history of the growth of ecumenical organizations. Rather, it is about a global dimension to our understanding of the church and the people of the world, which requires changes in our perception of the educational task. The challenge to those planning for education by churches around the world is to provide for learning with global dimensions:

186

- learning which enables people, while remaining rooted in one tradition of the church, to become open and responsive to the richness and perspectives of other churches, so that they become more active in seeking unity, openness, and collaboration between churches;
- learning which enables people of one country, language, ethnic group, class, or political and economic system, to become sensitive and responsive to those of other countries, ethnic groups, and political and economical situations, so that they become active participants in action for a more just world.

Another way of thinking about ecumenical learning is to understand it as a process by which

- diverse groups and individuals,
- well-rooted in their own faith, traditions, cultures, and contexts,
- are enabled to risk honest encounters with one another before God,
- as they study and struggle together in community,
- with personally relevant issues
- in light of the Scriptures, the traditions of their faith, worship, and global realities,
- resulting in communal action in faithfulness to God's intention for the unity of the church and humankind, and for justice, peace, and the integrity of creation.[9]

Components in Effective Ecumenical Learning

In June 1986, a world consultation on ecumenical learning was held at the Ecumenical Institute at Bossey in Switzerland. All participants coming to the workshop contracted to describe and analyze examples of effective ecumenical learning in their own countries. The two statements of what is involved in ecumenical learning set out above were used as the working definitions.

187

Most examples of significant ecumenical learning deal with issues of some urgency in the lives of people, rather than with consideration of abstract theory. Frequently, there is a close link between action and learning; much learning is the result of reflection on action or leads directly to action. These are familiar conclusions for educators, but remind us that the starting point for dealing with world issues is nearly always local and is therefore more realistic than may at first appear. A useful guideline is to assist people to act locally, while thinking globally.

The global dimension, or at least the recognition and acceptance of perspectives broader than one's own tradition or culture, comes most frequently from meeting with people of other traditions and cultures. Acceptance of more diversity than is common in one's living or worshiping group is frequently a step toward changing perceptions of the church and the human family.

Providing for expression of conflict as part of the process is a key issue. Avoidance of conflict may be achieved by retreat to one's familiar cultural and religious boundaries. A group, or some members of a group with tolerance for an acceptable measure of conflict, is often a precondition for consideration of more global perspectives. The issues raised here are about relationships, but are also about theological understanding and perspective.

One of the conclusions that has emerged from discussions about openness to differing perspectives is that few people within their own tradition have opportunities to hear positive and affirming stories from other traditions. To hear people speak of what is of value to them, whether in person or in quotations, is a comparatively rare but significant experience for the people in our churches.

In a similar way, hearing Scripture read ecumenically— that is, listening appreciatively to the way people in other cultures and traditions experience its life-shaping message— opens new vistas of understanding the nature of the life of faith to which it bears witness. Again the issue is fundamentally

188

theological; it is about the nature of the church, the nature of the Bible, and its witness to the action of God.

In all countries, one particular difference needs to receive fresh attention—differences between living faiths. Around the world, there are religions other than Christianity. A global perspective on the human family involves contemporary Christians in the consideration of unfamiliar issues about the relation of the Christian faith to these other religions. This has been a field for highly specialized dialogue by experts, but not one in which the people of the churches who increasingly mix with people of other faiths on a daily basis have been given assistance and encouragement. To provide the understanding and skills appropriate to this situation, relatively new for Christians, will involve the churches in major theological and educational responses.

Educational Strategies

It is potentially perilous to extrapolate from the experiences of people from twenty-five to thirty nations to formulate suggestions for strategies applicable in particular nations and cultures. However, some pointers for practical educational action have emerged for considering Christian education in light of a global perspective on the church and the world.

Crossing Boundaries

In many countries, educational programs constitute a large part of the programs of churches. If these programs are planned solely within traditional denominational boundaries, the church is in danger of working against its understanding of its own nature and of missing powerful opportunities for developing changed understandings and attitudes toward its own mission. Encouragement of contact between people of differing denominations, cultures, and traditions is a practical expression of commitment to the global nature of the church.

189

In groups that deal with issues in society, study of the Bible, or tackling of mission tasks, we can set in motion life-changing forces by working *across* denominational and cultural boundaries, seeking cooperation and coalitions that reach beyond our own faith groups.

We can invite Christians from other traditions, or respond to their invitations, to identify, affirm, and celebrate our common response to the grace of God in Jesus Christ, to cooperate in mission tasks, and to listen together for the life-shaping Word, which needs to be heard afresh in our day.

Curriculum writers and editors, teachers in theological institutions and in church educational programs, can enrich their own and others' understanding of the church by including opportunities for people in a particular tradition to listen appreciatively to understandings of the church that arise from other races and cultures and confessions. This is not merely consistent with, but required by, the biblical testimony to the universal nature of the faith and the church.

Consideration of the reason why activities that reflect a global understanding of the faith either happen or do not happen in our local churches and educational programs could be a stimulating or disturbing theological reflection.

Crises as Opportunity

Human crises may be seen as opportunities for establishing new relationships, particularly for coalitions to serve those of the human family who have special needs. Though of course we do not wish for crises, when such disasters do occur, they can be seen as occasions when agreement about the desperate needs of other people creates opportunities for reaching across barriers of tradition, culture, race, and religion, to affirm a bigger truth about the worldwide nature of the church and the human family. Reflection on such experiences is the heart of an imaginative and powerful educational process.

Concepts and Language

Identifying and using ideas and terminology appropriate to a global perspective on the church and the human family must become an important task of educators and theologians. We need to review the church's operational theologies critically. The churches of which we are a part are not "our" churches, but are parts of the universal church of Jesus Christ. The true nature of that church is global; it includes regions, rather than being regional and excluding other regions.

If the true nature of the church is to be communicated in educational programs, primary attention must focus on the nature and mission of the church, rather than on its organization and structure. Organization and structure necessarily reflect cultural and historical peculiarities. The nature and mission of the church involve global perspectives, within which are a variety of organizational patterns and structures appropriate to the diversity of cultures across this planet.

Theologians, educators, and other communicators in the church can develop a new sensitivity to the key role of language. Just as in recent years we have been through complex, and at times painful, rethinking of the ways male-dominated language has distorted the inclusive nature of the church, so we now enter a period in which use of denominationally and culturally biased language distorts the globally inclusive nature of the church. When we use the word *church* we should be aware of whether the intended reference is to the worldwide church of Jesus Christ, or to a particular tradition or denomination. When we use phrases such as "the people of God," we can consciously check whether the intended or unintended outcome of such language may imply that some people are not the people of God.

A Community of Support

Designs for educational programs, from graduate theological education to children's learning, need to provide both

191

opportunities for personal reflection and provisions for the creation of supportive subgroups. It is not possible to tell one's own story unless it is accepted that it may differ from the stories of others. On the other hand, getting in touch with one's own story creates a readiness to appreciate the different stories of other people. Building a community of support and encouraging a group to accept new spiritual experiences is both an expression of the vitality of the church in a particular place and a step toward the affirmation of the universal church, in which people of diverse races, cultures, and ideologies together acknowledge one God and one worldwide human family as the people of God.

The imperialism of closed theological systems is sometimes demonstrated most clearly in a simultaneous exclusion from approval of both an individual's particular experience of spiritual reality and whole sections of the diverse worldwide church. The creation of settings for a very different and more affirming kind of education presents a particularly significant educational and theological opportunity.

One Faith, One World

The challenge to Christian educators to see the church and the human family in a more global perspective is an invitation both to recover ancient insights into the nature of the church and to respond to a distinctive mission imperative of the late twentieth century.

In our recent past, churches often have applied the world *ecumenical* to a small optional extra effort to be undertaken after the main expenditure of time, energy, and budget has been devoted to denominational activity.

Now a different and more pervasive ecumenical task claims the churches' attention: Does our Christian education adequately express our understanding of the nature of the church and the church's relation to the contemporary world?

Part V—Method

Foreword

How does one practice theology? A classical paradigm emerged for the church when it sought to guard against chaos by protecting the tradition. The tradition needed to be cherished, honored, and defended because it provided God's way of salvation. Yet, in the desire to protect theology, the need to reflect upon the experience of being accepted, called, and sent by God was taken from the people. The theologians, the scholarly professionals of the church courts or universities, became the guardians of that reflection.

How can the method of theology allow all the people access to the reflective wisdom of the Christian tradition? The church needs those who relate theology to academic knowledge and reflection, those who guard the tradition against distortion and bigotry. But the church also needs an approach through which the people of God can reflect and decide upon their vocations within the world. An open conversation among both the people and the scholars is essential. To lose either perspective is dangerous.

Throughout this volume we have seen evidence of changes in the classical pattern. Education is not just "applied" theology. The process of theology does not begin only within the tradition, with results applied to practice. Theology is a mutual conversation which begins both within the tradition and within the practice of Christians who seek to be faithful. In our conversation, both education and tradition are sources of theological reflection about the nature of God, the way God interacts with the world—particularly through

Jesus the Christ—and the vocation to which God calls the church.

Both of the following essays deal directly with the issues of method, and in each case the definition of the theologian is extended. Robert O'Gorman engages the experience of Latin American base communities, where worship and reflection, action and thought are combined as the people in community seek to understand God's will and role in their lives. He defines the theological method of those communities as an educational method which offers possibilities to the North American church. Richard Osmer addresses the contemporary conversation about the nature of theological reflection and, in particular, the shape of practical theology. He clarifies the two-way street from tradition to experience and from experience to tradition. Moreover, he focuses the theological issues that are at stake when a teacher of the faith enters a classroom to face persons who seek to know and to live faithfully. Both essays emphasize the role of the whole people of God in the act of theology.

CHAPTER 11

Latin American Theology and Education

Robert T. O'Gorman

For the past thirty years Latin America has been the scene of change in the Christian church, rivaling in magnitude the Reformation of the sixteenth century. Participants and observers alike are referring to this change, not as a new Reformation, but as the Transformation church—a new meaning of *church*.[1] The possibility of such a development in our day and time should not be surprising: a motto of the church is *Semper Reformanda*, Always Reforming. Throughout its development, the church has undergone significant transformations of its nature. The task of the church is to "get up-to-date." We are an evolutionary people, not static. We must live historically by participating in the events that shape the future.

The character of the church is shaped by its context. In this instance, that means "third world." The new church, the Transformation church, is emerging from the "underside" of history. It operates from a horizontal, rather than a vertical framework, a shift from the hierarchically structured church, in which clergy and professional leadership are dominant over the base, where the whole people are.

This chapter describes this transformation and reflects on the history that has produced it, with particular emphasis on the way education and theology are reconceived in Latin America. Here education and theology take place at "sunset," after the day's experience. The people's way of knowing begins with their expeience, the living presence of God in their midst, and allows for Scripture and tradition to be critiqued by that

195

experience. This way of knowing concludes in action and religious identity expressed as political activity, seeking changes called for by the reign of God. Here we may find educational challenges that can inspire the transformation of the church in North America.

A New Church

Some time ago in central Mexico's Cuernavaca, I lived with a family that belonged to a Comunidad Ecclesial de Base— CEB.[2] That family, in whose home a gathering of the CEB took place, lived on the fringe of the *colonia*, where there are no municipal services. The husband of the family, Simplicio, was a short, thick man with gnarled, rough hands.

We met in the bedroom of Simplicio and his wife, a simple room with a bare concrete floor, one outside window, a sagging but otherwise rather elegant bed, a bookcase, and an altar. A table displayed dazzling white lilies and other beautiful fresh flowers. The table was filled to overflowing with pictures, all of the same youth, a statuette of Jesus, and votive candles. It was a shrine to the youth, their nineteen-year-old son who had recently died.

Andres had been the pride of this family. Every spare peso was devoted to his education. Against all odds, he was admitted to the university, where he studied law. When he fell ill, he had but two years before completion of his qualifications as a lawyer. Andres was treated by his family for stomach problems. When he grew worse and became feverish, the family became alarmed and took him to the nearest social-security hospital. There they were turned away, though he was finally admitted to a small private hospital. But he died almost immediately of peritonitis.

By law, working persons in Mexico must be provided with membership in the social-security system—El Sequro Social —which guarantees basic medical treatment. But Simplicio's last employer, by bribing a government inspector, had avoided paying the employer's contribution.

196

The shrine and all it symbolized were an awesome basis that evening for our group's discussion of the parable of the sower (Mark 4:1-20). The parable and its meaning were clear to the group: Those who suffer and are oppressed, yet believe and act upon the Good News, are those who have been given the secret of the reign of God. It is not enough to be poor. But to be poor, to experience injustice every day, and to see in one's suffering the intentions of God, is to *be* the fertile soil. But people who fear and want only to become part of the middle class—these stand outside God's reign.

The seed of the gospel does not bring wealth; it brings conflict and pain, for it is in the good soil that God's reign is growing. The good soil is this life, this place, this condition, not the future and distant world of heaven and God's second coming. It is only because we are afraid to die—our lack of faith—that keeps the reign of God from appearing now. These Christians have, by means of their condition, recaptured Mark's intention. It is clear why repressive Latin American governments consider the Bible a subversive document.[3]

Since the early 1960s groups such as these have been meeting in Latin America. Typically, there are twenty members in a group composed of adults and young adults who meet weekly. Brazil and Chile have been in the forefront of CEB development. In Brazil today there are as many as 100,000.[4]

The first such groups were developed by peasants in the rural areas where violence connected with land problems was prominent. The idea made its way to medium-sized towns and eventually to metropolitan peripheries, where groups were developed by persons displaced from the land who now faced the complexity of urban life.

Marcello Azevedo, in *Basic Ecclesial Communities in Brazil*, has described the condition of peasants and the upheaval in their religious life due to migration to the city:

> Dislocating and uprooting them . . . shattered the rural patterns of their lives, split up families, and threatened to erode

197

> their religious life. . . . It radically changed their conception of time, space, family ties, and social relationships. . . .
>
> Urban life brought to the fore the effort of the lone individual, on which everything seemed to depend. . . . The religious legitimation of their earlier world was fragmented or pushed into the background. Life is no longer interpreted in terms of the same presuppositions.[5]

Modernity and its production of the autonomous individual has come full force upon Latin America in the past two generations, and the result has been the immediate and keenly felt loss of community. While the Anglo/Saxon peoples have more slowly, over a period of extended time, become used to and even championed individualism, to Latin Americans, this cultural change has come as a shock. The fracturing of community is thus much more apparent.

In the crisis resulting from this disruption, the old forms of church life no longer met the need. It became incumbent upon the people to recapture community in their church, thus the building of what are known as Basic Ecclesial Communities (CEBs). It is these communities which embody the transformation of the church in Latin America today.

Three terms designate the instrumentality of the new church: *community, ecclesial,* and *base.*

Community

In premodern society the individual was clearly connected to the group. In community, one received identity and meaning. From the thirteenth until the nineteenth century in the Christian West, the sense of community gradually was broken by the developing autonomy of individualism; the result has been anonymity, extreme competition between individuals, and deterioration of social relationships. New forms of domination and oppression were thus produced. In its early days, the church moved from an apostolic community to a highly structured religion of the Roman Empire. Basic Ecclesial Communities are an attempt to restore community to the Christian religion—the personal relationships as

198

preached by Jesus—to live together less anonymously, more personally.[6] Moreover, in Brazil, repression by the military government in the 1960s occasioned a new outlet, popular gatherings in small groups of prayer and protest, and these spurred the development of CEBs.

Ecclesial

These groups are church. They are not sectarian, isolated, or exclusive congregations. They are not separate from the church in its institutional expression. They are one with the church of Christ and its tradition. In Brazil, this unity was maintained because the institutional leaders of the church joined with the people in their struggle. Like the camel in the gospel going through the Eye of the Needle, they knelt down, touching the poverty and oppression of the people. They became one with the people.

Base

The people who make up these communities are those at the base of society, those stripped of power. The base community becomes the place where the human being can begin again, can become someone. Association in this community provides a new way to be human. Here, then, at the base, the church is assuming the position of the poor—stripped of power. Here the agenda of the church and the agenda of the people become one. As an expression of the inclusivity of the church, the CEB is open to all humanity. The transformation of society becomes central in the church's mission.

The Historical Context

The Transformation church arising in Latin America needs to be understood in relation to the historical developments in both church and society. Let me sketch the post-Columbian political and ecclesial history of Latin America and particularize it with a reflection on Mexico, whose history provides an overall example of Latin America's relations with Europe as well as with the United States.

In 1521 Spain conquered the Aztecs and began to make its wealth off the indigenous people. In 1820 the rich families who ruled for the Spanish gained their independence, but this resulted in no change for the masses. It was the time of the great haciendas. It was not until 1915 and the revolution of Emilio Zapata with land reform that the masses of people began to experience independence. However, in the 1940s during World War II, United States' interests halted the reforms of President Cardenes because of its fear of socialism. As a result, the United States picked up the role that Spain and the rich families had played in relation to the people—that of dominator.

The bottom line of political history is that the constant state of the people, except for the brief period from 1915 until 1940 (35 of the last 450 years), has been one of oppression and dependency. Moreover, economically, 30 percent of the Mexican people control 70 percent of the income. That is, for the same day's work, 70 percent of the people gain wages that keep them enslaved, while the other 30 percent gain wages that magnify their wealth.

The church needs to be understood in this context. From 1521 until 1531, European Christianity was rejected. After 1531, an indigenous Christianity took hold, and to this day, the religious life of the Mexican people is the strongest element of their self-image.[7]

The church as an institution, however, was not identified with the people, but with the political rulers, with the crown. As a consequence, in 1850, thirty years after the break with Spain, the church in Mexico was stripped of its wealth and eventually outlawed. One hundred years later, the Catholic Church under Pope Pius XII, in an attempt to regain its lost influence, called missionaries from all over the world to Latin America. In 1955 the Mexican church, along with the other Catholic churches in Latin America, met in Rio de Janeiro to reorganize in a new type of power as CELAM, Consejo

Episcopal Latino-Americano, the Latin-American Episcopal Conference.[8]

The Birth of a New Theological Method

Francois Houtart, a Belgian priest at the Catholic University of Louvain in Belgium, had been trained in the sociology of religion at the University of Chicago. In 1961, Monsignor Luigi Ligutti, the Vatican's observer at the Food and Agriculture Organization of the United Nations (FAO), commissioned Houtart to conduct a study of the condition of church and society in each country of Latin America.[9] Several of Houtart's Latin American students joined him at this work, and in an amazingly short period of time, they established centers of investigation in various cities. Today these continue as major centers of research, training, and theologizing.

At the request of CELAM, Houtart summarized the studies and translated them into English and French for distribution to each of the world's bishops who attended the Ecumenical Council, Vatican II (1963–1965).[10] Furthermore, Houtart was appointed CELAM's *peritus* (theological expert) at the Council and made significant contributions by providing sociological and economic descriptions of the Latin American countries.

Two major documents emanated from Vatican II: (1) *De Ecclesia* imaged the church as the people of God, rather than as the perfect society (a hierarchical institution); (2) *Gaudium et Spes* shifted the church's theological method.[11]

Traditionally, the church had theologized deductively—that is, beginning with rational principles or articles of faith, then applying these to experience. In contrast, *Gaudium et Spes* carried out theology inductively, starting at the "here and now" of experience; theological principles were engaged in synthesis before being applied. From this base (much of the information provided by Houtart), the church exercised a new mode of theology.

During this same period (from the late 1950s until the late 1960s), Houtart and the University of Louvain also were affecting the church in Latin America in another way. Since Europe had been viewed as the center of culture, the tradition in Latin American countries was to send rising intellectuals— artists, architects, philosophers, as well as theologians—to Europe for training. So generations of young theologians went to the great European theological schools to encounter the classic texts and bring theology back home to raise the religious level of Latin America to the standards of Europe.

In several of the great European schools, however, a shift in theological approach was taking place at this time. The devastation and disillusionment of World Wars I and II had caused theologians to question the viability of a deductive approach. A more inductive approach was required, a theology that started with the present realities, similar to the method later espoused at Vatican II.

At Louvain during those years, there were several theology students from Latin America: Gustavo Gutierrez, Otto Moduro, Enrique Dussel, Camillo Torres, Clodovis Boff, and others. Houtart, as a sociologist of religion, had been appointed to employ critical sociology as a theological method.[12] Rather than being given the huge tomes of the great classical theologians to use as their starting point in theological reflection, these students were invited "to look in the mirror"—that is, to begin with themselves as the place to locate the action of God.

This was most difficult at first, since the students had learned to think of the Latin American situation as an embarrassment, in comparison to the culture of Europe. Yet as they came to envision their situation as an experience of the presence of God, they began to find God in the very conditions of oppression so characteristic of their world. They began to accept this identity as a poor suffering people as their own identity. Thus their theology became characterized as a theology of liberation, since the gospel of Christ in the Latin American reality was the good news that salvation meant freedom from centuries of oppression.

It is also important to recognize that young university men

and women in Latin America had evolved, with the Young Christian Students movement of the 1950s and its method of seeing, judging, and acting, into a "Christian left" movement, with analysis and action on the structural level of society.[13] Thus the ground had been prepared for the reform of church and society. When the young clerics came back from Europe, there was a mutual validation of vision.

It would be improper to say that the theology of liberation had its origin in Europe; yet it can be said that Louvain and the other centers there did foster a "theology of temporal realities" which, as a generic theological methodology, can be specified in different contexts. In the context of Latin America, this theology became Liberation Theology.

Basic Christian Communities— Instruments for the New Theology

In examining the developments of the church in Latin America since Vatican II, it is apparent that the United States has not developed contextual theology as quickly as have the countries of Latin America. In the second and third major gatherings of Latin American bishops and theologians at Medellin in Columbia (1968) and at Puebla in Mexico (1979), Latin Americans both translated and contextualized the work of the Second Vatican Council, something churches in the United States have not accomplished with such deliberateness and consistency.

At Medellin, "people of God," the image of "church" that guided Vatican II, was translated in light of the greater need for community amidst the fragmentation and anonymity of modern urban life. In the ten years between Medellin and Puebla, "the Latin American Church forged its own distinctive profile, matured in personality, and shaped its own contribution to both the local Church and the universal world Church." It did this by incorporating the Basic Ecclesial Communities as *the* instrumentality for transformation of the church, the concrete expression of "the people of God." In this way, Latin Americans contextualized Vatican II.[14]

203

Particularly in Brazil, the hierarchy recognized these CEBs as the new form of church into which the institutional church needed to develop. The CEBs became part of the pastoral plan of the church in Brazil, part of its attempt to locally implement Medellin and Puebla (i.e., the reforms of Vatican II).[15]

Through the base community church, the people of Latin America are, for the first time, seeing a union between their religion and their church. They now say, "We are the church," not "We are *in* the church," a movement from being objects to being subjects. The church is no longer distant from the people but has become intimate with their experience. Latin Americans now view their experience (oppression) in religious terms: The rich-poor structure of their society is challenged by equality in the reign of God. Their religious and political identity become one. The dualisms between religion and church, faith and life, cease to exist. It is for this reason that the church in Latin America has become a most feared presence and the Bible is considered a subversive document.[16]

A New Education

The Transformation church elaborates both a new theology and a new education. Education and theology are defined differently than in the North American church. Education is at the heart of the new church; the CEB is an intentional process with a clearly discernible educational model.

Crucial to this education is its content—the Word of God. In the CEBs the Word of God exists not in the Bible as such, but in the interaction of what Latin Americans call the text, the pretext, and the context.[17] The pretext is the experience the people bring to a meeting of the community; the text is the Scripture; and the context is the community itself, where the issues from the experience are actively engaged.

This schema marks a shift in educational method. Instead of the scholars' exegesis of rational abstractions, the poor engage the text directly with their imaginations as a sacramental encounter, an exegesis of experience. This is fitting, after all, as major sections of the Bible are written by the poor about the poor. Marxist categories of social analysis do provide tools for dealing with the reality of the concentration of power, but it is the discovery of the power of religious language in the Bible that is the source of energy for overcoming the oppression of their experience.

One goal of CEB education involves listening to and sharing the people's experiences as the present action of God. Another goal is organization of the people—that is, the building of community wherein the Word of God takes flesh. A third goal is that of clarifying or posing the problems that impede justice—discerning the will of God. A fourth goal is to research and analyze resources that will address this problem. A fifth goal is that of action on behalf of justice, to carry out the ethical demands of God's revelation.

In contrast to North American church education, the purpose of the CEBs is not to spearhead the membership drive or to indoctrinate, nor is it limited to intensifying individuals' religious expressions. Its aim is to evangelize—to recreate society according to the model of the reign of God. Evangelism, in its best meaning, is education for action, public action—the transformation of society.[18] It is clear that education and church are one in the CEB, that the very acts of education—seeing, judging, acting—are ways of living and ways of being church.

A New Theology

In Latin American, theology also gains its form from the CEB. In fact, the whole relationship between theology and education is reversed from that of the North American church. In a typical North American educational setting, it is thought that people should learn theology in church education. This is not the case in the CEBs. Religious education is not merely the preparation of people for church membership, or even leadership; in CEBs, the religious education is *itself* the very development of theology.

The North American method does not take account the epistemological status of the poor. It assumes that only highly schooled people can minister the gospel with any authority of truth. Thus, only clergy who are first trained by accredited seminary professors, who themselves have been trained at the accredited universities, can mediate the revelation of God to the people. The Latin American notion of church, with its belief in the preferential option for the poor, rejects this hierarchical epistemology.[19]

Human experience is the key to theology. Theology has been powerless for most people, because certain other people (white, Western, male academics) have controlled the experience out of which theology comes. Theology has become irrelevant to the public because its base of experience has been too narrowly controlled. Therefore, theology has little to say to the broader issues of life in the experience of the masses, and the people know this. Classical theological research seems to be based on the capitalist division of labor: Some think; others work. At heart, this issue is a struggle over ownership of knowledge. An elite group has become the keeper of theological knowledge. In contrast, the focus of the CEBs is on people.

In Latin America, theology is written in community. The various centers which Houtart set up have evolved into centers not only for research, but also for training pastoral agents in the development of the base communities, and as places for theological reflection. Here the activities of organizing, teaching, research, and theology take place interactively. Such centers see educational ministry as organizing people for social transformation—that is, helping people to: (1) analyze the socioreligious context in which they exist; (2) articulate the meaning of their experience theologically so as to religiously empower their endeavors; and (3) train persons as creators and organizers of religiously empowered communities.

A center is not a place as such, but an action/reflection endeavor with a research component, a training component, and a documentation, or writing, component. The curriculum of such a center is framed within a theology of action. It takes place in and arises from the community where ministry materializes.

A center, then, is a community composed of scholars, pastoral agents, and people from the neighborhoods who are mutually training for organization and ministry; researching, theologically and sociologically, the nature of religious community and its educational task; and collecting and preparing documentation as reflection resources for the local churches and the church at large. It is from these centers that much of the literature of liberation theology has been written.[20]

People in the CEBs are *creating* theology, not just learning it. They are a people relating faith to life, worship to work, prayer to action, proclamation to protest. Sharing in the mission of the church demands sharing in its theological task. Latin America teaches us that theology cannot be carried out without people and their experiences; people must become the *subjects* of theology.

Thus, Latin American theology is Theology by the People; the poor, the people, are the very origin of the theological discussion. Here the professionally trained theologian works in the context *of* and *with*, not *for* or *from* the people. The people must be involved in formulating the policies and projects.[21]

Theology is an articulation of the life and commitment of the people. Professionals cannot presume to write theology by the people, because they do not have in their bodies the experience of the poor (the people). Theological language for the nonprofessional is that of story—oral and nonliterate images—not the propositions and rationality of the scientific method. Furthermore, stories of the poor are told in sociopolitical-economic language. This theology is a body language; the people's commitment becomes "words into action," and their actions become events for reflection, the creation of stories.

207

In Latin America is being born a new sense of church, a new sense of theology, a new sense of education—all one and the same. Here dissolves the fruitless separation of theology and church and education. In the CEBs, theology loosens the tongue of the people to speak the truth of their experience.

Re-forming Education

We must be careful. It is the typical North American custom to buy what we want in the Latin American markets at "bargain" prices. Approaching the Transformation church with this attitude may cause us to trivialize and miss its challenge. We, however, need to risk. I do believe that certain challenges exist here for the North American church. This situation changes the possibilities for *transformation*.

Community—The Aim of Education

Community is crucial to the Transformation church. From this experience of life together, certain goals for education can be articulated.

1. *Both church and society are objects of transformation.*

Reflection on the development of the Transformation church in Latin America shows clearly the connection between the church and the politics of society. One is an expression of the other. There cannot be a new church without a new society. North America cannot be characterized by the Transformation church until there is a moral revolution in its society.

The Transformation church in Latin America is threatening because its religious revolution is a societal revolution—a radical reworking of a whole network of political, economic, agrarian, legal, educational, and cultural structures. At heart, it is an attack on the mind-set that one has the right to consume as one pleases without care for the whole. The church cannot be transformed alone. The oneness of faith and life go hand in hand. Leaven acts as leaven only if it is inside the dough. Thus, a goal of education to be learned from the Transformation church must be to transform the society.

208

2. *Education, as praxis, is the creation of community.*

The key to the transformation of society is the creation of community.[22] The church changed in Latin America because masses of people, in a very short period of time, underwent massive dislocation. When community broke down, individuality emerged. Moreover, Latin America has been profoundly affected by the technological control in North America and northern Europe. The "first world" society, after several generations of "modernization," experienced breakthroughs: air transportation, television, prefabricated housing, birth control, control of infections with antibiotics, electronic business machines, air conditioning—all moved life beyond a subsistence stage of living. This technological shift has produced major dislocations in life and a transition to a new world order, with the need to manage new world relationships, new pluralisms of countries, new forms of buying and selling, dislocation of labor pools, and the reallocation of capital and other resources from underdeveloped countries to those where resources have become depleted.[23]

The experience of modernization in Latin America points out the cost of North America's development of individualism. The way the church served people in an earlier world is inoperative in the new world. The Transformation church has emerged as an attempt to restore *community* to the Christian religion. The personal relationships preached by Jesus Christ—to live together less autonomously, more personally—this is what we need.

Have North Americans become aware of this transition and its effects? Social commentators are challenging a reevaluation of the individualism and privatism of contemporary religion and society. Religious writers are reexamining church—from its function to serve the formation and development of individuals to its concern with the formation of community, of a people.[24]

Latin American praxis is not only action; it is basically a relation of persons to persons: "To be together in a community is the fundamental praxis that anticipates the kingdom of

God."[25] Gathering people together in God's name is the originating religious experience, an act of community organizing. Thus a second goal of education from the Transformation church is to transform the alienation and aloneness of individuals into personal community.

Ecclesial—
The Nature of Teaching/Learning Interactions

The Transformation church suggests a new definition of church and new strategies for the relationship of church and education.

3. Education is central to the church.

The CEBs are a new way of living, being, and acting *as church.* They are not *programs of* or *movements in* the church.[26] The North American experience of church is highly institutional, and thus it is difficult for us to imagine *church* as a lived experience except as an individual expression, or as a sect or separatist group. The experience in Latin America, however, is not an experience of the growth of the new form of church, in opposition to or separate from the institution. In Brazil the hierarchy recognized CEBs as the form of church into which the institutional church needed to develop. And CEBs became part of the pastoral plan of the church, part of its attempt to implement Vatican II locally. Furthermore, the hierarchy reformed the curial offices to become a support network for this model of church.[27]

Education is central to the activity of the church. It is not a by-product or only one of many church ministries. The goals and visions of education itself must become the goals and mission of the church itself. In other words, education cannot be *program.* The church, at the national level, must deliberately attempt to translate the renewal of the church and, furthermore, contextualize this translation by incorporating the instrumentalities that arise from the people. We must take seriously the declaration that "We are the church." Only by doing so is the eventual union of religion and church in North

210

America possible. A challenge from the Transformation church is that church education cannot be separated from the institutional life of the church, but is central to it.

4. *In Latin America, religious education is a unity of theology, organizing, research, and teaching.*

Religious education arises from persons' action or ministry experience. These become the base for peoples' biblical and theological reflection, and thus produce transformation—their own, the church's, and society's. The task of religious education is not so much content mastery as lived ministry.

Religious education concentrates on (1) entry or listening skills—how to hear the experiences of people; (2) articulation skills—how to help people express their experiences through biblical, theological, and psychosocial analysis; (3) organizational skills—how to help people empower themselves to carry out the ministry or action of transformation called for by their vocation as religious people.

As education is redefined as empowerment, a new form of educator emerges: the pastoral agent, a person who discovers the secret of giving self to a community so that the community can discover who it is and what it can do. Latin America challenges religious education to new dimensions—analysis, articulation, organization.

5. *Present realities, as well as those of the past tradition, are matters for teaching/learning interaction.*

The experience of education in Latin America demonstrates a methodological shift from the vertical approach (beginning with tradition and applying it to the present) to the horizontal approach (equally honoring and considering the here-and-now and the tradition). The task of education is not merely to consume the theology of scholars, but to produce the theology of the people—an interplay of use of knowledge and generation of knowledge.

History must be made before it can be written; theology is first enacted, then reasoned out and refined. We cannot write a theology of the new church for North America until we first

211

experience it. The church must first live historically, "catch itself up to date" with God.[28] This is a new way of defining church and church education: church as a product and church education as a process which emerges from action. It is a new way of defining theology: "constructing and articulating a faith by which people can live," giving voice to the revelation made to the marginal.[29]

Following the lead of the Latin American church, the North American church can search for a theology of present realities, which must be honored equally with past tradition. Education has a generative, not simply a transmissive task.

6. *In Latin America, religious education operates from an iconographic, or imaginal, pedagogy.*

In the CEBs the people respond to the experience the text evokes at the level of picture, or image. This level is closer to experience than the conceptual or abstract level typical of North American pedagogy, and as an expression closer to experience, a more sacramental response.

In Latin American epistemology, imagination is not viewed as inferior to conceptual or critical knowing.[30] The Western experience of distance between the knower and the known does not characterize Latin American thinking. Latin Americans have retained the pedagogy of the middle ages, when the statues in the great cathedrals were the people's catechism.

For this reason, when Protestants brought the Bible to Latin America, it did not have the effect it did when the Catholics finally brought it after Vatican II. Protestants brought the Bible with the ideology of higher criticism, conceptual pedagogy. After Vatican II, when the Catholic leadership opened the Bible, it allowed for interaction of the biblical images with the people's experiences.[31]

Latin America offers us the ideal of a radical pedagogy for North America, an iconographic pedagogy. Religious education needs to involve the image and picture, or icon, found in the people's experience, as well as the concept taught through tradition. The image, of the nature of sacrament, connects us to the "religious."

Base—The Context

Education in the Transformation church calls us to honor the context of people's lives—the base from which religious experience emerges.

7. *Before liberation is possible, we must discover the base on which society is formed.*

The Transformation church is a church at the base of society—the poor, those stripped of power. To accept the poor as the preferred option for church education means that we recognize "the privileged status of the poor as the new and emerging historical subject which will carry on the Christian project in the world."[32] An assumption underlying this project is that the experiences of the Holy in the religious lives of marginal peoples are the immediate sources for theological construction. Thus, we must understand the meaning of religious education as it relates to life in solidarity with the poor, those who are society's powerless.

There are two issues to uncover in this focus on poverty. Poverty is a paradox, in that one expression of poverty is the material condition of want, not having the wherewithal to sustain life—that is, having little power over life. This is a poverty contrary to the reign of God which Jesus preached. But there is also poverty as a spiritual childhood which entails a radical openness to God—not being attached to material odds; or poverty as total availability to the Lord, the realization that we suffer because we are attached to things.[33] North Americans must ask, What are the attachments that keep us from being poor (free)? How do these relate to material poverty, the poverty that is contrary to the reign of God?

It is the people's religious instincts that create the beginning of a new theology—a lived experience of the numinous. "When people share in a process of liberation on the basis of faith, they have a hitherto unknown experience of the numinous—this flows back to give new content and form to their religious symbols and customs."[34]

The Transformation church offers us the discovery of the base of experience from which we should operate—that is, poverty in the sense of freedom from the attachments which oppress us. The key to this principle is to engage the base of our *experience* and to look at that which keeps this freedom from happening. Education must seek the base of human existence as its starting point.

Conclusion

Reflections on the Christian religious education in Latin America have suggested seven challenges to enrich North American religious education in the transformation of the church and society.

For education to transform, it needs to be oriented outward from the church, toward the transformation of *society*. This is done by the cultivation of community. Community development and organization become the tasks of religious education, expressions of the building of God's reign. Understood as such, then, education is central to the mission of the church. Its role is not merely functional (to gain numbers), but is generative (to renew the church's very meaning and mission). Iconographic, or sacramental, knowing is valued as maintaining the human connection to the material and organic elements of life, rather than their separation into abstract categories. Human community is a community of history, of material and flesh. Finally, and most challenging of all is the poverty basis, from which religious education connects with the source of revelation. Perhaps it is the story of Jesus and the rich young man that provides the challenge for our relationship with the Transformation church.

Ecclesiologically, this chapter contrasts two expeiences. One is the church as hierarchical, not part of daily life, unable to mediate the gospel so important to our lives. The other is the church as communal, people and leaders mutually searching the present realities for their religious dimension.

In the Transformation church, theologians are confronted by a different method. Church leaders can see the importance of the operation of a pastoral plan. Community workers are affirmed at their central task of community organization as incarnating the reign of God.

Comparing theology and education in North America with that of Latin America demonstrates that the churches in North America are clearly underdeveloped. They have failed to translate and contextualize the developments of theological and ecclesial reform represented in the Second Ecumenical Council—Vatican II. The gift of Latin American churches is the vision of a new Christian life, with a model of its operation.

Thus, the task in North America is to find a way to cultivate a new sense of church within the institutional church. In the Brazilian experience, this happened when the institutional church got down on its knees and became one with the poor.

North Americans have fallen behind in our failure to get down on our knees. However, there are signs that this may be happening. During the past ten years, Catholic bishops and leaders of various Protestant denominations in the United States have issued major documents which focus the church on the present realities. And the Hispanic church has produced a national pastoral plan for the Transformation Church in North America.[35]

Concerns in theological and other scholarship, and in North American culture at large, show signs of hope. More stress is beginning to be placed on

> the public rather than the private, the social rather than the individual, liberation than liberty, equality than hierarchy, inquiry than authority, praxis than theory, the ecumenical than the provincial, the plural than the monolithic, the global than the national, the ecological than the anthropological.[36]

Our real task, if we are to participate in the transformation of the church, is to put ourselves in a condition that frees us to be in touch with our present realities—to find in our tradition, with its Scriptures, the religious language that empowers us to name our expeiences as religious people, and then to respond to thosc experiences by doing all that is necessary to call forth the reign of God.

215

CHAPTER 12

Teaching as Practical Theology

Richard R. Osmer

Method in Theology

Methodological reflection in theology is the self-conscious account of the way theologians carry out their work. Every theologian must answer a number of questions in the course of doing theology: What is the subject matter of theology? On what sources does the theologian draw? To what end is theology undertaken? What criteria can be used to evaluate its adequacy?

The need for methodological reflection has become especially pressing today because of the wide range of theological options that has emerged. Liberation, neoorthodox, and liberal theologies, for example, are based on very different assumptions. Most systematic theologians believe that part of their task is to articulate their own position on these methodological issues in order to set forth the basic assumptions which inform their work.[1] Such reflection also has become important during this period, as theology is divided into several distinct theological disciplines. Biblical theology, historical theology, systematic theology, and practical theology do not carry out theological reflection in the same manner. A variety of proposals have been made as to the distinct focus and interrelation of these disciplines.

This chapter engages in methodological reflection on practical theology as it informs the teaching ministry of the church. Every teacher engages in a process of practical theological reflection: Is the primary purpose of the church's educational ministry conversion, or a gradual process of growth in faith? What is the subject matter of church education—the Bible, personal religious experience, or church doctrine? What teaching approaches are consistent with the purpose and subject matter of church education?

All teachers give answer to these and other important questions, whether they do so self-consciously or not. Their *actual teaching* is theory-laden or, perhaps better, *theology-laden*. Methodological reflection can help teachers become aware of the important questions they face and the answers they are giving already in the course of their teaching. This chapter is designed to assist them in this task. A brief history of the rubric "practical theology" will help teachers become aware that theology has not always been viewed as the work of academic specialists, but as part of the vocation of every Christian. Then a particular view of practical theology will be set forth—one that describes it as a hermeneutical process closely related to interpretation and action in particular contexts of experience. Last, the theological significance of five dimensions of teaching will be explored, identifying the important questions all teachers face as they participate in the church's educational ministry.

Theology as Practical

Practical theology became widely used at the end of the nineteenth century, when theology was located in the universities. Its history predates that period, however, and continues after it. "Practical theology" cannot be taken over from the past in an unreconstructed fashion, for no singular definition of this category emerges from its history. Rather, we discover a number of important clues as to what has been at stake in the gradual emergence of this way of viewing theology.[2]

An important problem immediately apparent is the implication that only practical theology is practical, while all other forms of theology are not. Such an assertion would fly in the

217

face of Protestant and Roman Catholic understandings of the entire theological enterprise, as being concerned with the formation of the life and work of the church—a very "practical" activity.

The most adequate way to respond to this concern, I believe, emerges from the recent discussion of theology as *hermeneutical*, something that will be explored more fully in the following section. For the present, it is enough to point to the common-sense recognition of the need for some specialization within the theological enterprise as a whole. Just as we would affirm all theology as grounded in the Bible, we still recognize the need for the special forms of inquiry pursued in biblical studies. In a comparable fashion, we can affirm the inherently "practical" nature of all theology, while recognizing the distinctive focus of something called *practical* theology. But what is that focus? No clear and simple answer emerges from the history of practical theology. Rather, what this history discloses is a series of phases in which certain methodological concerns came to the fore in the attempt to define what practical theology is and how it properly pursues its work.

Practical theology first appeared in conjunction with the emergence of moral theology, or what Protestants have come to call Christian ethics. In Roman Catholicism, moral theology gradually emerged out of speculative, or dogmatic, theology in the sixteenth and seventeenth centuries, in response to the need for reflection on the situation of priests in their assignment of penance.[3] *Ethics*, as a special form of theological reflection in the Protestant tradition, emerged around this same time in the face of Catholic charges that the Reformers' emphasis on justification undermined the basis of morality. A literature was spawned which sought to provide help for both *ministers and laypersons* in discerning the moral dimensions of their everyday lives, their vocations in the world. This literature was occasionally referred to as *practical* theology. While the practical nature of *all* theology continued to be affirmed, the need for this special form of theological reflection was clearly recognized.[4]

The relationship between practical theology and moral reflection simultaneously broadened and narrowed during the next phase. Gisbert Voetius, in *Selectae Disputationes* (1667), broadened practical theology by including under this rubric not only moral theology, but also ascetic theology (the practice of devotion) and ecclesiastical polity (including reflection on the church's constitution and the affairs of the ordained ministry).[5] This broadening of the scope of practical theology, however, represented a narrowing of its focus. Voetius viewed it almost exclusively in terms of its usefulness for the *leadership* of the church, especially its ordained leadership. Practical theology was now seen as focusing on the sorts of issues that confronted ministers in their work in the congregations.[6]

This focus became dominant during the third phase in the history of practical theology. During the latter part of the eighteenth century, theology was located in the newly emerging universities in Germany and began to define itself along the lines of an academic discipline.[7] Four specialized forms of research and teaching became normative—biblical studies, church history, dogmatic theology, and practical theology. As theology was divided into these discrete disciplines, it became more and more difficult to see how the different branches were interrelated. A specific genre of literature arose to respond to this concern—the theological encyclopedia.

In this literature, practical theology was largely given the task of relating to the work of the ordained ministry the theological insights generated by the other disciplines. This does not mean, however, that it was consigned to viewing itself as "applied theology," as is sometimes supposed. In the thought of persons like Friedrich Schleiermacher, practical theology was viewed as having a constructive role in its own right.[8] Its task was to formulate "rules of art" which could guide ministers and church leaders in carrying out their work.

219

General principles and ideas from the other branches of theology were conjoined to the accrued wisdom of past practice to provide church leaders with an integrated, coherent orientation toward the various situations they faced. In providing rules of art, practical theology represented theoretical reflection designed to guide thought and action as they occur in the actual practice of ministry.

While Schleiermacher did not, in principle, confine practical theology to the work of the ordained minister, but focused on the leadership function of the whole church, those who followed his thought increasingly came to limit it to the tasks and functions of the clergy. This represents the fourth stage in the history of practical theology.[9] The specialization of the theological encyclopedia continued, with practical theology's task viewed as helping ordained ministers gain a proper understanding of the purpose and practice of preaching, teaching, and the cure of souls.[10] Methodologically, the constructive role of this form of theology became more and more unclear. In the encyclopedia period, the following questions were not being addressed adequately: What contribution does practical theology make to the larger theological enterprise? Is there a place for original research and theory-construction in this discipline, as in the other theological disciplines?

During the fifth stage in the history of practical theology, these two issues were addressed directly by practical theology in dialogue with the social sciences, as it will be called here. The religious-education movement and the pastoral-care-and-counseling movement are representative of this period. Both emerged as potent forces during the first part of the twentieth century and focused on incorporating the findings of the social sciences into their practice. Representatives of both movements articulated a much stronger role for theory and research in the practical theological disciplines. At the same time, they developed a far more dynamic understanding of the theory-practice relationship than was present earlier.

The result was a major shift methodologically. Persons like George Albert Coe, Anton Boisen, and Seward Hiltner were not satisfied with determining the practice of religious education or pastoral care on the basis of theological concepts derived from the other theological disciplines.[11] Rather, they were empirically and clinically oriented, drawing on research in a newly emerging field, the psychology of religion. At the same time, they pointed to a method in which theory and practice were mutually influential. Both Coe, in religious education, and Hiltner, in pastoral care and counseling, were influenced by John Dewey's understanding of the theory/practice relationship, in which thought emerges out of and reconstructs experience in an ongoing fashion.[12]

While Coe, Boisen, Hiltner, and others in these movements were more theologically inclined than is commonly acknowledged, the central methodological problem which emerged from this period was an overreliance on the social sciences as a *source* of substantive theological reflection. In general, a liberal confidence in the immanence of God in history led people to look to human sources of understanding to define the nature of humanity and the Godhead. And ultimately, a recognition of the distinctive source and purpose of practical theological reflection as a form of *theology* suffered.

It is precisely this weakness that was clearly recognized in the next stage of practical theology: practical theology as formulated during the ascendancy of neoorthodox theology. During this period (1930s and 1940s), a strong affirmation of theology's grounding in revelation provided a clear basis for distinguishing it from other forms of human reflection. The social sciences were rightfully seen as grounded in empirical research. Theology, in contrast, was thought to look to Scripture's account of salvation history, especially God's self-disclosure in Jesus Christ, to discern the nature of God and the world in relation to God. Persons like James Smart and H. Shelton Smith mediated the insights of this movement to the practical theological disciplines.[13]

It was of the utmost importance to representatives of this

221

movement that practical theology remain *theological*, that it not sell its birthright to the social sciences or philosophy. Methodologically, this led to an intensive effort to hold together the various theological disciplines and, through practical theology, bring them to bear on the church's practice. James Smart, for example, used a theological method which began with biblical theology, moved to doctrinal formulations, and then set forth the implications of these doctrines for Christian education. Emphasis was placed exclusively on the internal dialogue *within* theology, which must take place if practical theology is to retain its integrity as theology. Two things are missing, however, in Smart's work, and in this stage in general: (1) an appreciation of the close relationship between thought and action (or experience) in practical theology; and (2) an understanding of the way that interdisciplinary work can properly be carried out in this field.

In large part, the recent interest in practical theology, which must be thought of as the seventh stage in its history, has been sparked by two trends. First, the "praxis epistemologies" of Marx and Aristotle have exerted a renewed influence on theology, the former taken up by liberation theology, the latter by the ethics of character.[14] Both have pointed to the need that thought be grounded in authentic forms of practice. Second, there has been an increasing sense of urgency about the need to move beyond the modern custom of confining theology to the highly specialized thought of professional theologians.[15] Theological reflection is more properly viewed as an inherent part of every Christian's vocation. While academic theology has a role in the church's life, it is not exclusive of other forms of and settings for theological reflection.

These trends and others have conspired to raise the question of the nature and purpose of practical theology with renewed vigor. While no consensus exists within the recent discussion as to how this rubric should be defined, one of the most important formulations to emerge has been articulated by those who view theology as a hermeneutical enterprise.[16]

222

Practical Theology as Hermeneutical

The term *hermeneutics* is closely associated etymologically with Hermes in Greek mythology.[17] Hermes served as messenger of the gods, charged with the task of transmitting divine communication into a form human intelligence can grasp. Retaining this basic meaning, hermeneutics in the modern period was viewed initially as a discipline concerned with the art and science of the interpretation of ancient texts in ways that were meaningful to people in the present.

Gradually, this understanding was broadened. An important step in this process took place when Wilhelm Dilthey argued that hermeneutics, which focuses on interpretation, is the proper mode of understanding in the human sciences, in contrast to explanation, which is proper in the natural sciences.[18] As historical, cultural beings, people can be understood, not explained. In this century, Martin Heidegger, Hans-Georg Gadamer, and Paul Ricoeur have gone one step further, arguing that hermeneutics is a constitutive dimension of human existence.[19] Human beings are constantly engaged in a hermeneutical process: From the moment they first begin to use language, they participate in a system which presents and interprets objects, persons, and events in a particular way. Humans can no more escape the process of interpretation than they can think and remember without using language.

A fundamental characteristic of this process is its temporality. The activity of understanding an object, an event, or even the whole of reality takes place within the constraints of time. It invariably begins with a certain "preunderstanding," or prejudice, in the present.[20] Even supposedly objective scientific methods reflect the present assumptions of the paradigms in which they work.[21] These, in turn, are grounded in and grow out of the past, constructing present understandings by drawing on cultural and linguistic traditions. Present preunderstandings and past traditions are not closed, however. They open out toward the future. Understanding, if it is

223

genuine, does not merely repeat the past in the present, but reaches out to achieve something new. It allows the person, object, or event being understood to reveal itself in a new light, opening up new possibilities for the future.

An important insight that has emerged from this recognition of the temporality of understanding is its circular character, frequently described as the hermeneutical circle.[22] In all interpretation, there is a reciprocal relationship between the parts and the whole. In interpreting one of Paul's letters, for example, it is necessary to begin with some sense of Paul as a person, why he is writing, and the general contours of his theology. Such preunderstanding in the present is based on inherited or accrued understandings of the past. Yet it is the different parts of Paul's letters which, in fact, make up the whole of his thought. The preunderstandings which structure one's initial understanding may be confirmed or denied by those different parts. It is precisely the experience of being brought up short that opens up the possibility of new understanding.[23]

There is an unavoidable circle here: The parts and the whole are mutually interrelated. To understand the parts is to presuppose some form of understanding of the whole. But the whole can never be known immediately and directly in its totality. It can be known only in and through its parts, which may open up new understandings of the whole.

This description of the hermeneutical dimension of human existence has influenced theology in a wide variety of ways. Two lines of thought are particularly important, with respect to our interest in practical theology: (1) an understanding of theology's task as hermeneutical; and (2) the use of the hermeneutical circle to grasp the interrelation of the parts and whole in the theological enterprise.

Drawing on the insight that human beings are constantly engaged in an interpretive process, certain representatives of hermeneutical practical theology view the theological task as an inherent part of the vocation of every Christian.[24] That task

224

is the *reflective dimension of piety*—the attempt to understand God and the world in relation to God. This is done with various degrees of self-consciousness and comprehensiveness in the Christian life, and it ranges from the idiosyncratic images of God formed by a preschooler to the highly technical proposals of a systematic theologian; both are engaged in a hermeneutical activity that is theological in nature.

While there is an important role for specialized technical theological reflection in the formation and transformation of this interpretive activity, it is a mistake to think of theology primarily as being sharply distinguished from the fundamental theological interpretation that takes place in the lives of ordinary Christians. Such a distinction has been drawn in recent years on the basis of an analogy between theology and grammar.[25] Theology is viewed as related to "first-order" religious discourse, in ways that are similar to grammar's relationship to everyday language: It sets forth the rules governing the proper use of religious language. As such, theology is viewed as "second-order" discourse, one step removed from the hermeneutical process carried out by ordinary Christians.

This sort of analogy works best with only one type of theological reflection—systematic theology. The task of such theology is the systematic presentation of Christian doctrine in an attempt to show the internal relationship of a wide range of theological beliefs important to the Christian life. It is a mistake, however, to argue that this is the *only* task of theology. The different forms of reflection involved in both historical and practical theology are not well suited to the analogy with grammar. Historical retrieval in biblical studies and church history often poses challenges to systematic theologies. Ideas are placed in their original context; generalization from one historical particular to another is not always easy, nor is it necessarily systematic. The theological task is to discern both continuity and discontinuity in past expressions of the Christian faith, as found in Scripture and tradition.

225

Similarly, the task of practical theology is not best understood in terms of the analogy with grammar. Those persons who describe practical theology in a hermeneutical mode view it as the sort of theological reflection used to guide action in the midst of deeply particular, dynamic contexts of experience. It is not so much an effort to stand back from a situation and identify a relatively constant set of rules, as in grammar, as it is a process of reflection which develops as it interacts with an unfolding situation. Reflection functions as an instrument *in* a situation, influencing the course of events and, in turn, being influenced by them.

To the extent that rules enter into this sort of reflection, they resemble Schleiermacher's rules of art. They do not stipulate the proper action to be taken (as grammar governs linguistic expression) but function as *illuminative* principles which tentatively project a way to interpret a situation and to proceed in it. Based on cumulative experience (or past practice), such rules serve as the starting point for reflection and engagement of a situation in its concreteness. They will be confirmed or disconfirmed as the situation unfolds through time. In no case will they simply be applied.

The basic presupposition here is that *all Christians and congregations should carry out this sort of theological reflection as they attempt to interpret their present existence in relation to God.* Christians, as they pursue their vocations in the world and come together in congregations, are not totally nonreflective, as the analogy with grammar seems to imply. Nor does their reflection lack biblical and theological substance. They reflect upon the various situations which confront them in the present, in an attempt to discern God's will and shape their commitments, relationships, and actions accordingly. Such reflection does not strive for the logical coherence of a systematic treatise. Rather, it is reflection which seeks a deeper understanding of concrete situations, attempts to identify relevant theological and ethical issues, projects possible ways to proceed, enacts concrete courses of action, and reflects upon the consequences these actions engender. *In short, practical theological reflection is an interpretive process which takes place in the midst of unfolding situations and seeks to understand and shape those situations according to the discernment of God's will.*

What is the relationship of this sort of reflection to the sort carried out by other forms of theology? This brings us to the second influence of hermeneutics on practical theology: It views the interrelation of the various modes of theological reflection in terms of the hermeneutical circle. Each form of reflection represents part of a larger whole. The parts are mutually dependent; they represent necessary moments in an integrated theological interpretation of God and of the world in relation to God.

In Protestant theology, this can be conceptualized in terms of movement from the Bible to contemporary life.[26] This is inherently a hermeneutical task, which involves persons in the task of interpreting texts formed in past historical contexts, in ways that are meaningful in the present context. That interpretation involves several distinct "moments" which are parts of a larger whole.

Traditionally, Protestant theology was viewed the Bible as the norm in the church. As such, all theological interpretation must include a "moment" of biblical interpretation, which incorporates the findings of biblical scholarship. Biblical interpretation, however, does not take place in a vacuum. It presupposes a tradition of interpretation embodied in the past expressions of the Christian community. Scripture and the history of its interpretation in church tradition stand in a dialectical relationship. The former cannot bypass the latter; the latter cannot determine the former. Within the historical moment of theological interpretation, both are necessary.

Historical interpretation in turn gives way to the present. Drawing on the investigation of Scripture and church tradition, contemporary theologians must forge a constructive statement of the Christian faith which articulates its various dimensions. Here, theological interpretation achieves a

227

systematic moment. At this point, the inner coherence of theological interpretation is at stake—the fact that a commitment to certain doctrinal perspectives in one part of a person's thought implies commitment to related doctrinal perspectives in other areas. A commitment to the doctrine of justification by grace, for example, excludes a commitment to a Pelagian view of human works—or at least it should! Systematic reflection upon the entire range of theological doctrines is necessary to prevent unwitting contradictions in a person's beliefs and actions as a whole.

This systematic moment in theological interpretation gives way to present Christian existence in its concreteness. Individual Christians and congregations interpret the circumstances of their lives and enact faithful responses, not in general, but in very particular situations. *They do not strive to articulate a systematic treatise, but to live lives of faith and obedience.* This is the practical moment in theological interpretation: the reflection carried out by ordinary Christians and congregations as they attempt to live our their vocations in the concrete circumstances of their lives. At some point, theological interpretation must achieve this moment if it is to play its role in the life of the church. In the give and take of practical theological reflection as it unfolds in concrete contexts of experience, the insights of the other theological disciplines are tested in the matrix of Christian existence, and new insights are generated, which may reverberate throughout the entire theological enterprise.

Each moment is necessary to theological interpretation as a whole, and interpretation can legitimately begin at any point. Moreover, the parts are mutually influential; issues that emerge from present Christian existence can influence the themes investigated in Scripture and tradition, and comprehensive statements of the faith can lead to the alteration of present practices in the church. Thus theological interpretation in a hermeneutical mode is best viewed as a circular process, in which the various forms of theological reflection represent necessary parts of a larger whole.

228

Hermeneutical Practical Theology in the Teaching Ministry

Though part of a much larger interpretive process, practical theology begins with the present life and thought of the church and its members. Its primary text is the present context in which Christians live out their vocations in the world. However, primary attention here will be given to the leaders of the church and the way practical theological reflection takes place in conjunction with their guidance of the church's educational ministry.

To begin, a distinction between teaching and education is needed. Education involves a community's systematic and intentional effort to transmit and evoke worthwhile knowledge, attitudes, values, and skills.[27] It focuses on a *community's* moral vision, its attempt to identify those portions of its heritage and present knowledge that are important to hand on to the next generation, that are necessary to the continued well-being of the community and its members.[28]

Teaching, in contrast, has a more limited role. It focuses on those *specific occasions* in the life of the community through which education takes place. Teaching always involves particular people in specific settings. It is an event. At the heart of teaching is an increase in *understanding* of the subject matter on the part of the student.[29] Here *understanding* refers not only to cognitive apprehension, but to a gestalt of thought, emotion, and behavior by which meaning is constructed and expressed. Communities have the right and responsibility to determine the knowledge, skills, values, and attitudes that should be handed on, but in the actual event of teaching, they must be handed on in a manner that respects the learner.[30] The goal of teaching is not indoctrination, but an increase in *understanding*.

Those who undertake the activity of teaching inevitably engage in a rich and complex process of interpretation which involves certain key dimensions. As we shall see, each of these dimensions has to do with decisions and understandings of a theological nature, which methodological reflection attempts to clarify. While not exhaustive, this list of key dimensions includes the subject matter being taught, the context in which teaching takes place, the person(s) engaged in learning, the broader curriculum of which this particular teaching is a part, and the teaching approach chosen for each particular occasion.[31]

In any teaching occasion, the teacher may focus attention on one or two of these dimensions at any given time. However, at every point, there is some interpretation of each dimension. It is helpful to think of the interrelation of these dimensions in terms of the hermeneutical circle. The various parts, or dimensions, of teaching are mutually interdependent and make up the whole. Interpretation of the context in a particular way, for example, may influence the teaching approach chosen. Or if the learners are interpreted as possessing certain cognitive abilities, the subject matter is likely to be presented in a particular way. In a very real sense, a circular process takes place, since the parts and the whole are interrelated. This circular process, moreover, is located within the larger hermeneutical circle of theological interpretation.

It is especially important to grasp the *theological* nature of each dimension. While it is legitimate and even desirable to draw on nontheological resources (e.g., education, developmental psychology, cultural anthropology, etc.) in forming interpretations of persons, context, subject matter, curriculum, and teaching approach, it is crucial that the theological nature of these dimensions be grasped in practical theological reflection. The way theology and nontheological resources are to be related is one of the most important methodological decisions made by every practical theologian.[32] For our purposes, it is enough to point to the theological element at stake in each of these dimensions. As will become apparent, each dimension opens out to the kind of reflection that takes place in systematic theology and in the historical retrieval of biblical studies and church history. In practical theological reflection, these dimensions point to the kind of theological interpretation that *guides the practice of teaching* in concrete settings and over time.

Methodological decisions of great import are involved in the dimension of *subject matter*—the knowledge, values, skills, and attitudes deemed worthy of attention in the church's educational ministry. Obviously, this definition includes much more than knowledge. It is quite possible that the activity of teaching at any given time could focus less upon the transmission of information than upon the forming of certain attitudes viewed as central components of Christian piety. Three decisions in regard to subject matter are particularly important in teaching that takes place in the church and that involve the teacher in a process of theological interpretation: (1) How is the subject matter related to Christian truth? (2) Who has the authority to determine the knowledge, skills, values, and attitudes that are the proper focus of teaching in the church? (3) What is the teacher's personal relationship to the subject matter?

The relation of subject matter to Christian truth is perhaps the most important interpretation. At stake is the teacher's understanding of Christian truth and the relation of that truth to the subject matter of a specific teaching event. Teaching in the church can focus on a wide variety of subjects, ranging from the content of Scripture to the official doctrines of the church, to personal experiences of the Holy Spirit. Sometimes the subject matter is suggested by provided printed material. Sometimes the congregation and individual teacher must make this determination themselves.

In any case, the teacher faces these questions: What is the primary means by which Christian truth is known? Does it determine the knowledge, skills, attitudes, or values included in the subject matter of this particular teaching event?[33] If revelation is viewed as closely bound to Scripture, for example, it is highly likely that the content of Scripture will be an important part of the subject matter. Similarly, if personal experience of the Holy Spirit is viewed as primary, the subject

231

matter will include the sharing of such experiences. Frequently, teachers experience tensions between their own understanding of Christian truth and the printed literature the church provides. They may believe strongly in a linkage of Christian truth and Scripture, for example, but find that the printed material focuses almost exclusively on social and ethical issues. They are faced with a dilemma of theological import.

This leads to a second issue of theological interpretation inherent in subject matter: Who has the authority to decide the proper subject matter?[34] It should not be automatically assumed that each individual teacher has this right. Throughout most of church history, teaching authority has been invested in a variety of roles and agencies beyond the local church—representative bodies, denominational leaders, confessional statements, theologians, seminaries. Across the centuries, it has not been up to each individual teacher, for example, to determine the contents of the catechism. This was seen as the right of representative bodies working on behalf of the entire church.

Each teacher in the church must decide, on theological grounds, what sort of authority he or she has in relation to the broader constellation of teaching authorities affirmed by many church traditions. What part does the teacher legitimately play in determining the subject matter? Is this largely a matter of the individual's own conscience, a function of congregational leaders, or is the priority of bodies and/or leaders representative of the entire denomination? Teachers should not assume that they can reject the printed material of the denomination, or that this material accurately reflects Scripture and the heritage of the denomination. These are theological questions to be engaged.

This poses a third issue of theological import: What is the teacher's personal relationship to the subject matter? Put another way, who is qualified to teach in the church? If the subject matter is closely related to Christian truth, does this imply certain things about those who teach it? Can Christian

232

truth be taught by someone not personally engaged by that truth? Must teachers subscribe to theological standards representative of their church's tradition, standards which exercise control over the subject matter? Can teachers really grasp the subject matter of Scripture without a prior commitment to and involvement in transforming action on behalf of the poor and oppressed? Teachers invariably answer these questions according to the way they view their role in teaching and their relationship to the subject matter they teach. Explicitly or otherwise, they do engage in a process of theological interpretation.

The second dimension of interpretation is the formation of an understanding of the *learners* involved. This takes place on several levels. On the most immediate level, the teacher must ascertain the present or potential capacities of those being taught. If teaching is an attempt to increase the learners' understanding of the subject matter, it would be contradictory to teach in a manner that surpassed their present ability to interact with the subject matter in meaningful ways. Here many educational and psychological theories may prove helpful to the teacher: developmental theory, learning theory, research on differences between men and women in the construction of knowledge, and so forth. These are powerful tools for interpreting the skills learners bring to the teaching event.

The use of nontheological resources brings into focus a more fundamental level of interpretation inherent in this dimension—a theological interpretation of the pattern of Christian existence. Traditionally, this pattern has been dealt with under the doctrinal rubrics of humanity, justification, and sanctification. What does it mean to be created in the image of God, to fall, to be justified, and to live a sanctified life?

It is not enough to employ the insights of the social sciences in church teaching. Inherent in these sciences are important assumptions about what it means to be human, assumptions which may or may not be consistent with the teacher's theological understanding of the human condition.[35] All too

233

often, teachers base their interpretations of the learner on an uncritical use of nontheological resources which leads them to view the pattern of Christian existence in a certain way. A greater awareness of the theological issues at stake is needed in interpreting the learner along certain lines. It makes a great deal of difference whether the pattern of Christian existence is viewed primarily in organic, developmental terms; in terms of in-breaking, transforming crisis events; as a matter of each individual's free will; or as the ongoing, paradoxical struggle between God's forgiveness and human sin. Teachers inevitably are forming interpretations of the learner. In these interpretations, issues of great theological significance are at stake.

A third dimension inherent in all teaching in the church is an interpretation of the *context* in which the teaching is taking place. Context represents the network of systems, existing through time, which are relevant to the teaching activity. This can range from familial relationships to the culture of the congregation, to the national and even global ecology of institutions and relationships which impinge upon persons. As used here, context also has temporal dimensions, pointing to the fact that the systems which constitute the context of teaching exist through time. These have a "giveness" about them which the teacher must take into account.

Interpretation of context is important for two reasons. First, the learners cannot really be understood in isolation from the relationships, institutions, and history of which they are a part. It is very important for the teacher to move beyond the behavior and attitudes presented by persons during the actual teaching event, to a richer understanding of the context that lies behind those attitudes and behaviors. It is not uncommon, for example, for teachers to discover that behavior problems during teaching activities are closely related to things going on at home. Only when this context is understood can an accurate interpretation be formed. A wide variety of contexts is important in this regard—social class, nationality, sex roles, family systems. At any given time, the learner is participating in multiple contexts. One of the decisions the teacher faces is to decide which context(s) is most important to the teaching at hand.

This brings us to the second reason contextual interpretation is important, a reason that is more explicitly theological. Why is it important that the church struggle to understand the context in which it carries out its ministry? Why not simply preach the Word of God and administer the sacraments, and let the Holy Spirit do the rest? To willfully ignore context in this fashion is to imply that the church's ministry escapes the limitations of finite existence. The church's teachings are viewed as rising above the constraints of their social and historical context. Inevitably, this leads to the elevation of church teaching (and the one doing the teaching) to a position that is properly reserved for God alone.

Acknowledgment of context is based on the recognition that church teaching is a finite, fallible activity, subject to the limitations of time and place. It inevitably participates in historical and social processes. Teachers can no more escape from the constraints of context than a fish can live out of water. Rather than pretend that contextual factors do not influence their teaching, they should attempt to understand, in a self-conscious fashion, the contextual interpretation operative in their teaching at any given time. This allows them to bring into awareness an element of their preunderstanding which often exerts influence at an unconscious level, diminishing its power to direct their teaching in ways that distort their understanding of the subject matter or the learner.

A fourth dimension of teaching is the *curriculum;* which stands between the community's educational vision and institutions, and the specific teaching events. The etymology of curriculum is "course of study," or "race to be run," both of which capture the essence of this dimension. Teaching occasions are part of a longer and broader process through which a community hands on the knowledge, attitudes, skills, and values it deems worthwhile. It is not possible to teach everything of importance all at once. Rather, communities

235

devise a course of study, or curriculum, by which they structure teaching and learning over a period of time. Certain portions of the Bible are covered during certain grades; abstract theological doctrines are covered at other points. There is a sequencing of the subject matter, based on both the integrity of the subject (some things are best learned before others, serving as their foundation) and the capacities of the learners.

All teachers make certain important interpretive judgments about the relation of their teaching to the larger curriculum of the community. Two issues of theological import are at stake in this regard. The first was pointed to earlier, focusing on the authority granted the larger church community in determining the subject matter. What role does the community have in determining the curriculum? How free is the teacher (or the congregation) to replace or modify the curriculum the community has set up? Is the curriculum true to the community's heritage? In answering these questions, teachers are forming an interpretation of the teaching office and their role within it.

In many mainline Protestant churches, for example, the community is seen as playing an advisory, consultative role by offering written material which organizes the subject matter over time and by suggesting teaching approaches appropriate to the learners' capacities. Teachers are encouraged to adapt the material to their context, interpreting it in ways that are consistent with the particularities of their own situations. But they are not encouraged to disregard it altogether, disrupting the sequence of learning the curriculum proposes, or substituting their own theological perspective for the one the curriculum advocates on the basis of communal traditions. Invariably, teachers must decide on their stance toward the community's curriculum. Are they primarily agents of transmission, of adaptation, or of correction? These questions become particularly pressing when teachers do not agree with the curriculum's proposals.

A second issue of equal importance has to do with teachers'

ability to locate their own teaching within the ongoing, open-ended process of learning to which the curriculum points. Learning in the Christian faith is never completed. It is not like graduation from a school upon completion of certain requirements. In the church, the subject matter is ever before the learner, for it deals with God and with the world in relation to God. The curriculum symbolizes a lifelong process of openness to divine instruction.

Teachers must make another important judgment: What does their own teaching contribute to this lifelong process? At some special "teachable moments" in the lives of individuals and communities, they are particularly open to new truth and transformation. At other times, growth and learning seem to plod along with few visible signs of change. The way teachers interpret the apparent growth or stasis of their students says much of theological importance. What role is the Holy Spirit seen as playing in this lifelong curriculum of faith? How far can teachers legitimately go in pressing students in certain directions? What is the role of the church community as a whole in nurturing the seeds of learning planted in teaching? Teachers of the church cannot avoid answering these questions, if only implicitly.

The final dimension of teaching focuses on the *teaching approach* chosen to structure a particular teaching event. In light of their interpretation of the context, subject matter, learner, and curriculum, teachers must make a range of decisions: What are the appropriate goals for the session(s) being taught? What are the best teaching methods to achieve these goals? What sequence of activities is most appropriate? In order to answer these questions, teachers must develop a repertoire of teaching approaches appropriate to different teaching goals and styles of learning. Recent efforts to form a taxonomy of teaching have identified five such approaches: information processing, group interaction, indirect communication, personal development, and action/reflection.[36] Each approach has a particular emphasis—the transmission of

237

information, for example, or the enhancement of the individual's development.

At their best, teachers are like artists in their use of approaches.[37] Drawing on a rich repertoire of knowledge and skill and a fund of practical wisdom, they craft teaching events that are appropriate to context, person, subject matter, and curriculum. They have the capacity to ask questions which integrate the various dimensions of teaching: Why teach this subject matter to these persons in this context? What teaching approaches best communicate the subject matter that is the focus of this part of the congregation's overall curriculum? What teaching approaches work best with these persons? Artist-teachers begin to operate with a high degree of intentionality and are able to translate this intentionality into meaningful planning. While forming a teaching plan to guide them, however, they do not allow such plans to determine their actual teaching in a slavish, mechanical manner. Artist-teachers constantly make on-the-spot judgments and introduce improvisations. They engage in a process of interpreting what is going on and adjust their teaching accordingly: This method appears to be working well and should be given more time; that person seems to be left out and needs individual attention. In short, they engage the hermeneutical task in its concreteness as they teach.

Teaching is a living transaction which involves many dimensions. A great deal is at stake theologically in the ways teachers carry out this ministry of the church. Many teachers in the church already engage in the kind of practical theological interpretation that has been outlined here. It is the goal of methodological reflection to help them become self-conscious about what they are already doing, and to provide the opportunity to deepen the interpretations that inform their teaching.

Living into a World of Confessional Pluralism: The Partnership of Education and Theology

Donald E. Miller and Jack L. Seymour

What is the place of theology in Christian religious education? In chapter one we defined theology as reflection within the community of faith, seeking to understand and respond to what it means to be accepted, sent, and called by God into the brokenness of the world. It is our contention that Christian education is more than the initiation of persons into a faith that is already delivered in a relatively completed form. Learning is more than remembering or re-creating; learning is also membering and creating. The process of learning the faith that was delivered to us is a process of interpreting during the act of receiving.

As long as instruction in the faith is understood as simply the transmission of what has been received, then the art of education is merely that of helping people comprehend what is already given, and theology is relevant principally to shape the belief that is to be learned. Theology and education then have very little direct influence upon one another.

When, however, instruction in the faith is understood as a process of interpreting what is being received, and when learning is an act of creation as well as re-creation, then the art of education is more than simply transmission, and the tradition is being shaped in the process of being learned. The shaping of the tradition is then disclosed as an essential part of the tradition itself. The relationship between education and theology becomes much more one of interdependence, and the exploration of that interdependence is the central concern of this book.

239

Framing the Issues

Let us rephrase the issues to bring out the partnership of education and theology. With regard to tradition, we may ask, what is the nature of tradition, in that the tradition itself is born in a constant process of interpretation? In a similar way, what is the nature of the church, in view of the fact that the church lives in a constant process of interpretation? What is the nature of the person, and the nature of the church's mission in the world, in view of the process of formation and transformation? And what is the nature of theological method, in view of this constant interpretation of tradition?

We need a fundamental concept of education, wherein teaching is a theological activity, empowering the people of God to be agents of the new community within the public world of God's presence and power. Such education participates in the dynamic process of understanding, interpreting, and living in relation to the Holy One, the horizon of our being. Understanding arises from action, and action arises from understanding, so that education is an ongoing praxis.

We need a fundamental concept of theology, wherein theology is a constant process of interpretation and discovery in view of the actual experience of people, so that they may become agents of the new community within the public world of God's presence and power. Such theology allows the dynamic process of understanding, interpretation, and praxis to be essentially included in the living relationship to the Holy One, the horizon of our being. Theological understanding arises from the process of learning and is shaped by it, while theology gives significant guidance to learning, as it, itself, is being transformed.

God's will, as made known in Jesus Christ, is not independent of the experience of those who were and are being transformed by God's will. God's revelation is not independent of those who were and are being created by that revelation. The apostle Paul speaks of having the truth of God in earthen vessels. Part of that earthen quality is the ongoing process by which we constantly interpret and reinterpret, embody and reembody, in order to understand.

A more intrinsic interrelationship between theology and education will require a new language for both disciplines. The traditional terms cannot merely be stretched to include the new. Like the theological language of the past, the new language will be created more by common use than by formally constructed ideas. Just as the New Testament is written in the common language, Koine Greek, so the language of faith most often arises from the experience of the people.

It is our conviction that the new language for religious education should be developed in the public arena. The language of faith develops in the struggle with idols of culture. At the close of the twentieth century, it is in the public arena that many of the basic questions of the meaning and nature of human life are being debated. And there the new language for both theology and education will be born. The expression of Christian faith is private only when circumstances force privacy upon it. Otherwise, the Christian faith reaches for public expression.

Tradition

What is the nature of the tradition with regard to its transmission? The tradition is a community forming reality. In a real sense, community is the tradition in embodied form. At the same time, the community carries the tradition. Protestantism has emphasized the importance of Scripture as a source of the Word of God, while Catholicism has emphasized the ongoing tradition. However, we know the relationship is dynamic. Scripture itself is formed in the process of continual reinterpretation of tradition.

A classic twentieth-century interpretation of faith is that of Dietrich Bonhoeffer, who understood faithful living to be a Christlike openness to the neighbor, a willingness to accept the guilt of the neighbor. Faith is a spirit of openness toward one

241

another, such openness being possible only in the grace of God through Jesus Christ.

The tradition becomes a living reality in a community where there is openness toward one another and toward all whom Christ loved. For such a community the scriptural traditions become a vibrant reality. The traditions are carried by a living community and become an essential part of the community, forming a reality which nourishes the community.

The tradition lives and is carried and expressed in various ways—in worship, study, service. These expressions give voice to the tradition, but are themselves meaningless unless they manifest Christlike openness in and beyond the community of faith that evidences God's grace. The process of interpreting and reinterpreting is thereby taken into the heart of the meaning of a living tradition. Furthermore, the interpretation process takes place in the setting of openness to a world that is the wider focus of God's presence and power.

As Marianne Sawicki notes, the tradition comes in the written word, the sacraments, and in ministry to the little ones. And as Melanie A. May and Mary Elizabeth Mullino Moore clarify, tradition is always dynamically being formed. Protestant or Catholic, the importance of the living relationship, a manifestation of God's grace, is the reality within which tradition is carried. At the same time, the interpreting and reinterpreting of the tradition in worship and sacrament, in service and study of Scripture, is an essential expression of a living faith. There is both a paradoxical and a mutually interactive relationship between the processes that nurture the tradition and the living relationship to God and to one another.

Since theology is a part of the tradition, theology itself, as much as education, is caught up in the paradoxical relationship to the living Christ. Theology and education carry out their parallel efforts to reinterpret the tradition within the prayer, hope, and faithful expectation that God will grace these efforts with the vitality of God's new humanity. Therefore theology is more and more inclined to take into itself

242

the dialogical character of communicating the faith, and education is more and more inclined to converse with theology to uncover the relationship of the content of faith, the process of meaning-making, to the living relationships of a faithful community.

Many church educators have emphasized that the quality of Christian education depends upon being good education. Behind this view are the generations of theology's dominance over church nurture. Many educators do not want to run the risk of handing education back to a theology that is devoid of any educational insight. While such a warning is worthy of note, the discussion must process beyond such turf protection. Theology itself is searching to discover why meaning itself is carried in a constant process of reinterpretation. Education cannot focus simply upon the process of meaning-making without asking the fundamental questions about what is meaningful. To do so is to court the trivial. So theology and education are drawn into a mutually supporting dialogue, which itself is paradoxically related to God's graceful presence in the relationships of the new humanity.

Church

What is the nature of the Church with regard to the nurturing and meaning-seeking activities within it? The Pauline reference of the church as the Body of Christ describes Christians as joined together in a community of belief. Christianity embodies a distinctive call to community.

Yet, contemporary expressions of voluntarism undermine the church in two ways. Individuals come to the church simply in order to have their individual needs met, rather than in a self-giving relationship to the larger community of faith. Furthermore, individuals now have the option not only to choose different expressions of community, but to decide whether any community at all is necessary. The latter choice violates the distinctive character of the Christian life.

A primary task of Christian religious education is to serve as a vehicle for the divine calling of the church to be the Body of

243

Christ. To fulfill that task the church must seek to initiate people into the stories and traditions of the community—what Foster calls mediation; Matsuoka, identity. Moreover, the church must seek to witness to the power of the Word of God in the midst of the world. To continue to sing the Lord's song, even in a foreign land, is the courage of the faith.

Foster and Matsuoka have addressed the question of ecclesiology from majority and minority perspectives. Both assume that the church is a community forming reality, the Body of Christ. Both assume that Christian religious education will enhance the formation and reformation of the community. Oddly enough, from the two perspectives, the problems are not so different. Foster believes that radical individualism in today's Western societies challenges the very community character of the Church. Matsuoka has found that the dominant culture makes the discovery of a new ethnic identity extremely painful. In fact, the whole church contains elements of minority situations with regard to the majority culture.

Majority Christians may speak of addressing injustice, but seldom with the sense of suffering injustice. The majority experience is aware of the importance of reinterpreting the tradition, but without the sense of holy insecurity. A community theology is aware of the educational tasks of mediation, but without the sense of discovering a tenuous, fragile, common thread.

In its effort to speak to actual need and find real interests, Christian education is especially prone to promote a narrow provincialism or an idolatrous culturism. Education within a faithful community remembers a life-giving past in order to be open to the possibilities of a promise-filled future. The minority church's contribution to ecclesiology is to remind everyone that a faithful community strengthens the courage to live in holy insecurity as a people, to seek a promised identity often full of ambiguity, and to reach out into the public arena in ways that are often merely fragile threads. Such a theological perspective may help Christian education to be faithful to the reality of the Body of Christ.

244

The Word of God is a community forming reality, the context of our lives. The Word nourishes and recreates us in loving forgiveness, comforts and strengthens us in hope. The Word comes to us as gift and promise, encouraging us to remember when we are God's people, helping us anticipate the overcoming of our marginality, and enabling our ethnicity to be a blessing to all people. The Word comes as an openness toward the neighbor, overcoming the enemy with love, welcoming the stranger with hospitality, and taking on the guilt of the neighbor. A nurturing, remembering, anticipating, sharing, hospitable, publicly engaged community of faith is both the context and the goal of Christian religious education.

Person

The majority culture nurtures an atomistic, autonomous model of individual personhood. Yet to be faithful is to be possessed by the Story and true to the character of reality. We are rooted in bodily, historical existence. We exist in relation to all that God creates and loves. The fundamental sin is that we attempt to prosper without God, who alone can free us from our self-captivity.

Christian character is the goal of Christian formation. Sanctification is the lifelong formation and transformation of individual character. Participation in the Christian community is the primary means of grace by which character is transformed. Sanctification, the transformation of character in view of the image of God, is an immersion of believers in the spiritual disciplines of a dynamic faith community.

Romney Moseley further defines the meaning of the image of God by focusing on Jesus Christ—the incarnate One who emptied himself of power and glory in order to take on the form of humanity. In contrast, contemporary Christian education has been bound by developmental psychology. The result is that symbols of faith are demythologized according to their stage of development; thereby the imaginal content of faith loses its seriousness. Furthermore, a community of faith

245

should not be so concerned that individuals move through a prescribed sequence, but rather that they live with the paradoxes and differences that arise in the Christian community. Theories that emphasize progressivism at the expense of human suffering need to be measured by a kenotic Christology, one that emphasizes the pain and self-emptying of God within humanity. Such a theology reminds us that we all are imperfect and in need of grace before the ultimately gracious One.

The critical anthropological conception for education is the Imago Dei (image of God). This self-emptying (kenotic) conception of incarnation leads to a concern about the formation and transformation of character through an immersion in spiritual discipline. Emphasis is upon worship, praxis, and instruction in the community of faith, as well as upon the imaginal content of faith, especially with regard to those who are poor, dispossessed and powerless.

The Christian educator's theological conception of mature personhood shapes consequent educational theory and practice. A conception of personhood that is educationally and theologically adequate must recover the sense of God's presence so that education becomes an exercise in spiritual discipline. Education then will give its primary attention to the imaginal content of faith. How each individual feels and acts about God's presence and power becomes more important than whether it is expressed as stage-three or stage-four morality. God's self-emptying and humiliation within humanity give unequaled significance to the most despised people. Groups that do not score well on moral development tests are as worthy in their reasons for belief as are those who do score well.

Such a reversal of priorities does not mean that faith-development literature is to be ignored, but that primary attention is to be given to a person's actual sense of spiritual reality, the actual way a person feels the presence and power of God, the moving moments of worship and prayer, the deeds of mercy done in the name of Christ. Such an approach to education brings the educator's attention back to God's presence and power in life, back to Christ's self-giving, back to education as a spiritual discipline.

Mission

An adequate doctrine of mission is one in which the church will be continually engaged in dialogue with the critical issues of the contemporary world. The modern world has adjusted to social, political, ideological, economic, and cultural pluralisms, but not to religious pluralism. Should not the church look behind the celebrations of other religions, to sense what is being celebrated at the most profound level? If a Hindu festival is a celebration of life, then it may have affinity with the celebration of life in the resurrection of Christ. Choan-Seng Song reminds us that religious educators should look at the ultimate concern of all cultural stories and learn to resonate with the genuine longings of the human heart. God's self-disclosure is not only in the life of Israel, but also in the lives of people of other religions.

To be adequate, the mission of the church must be approached from a global perspective. While it is true that the local congregation is a context for Christian education, it is more true to say that the worldwide church is the proper context for Christian education. The task of the educator is to equip all of God's people for ecumenical understanding, for renewal of the whole church in its outreach to the whole human family. Global education will necessarily be open to many other perspectives and will necessarily be ecumenical.

The full range and breadth and depth of human experience is to be addressed in the doctrine of the mission of the church. But that mission may be defined too narrowly, thereby severely limiting and distorting it. The church is chosen, called, and sent to live in the world as the Body of Christ, the sign and witness of the coming of God's reign of justice and peace, the presence of God in all places and for all peoples. Furthermore, the church is to be such a witness and engage in such a mission as those who experience the range, breadth,

247

and depth of human experience, allowing that experience to shape and reshape the measure and the content of its self-understanding.

Such a mission implies a concern on the part of various traditions to learn about other traditions; it requires a penetration to the deeper issues of those traditions. It means testing the Christian story by the measure of others' experiences.

The mission of the church raises questions about the sense in which Christ's call is inclusive and exclusive. What human experience is not included in the church's mission? How far does the Christian go in being sensitive to the issues found in the celebrations of non-Christians?

While no quick answer can be given, these questions cannot be dismissed out of hand. They must be addressed in dialogue with the variety of human experiences. The mission of the church is to ensure that all humanity might be touched by Christ, while those who are called and sent continually reinterpret their calling in view of the range of human experience. In particular, the mission of the church is to be publicly engaged in the cultural issues of the time.

Such a view puts a priority upon education as a primary instrument of dialogue. In this view, education is at the heart of the mission of the church. At the same time, education is stretched beyond the narrow transmitting of the tradition. Education must itself become concerned about the range of human experience. It must become involved in the debate about the cultural issues of the time. The mission of the church calls Christian education into engagement with the fundamental public cultural issues, thereby empowering people to respond.

Method

The experiences of the church in Latin America confront us with suggestive forms. One finds there a shift from a hierarchically structured, professionally dominated leader-ship to a leadership of the whole people. The people of God search Scripture and tradition through the present action of God in their midst, which is then expressed as political activity. The goal of Christian education is to listen to the experience of the people, build community, clarify problems that impede justice, then act in behalf of justice. Education is not for the sake of indoctrination or increasing church membership, as it so often is in North America.

Theology is a community enterprise of the whole people of God, not just those who are professionally trained. Theology is carried out in conversation between the scholars and the people, as they address the injustices the people face. Theology and education are closely bound together in the people's search to discern the meaning of Scripture for their own immediate experiences of injustice.

Moreover, theology is practical. Discernment in the midst of unfolding situations gives it a practical character; Christian education is an example. As Richard Osmer notes, any religious teacher is engaged in an exercise of practical theology, for such teachers seek to understand and shape a learning situation according to their understanding of God's will. Established theological truths are not applied to particular situations, as perhaps geometry is applied to architecture. Rather, communities of people living and studying together bring the combinations of their "preunderstanding" to bear upon a further understanding, to shape both the religious tradition (the gospel) and their contemporary situation.

Practical theology may be primarily addressed to either the church or the world. Further, it may use the methods of social science or theology, or a dialogue between social science and theology. We are calling for a confessionally dialogical approach addressed primarily to the wider cultural issues. One comes with a precommitment from one's own tradition, but willing to reinterpret that tradition within the context of other Christian traditions, be in dialogue with the cultural disciplines, and engage the wider cultural issues.

Christian education needs a hermeneutic of life situations within the context of interpreting the Story and the hope of the tradition, and within an ongoing covenantal relationship. Theology is the process of discerning the will of God in the present situation, in view of the tradition. When one features the awareness and expression of God's will, the theological moment is primary. When one features the tradition and the contemporary situation, then the educational moment is primary. A liberating Christian religious education, acting in the grace and hope of God's will, requires both moments. Such education births the life of faith.

The Emerging Partnership

Our discussion suggests that at the close of the twentieth century, the church is coming to a new understanding of its mission and purpose. As a part of that new understanding, Christian educators are beginning to see their calling differently. Nineteenth-century Christian educators sought to bring the gospel to new communities in North America while addressing the problems of a rising industrialism. Twentieth-century educators have sought to incorporate the understandings of the social sciences, especially those regarding human development and group interaction, and to free the gospel from cultural prejudice. However, the close of the twentieth century finds the North-American church caught in the perpetuation of a radical individualism and other dominant cultural idols. The task of educators, and of the whole church during the twenty-first century, will be to find an understanding and praxis that allows the gospel truth to be expressed in new ways which are faithful to God's purposes.

An emergent approach to Christian education will find a way across many of the separations that have developed during the past century. One fundamental separation, the one to which this whole book is addressed, is that between theology and education. When the gospel is most alive in a continual process of reinterpretation within a community of faith, then theology is both guide to and guided by that process, in one and the same moment. Theology and education

250

join hands to serve the church in its mission. The tasks of educator and theologian cannot be divided according to form and content. Rather, the message is being constantly reinterpreted in a process that requires a partnership between educator and theologian.

Neither can the division between confessional and ecumenical education be maintained. Ecumenical education is not an alternative to confessional education. Rather, the ecumenical vision lives in the dialogue between the various confessional traditions. Individual confessional traditions will die unless they are in dialogue with other Christian traditions around the world. They will die also if they lose their distinctive contribution to the dialogue. All Christian education needs to be informed by dialogue with other traditions. The ecumenical and the confessional belong to each other.

Moreover, the relation of church to public is crucial. Modern individualism has so captured the Western world that it erodes the reality of the church as the Body of Christ. The liberal senses maturity as the goal of education; the conservative, salvation. Yet both have lost the corporate sense of being the Body of Christ. Congregational life has suffered the onslaught of twentieth-century life, with many scars. The larger sense that Christians are bound together in Christ is very fragile. To the extent that education has tried to prop up congregational life, it has great difficulty in addressing the issues of the wider community. Educators need a doctrine of the individual within the community that would heal the separation between the two.

Theology during much of the twentieth century has attempted to move away from the nineteenth-century effort to develop a culturally relevant theology. The scars of fascism and colonialism have led the church to seek a theology free of cultural bias. The result has often been that Christian educators have drawn away from addressing the larger cultural issues. It is now clear that the best resources of religious education are needed to address the issues that will threaten the earth in the twenty-first century. If the church's effort to be relevant can be trapped by bigotry, the church's silence can contribute to the decline of the public. Christian education must again address the cultural issues of this day.

Another crisis that calls out to be addressed is that between human culture and the creation. The church has helped to perpetuate the view that human culture is God's primary concern, while the creation may be given over to whatever the human imagination invents. Recent biblical study suggests that both humanity and human culture are parts of the divinely created order. When humans poison the creation, we poison ourselves. Humanity is an integral part of the creation and shares its destiny. Christian educators are called to teach a reverence for creation that does not separate and exempt human culture.

The struggle between salvation and liberation must be overcome in the years ahead. Salvation has come to mean transformation of the individual by the power of God's grace, and certainly all individuals need God's transforming power. Liberation has come to mean the overcoming of social injustices, and certainly the cries of the oppressed fill the earth. We need an attention to transformed lives that is, at the same time, an attention to transformed communities. There may be no easy answer for a separation that has plagued Christianity throughout the twentieth century, yet Christian educators must reach for a healing between proponents of salvation and liberation.

Another contradiction has arisen in recent years—that of faith and maturity. Faith cannot be reduced to a set of stages through which everyone moves more or less, even though those stages of human development must be constantly in the purview of the educator. The imaginal content and commitment of faith is of equal importance with, or even more important than its formal stage characteristics. Christian educators need to turn their attention to the nurture and development of the spiritual as an expression of the image of God in the human spirit.

Finally, a paradox to be addressed is that between reflection and practice. Whereas twentieth-century Christian education has sought to allow learning to be experiential, in fact there is a continuing hiatus between learning doctrine and putting it into practice. In more recent years the North-American church has been influenced by the Latin American emphasis upon the interaction of reflection and action. When the church addresses the larger social and ethical issues more directly in order to bring about a more viable human community, then the relationship between reflection and practice will be healed.

The dialogue between theology and education calls for a new understanding of the goal, context, and method of Christian education. Such education will be more oriented toward the language of faith, more concerned about the image of God in the human spirit, more focused upon the self-giving incarnation of Christ, more concerned about the Body of Christ as a community forming reality, more attuned to the self-giving of Christ within an ongoing grace-filled creation. In the dialogue with theology, Christian education plays the role of an equal partner.

Here is a proposal for the new role of Christian education in a world of confessional pluralism:

Context	Embeddedness in God's Creation
Goal	Life in the Risen Lord
Method	Kenotic Self-giving

The Context

The context for Christian education in the twenty-first century is embeddedness in God's creation. For two millennia Christians have taught that the creation is to be under the dominion of humanity, and faith has sought to escape this evil world. Now we must come to realize that humanity is a part of the creation. As the creation goes, so goes humanity. The web of human relationships belongs to the creation. Jesus' prayer was that God's will be done on earth—in the creation—as in heaven. A sense of the wholeness of creation is basic to faith.

Embeddedness in God's creation points to God's sovereignty. Christians have long assumed that God is primarily concerned about humanity and human culture. The embeddedness of humanity points to the concern of God for the whole of creation. Humanity may not be God's only, or even the principal enterprise, which does not negate the fact that God so loved the world that God's very embodied self was given for the world. God's concern for the world is much broader than we had thought.

The wider context of the church's mission is found in the globe. Christian religious education thereby becomes global education, which includes a concern for both the whole earth and the whole human family. To be faithful, the church should become much more concerned about the environment. In addition, modern individualism that erodes the community character of faith is to be challenged. The concerns of the marginalized, the oppressed, and the poor especially must become the concern of education.

The most prevailing characteristic of modern culture is its pluralism. Christian educators cannot avoid the multiplicity of pluralisms. Rather than overcome pluralism by converting the other to our truth or tolerating the difference, the doctrine of embeddedness in God's creation calls for acknowledgment of other cultures, from which all of us can both give and receive.

If the wider context of religious education concerns the whole globe, the more immediate context is the whole church. The church is an embodied tradition in the process of being continually re-created. In the reinterpretation of the tradition within the circumstances of daily life, the church remains in touch with God's ongoing creativity.

God intends that the church should recover the connectedness of life. The connectedness with other persons of faith is given in the risen Lord and the Body of Christ. However, the individualism of the modern world is so corrosive that the church loses its connectedness also. The immediate context of Christian education is to reestablish the connectedness of life, no matter how tenuous. That tenuous connectedness belongs to all those within the church; to the wider community, with its often dominating culture; and to the whole of the creation that is so threatened in this day.

The Goal

The goal of Christian education is life in the Risen Lord. This turns the focus of faith from maturity, or development, to the imaginal content of faith; from being saved to living; from maturity to abundance of life. The goal is meant to be both individual and communal, both confessional and active. It is very much centered in the gospel, especially the Pauline concept of resurrection, but is, at the same time, engaged in ongoing reality.

Life in the risen Lord is spiritual and devotional. Christian education reinterprets the stories of faith, scriptural and contemporary, to encourage spiritual discipline. Prayer and worship are at the center of education in the church. The devotional life, individually and as a group, is important. Faith is an encouragement of things hoped for in the midst of the tenuousness of life. As a confessional conversation within the multiple pluralism of life, faith is holy insecurity. As a liberating and releasing reality, faith leads persons to the edge of that which holds them back, and the spiritual center of church education is thereby restored.

Life in the risen Lord is also liberation from oppression. It engages the issues of our time, the prevailing cultural dilemmas. The way in which our community is an oppressed or oppressive community is reinterpreted in order that the oppression might be driven out. Communities are empowered to live in the abundance of life that God intended for them and for all creation. This calls for mutual participation in the human family, dialogue with our traditions. Life in the Risen Lord is simultaneously active and reflective.

It addresses both the pluralism and the embeddedness of life. Pluralism is addressed in conversation with the secular and religious traditions that make up our communities and our world. The embeddedness of life is addressed by caring for the creation. Part of the goal of Christian education in the twenty-first century must be more than caring for the community of faith. Nothing less than care for the whole creation is adequate to faith. In the response to pluralism, committed cultural conversation must replace hostility, isolation, or domination.

Life in the risen Lord is a connected life, tenuous though it may be. The risen Lord is a community-forming reality which overcomes the extreme individualism of our time. Persons in the community of faith reach out for relationships within and beyond the community. The community understands itself to be forming relationships with other groups within the total human family, no matter how tenuous those relationships. Peace and reconciliation become the primary goals in the risen Lord. The goal of Christian religious education is to partici-pate in the reinterpretation of the tradition (the gospel) within this time, within this pluralistic and oppressive world, and within God's ongoing creativity.

The Method

The method of Christian education is that of kenotic self-giving. Again, the biblical image shapes the method of education as it did its context and its goal. Now is the time to move away from the concept that truth is to be imposed upon a waiting and unenlightened object. Truth is rather to be found in the self-giving love of the incarnation. The image is vividly picked up in the Pauline concept of self-emptying, kenosis.

The primary characteristics of kenotic self-giving is that of hermeneutical praxis. The tradition is studied in order to be reinterpreted. Furthermore, the reinterpretation of the people, with their many experiences, is fundamental to academic reinterpretation. Hermeneutic praxis includes the reading of the present situation in order to newly understand and act within it. Such a reinterpretation is a praxis, in that it seeks a change in the oppressive conditions of the current situation.

256

Another characteristic of kenotic self-giving is its connectedness. Self-giving does not occur within itself, but for the sake of the other. The educational method includes a community of interpretation, reaching out to engage other communities of interpretation. The connectedness is not only to the faith community, but to the wider human community; not only to human culture, but to the whole creation.

The method of kenotic self-giving is imaginal and mutual. The focus is not only upon rational consistency, but also upon imaginal insight. The life of faith is richly imaginal, but so also are the discovered possibilities of human community. The imaginal method is not closed within itself, but is mutual. It is given over to the enrichment of the wider human family and the care of the creation.

The kenotic method is liberating, in that it addresses arenas of oppression. Oppression is addressed not in order to destroy the oppressor, but in order that there be transformation. Oppression is also destructive to the oppressor. In an open self-giving confrontation, oppressor and oppressed can be mutually empowered.

The kenotic method is one of confessional pluralism. The method is one of dialogical engagement with other traditions and beliefs, at the same time acknowledging one's own beliefs and commitments. It does not try to find wholly neutral ground or to construct some third area of belief. Nor does faith require that all else must conform to one's own understanding. Kenotic faith gives itself in open conversation with other traditions and other situations, at the same time acknowledging its own faith commitment.

Conclusion

Theology and education inform each other as equal partners in a conversation. The possibility of such mutuality arises from the way doctrine has become the interpretation of the tradition and the present reality, in the midst of addressing the broader global issues within God's grace-filled ongoing

257

creativity. The experience, conversation, and praxis of the people of God are fundamental to doctrinal formulation. At the same time, Christian education's role of interpreting the tradition and the present reality needs a partnership with the theological disciplines. A common task of educators and theologians is to develop such a partnership, so that the gospel might find a powerful voice in this day.

The emerging and special role of Christian education includes discerning its context as one of embeddedness within the creation. Such an understanding awakens us to the reality of the connectedness of humankind with the creation, the multiple pluralism of world cultures, and the grace-filled ongoing creativity of God.

The goal of Christian education becomes one of living in the risen Lord, spiritual growth in the gospel, confessional conversation within cultural pluralism, holy insecurity within tenuous communities, liberation from poverty and oppressiveness, and living toward the grace-filled future that is given by the Creator.

The method of Christian education is being transformed into kenotic self-giving. Such self-giving is marked by its ongoing reinterpretation of both the tradition and the present realities, its connectedness to the human community and the whole of creation, its imaginative mutuality and confessional pluralism, and its concern for the empowerment of people as they care for the whole creation.

This new definition of Christian religious education takes up themes from the approaches of a decade ago and reinterprets them according to contemporary discussion and praxis. The role of Christian education can be enormously significant in the coming decades, if the directions indicated here are elaborated by the people of God as they address great issues of our time within God's grace-filled creativity.

Contributors

Charles R. Foster is professor of Christian education at Candler School of Theology, Emory University, Atlanta, Ga. He is a minister in The United Methodist Church.

Susanne Johnson is Associate Dean for community life at Perkins School of Theology, Southern Methodist University, Dallas, Tex. She is a minister of the Disciples of Christ.

Fumitaka Matsuoka is Academic Dean and associate professor of mission studies at Bethany Theological Seminary, Oak Brook, Ill. A citizen of Japan, he is a minister in Church of the Brethren.

Melanie A. May is ecumenical officer and executive of the Office of Human Resources for Church of the Brethren in Elgin, Ill. A Brethren minister, she is chair of the Commission on Faith and Order for the National Council of the Churches of Christ in the U.S.A.

David Merritt is executive director of the Joint Board of Christian Education and a minister of the Uniting Church in Australia. He is moderator of the Education Working Group of the World Council of Churches.

Donald E. Miller is general secretary for Church of the Brethren in Elgin, Ill. A Brethren minister, he was previously Alvin F. Brightbill Professor of Ministry Studies at Bethany Theological Seminary in Oak Brook, Ill.

Mary Elizabeth Mullino Moore is professor of theology and Christian education in the School of Theology at Claremont, Calif. She is a diaconal minister in The United Methodist Church.

Romney Moseley is associate professor of divinity at Trinity College, Toronto, Canada. Born in Barbados, he is an Anglican priest.

Robert T. O'Gorman, a Roman Catholic, is associate professor of pastoral studies and coordinator of the Master of Divinity program at Loyola University of Chicago.

Richard R. Osmer is assistant professor of Christian education at Union Theological Seminary in Virginia. He is a minister in the Presbyterian Church (U.S.A.).

Marianne Sawicki is guest professor of Christian education at Princeton Theological Seminary (1989–1990). A Roman Catholic, she has taught theology and religious education at Loyola Marymount University and at Lexington Theological Seminary.

Jack L. Seymour is professor of religious education at Garrett-Evangelical Theological Seminary in Evanston, Ill. He is a minister in The United Methodist Church.

Choan-Seng Song is professor of theology and Asian cultures at Pacific School of Religion in Berkeley, Calif. Born in Taiwan, he is a United States citizen and member of the Presbyterian Church in Taiwan and of the Reformed Church in America.

Notes

Acknowledgments

1. Jack L. Seymour and Donald E. Miller, eds., *Contemporary Approaches to Christian Education* (Nashville: Abingdon Press, 1982).
2. H. Richard Niebuhr, *Christ and Culture* (New York: Harper & Row, 1951), p. 37.

Chapter 1—Openings to God

1. See Gordon Kaufman, *Theology for a Nuclear Age* (Philadelphia: Westminster Press, 1985); Sallie McFague, *Models of God: Theology for an Ecological Nuclear Age* (Philadelphia: Fortress Press, 1987); David Tracy, *Plurality and Ambiguity: Hermeneutics, Religion, and Hope* (San Francisco: Harper & Row, 1987).
2. Kaufman, *Theology for a Nuclear Age;* Joseph Hough and John Cobb, Jr., *Christian Identity and Theological Education* (Chico, Calif.: Scholars Press, 1985); Edward Farley, *Theologia: The Fragmentation and Unity of Theological Education* (Philadelphia: Fortress Press, 1983); Jack Seymour, Robert O'Gorman, and Charles Foster, *The Church in the Education of the Public: Refocusing the Task of Religious Education* (Nashville: Abingdon Press, 1984).
3. Marianne Sawicki, *The Gospel in History: Portrait of a Teaching Church: The Origins of Christian Education* (Mahwah, N. J.: Paulist Press, 1988); Mary Boys, *Educating in Faith: Maps and Visions* (San Francisco: Harper & Row, 1989). For an excellent survey of the engagement of Christian education with theology, see Sara Little, "Theology and Education," *Harper's Encyclopedia of Religious Education*, ed. Iris V. Cully and Kendig Brubaker Cully (San Francisco: Harper & Row, 1990), pp. 649-55.
4. See Edward Farley, *The Fragility of Knowledge: Theological Education in the Church and the University* (Philadelphia: Fortress Press, 1988), p. 101, for his discussion of the typology presented in *Contemporary Approaches*. Farley is correct when he names these approaches as approaches "to the 'discipline' or field of Christian education as a literary, pedagogical undertaking."
5. For other typologies see Mary Boys, *Biblical Interpretation in Religious Education* (Birmingham: Religious Education Press, 1980); Boys, *Educating in Faith;* Harold Burgess, *An Invitation to Religious Education* (Mishawaka, Ind.: Religious Education Press, 1975).

261

6. A Korean edition edited by Yong Kil Maing appeared in 1982, published by the Department of Education, Presbyterian Church of Korea. A Japanese edition, translated by Kazuhiro Okuda and Tsugikazu Nishigaki, was published in 1987 by Skinkyo Shuppansha (Protestant Publishing Co.).

7. The tenth anniversary meeting was held in Allison, Ontario, Canada, October 7–11, 1983.

8. See National Pre-test "Christian Education Effectiveness: A National Study of Protestant Congregations," Search Institute, 122 W. Franklin Ave., Minneapolis, MN 55404. The final results of the study have been published in Peter Benson and Carolyn H. Eklin, *Effective Christian Education: A National Study of Protestant Congregations. A Summary Report on Faith, Loyalty, and Congregational Life* (Search Institute, 1990).

9. See the work of Joseph Crockett on educational approaches in the African-American community, "New Strategies in Christian Education," *Interpreter* (July-August 1989):19-21. Crockett's research will appear in a book published by Discipleship Resources, Nashville, Tenn., in late 1990.

10. *Contemporary Approaches* was intended to be a historical description of current approaches, not a philosophical articulation of ideal types. While we tried to find as much typological consistency as possible, we did not want to separate ourselves from the actual dialogue in the field. This resulted in sometimes-overlapping metaphors of emerging alternatives in Christian religious education. We attempted to communicate that all five approaches were equally important. We did not believe that any one approach captured the direction for the future.

11. Sara Little, "Religious Instruction," *Contemporary Approaches to Christian Education*, ed. Jack L. Seymour and Donald E. Miller (Nashville: Abingdon Press, 1982). See also her helpful clarification of teaching models in *To Set One's Heart: Belief and Teaching in the Church* (Atlanta: John Knox Press, 1983).

12. George Lindbeck, *The Nature of Doctrine: Religion and Theology in a Post-Liberal Age* (Philadelphia: Westminster Press, 1984); McFague, *Models of God;* Kaufman, *Theology for a Nuclear Age;* Farley, *Theologia.* See also Sallie McFague, *Metaphorical Theology: Models of God in Religious Language* (Philadelphia: Fortress Press, 1982).

13. Farley, *Fragility of Knowledge,* chap. 2.

14. Ibid., p. 99.

15. Craig Dykstra, "No Longer Strangers: The Church and Its Educational Ministry," *Princeton Seminary Bulletin*, New Series 6:3(1985):189.

16. Ibid., pp. 191-93.

17. Charles Foster, "The Faith Community as a Guiding Image for Christian Education," Seymour and Miller, *Contemporary Approaches*, pp. 54-58. See also his discussion of being children of God in *Teaching in the Community of Faith* (Nashville: Abingdon Press, 1982).

18. See C. Ellis Nelson, ed., *Congregations: Their Power to Form and Transform* (Atlanta: John Knox Press, 1988); Maria Harris, *Fashion Me a People: Curriculum in the Church* (Louisville: Westminster/John Knox, 1989).

19. Donald Miller, "The Developmental Approach to Christian Education," *Contemporary Approaches*, ed. Seymour and Miller, pp. 77-93.

20. Ibid., pp. 98-102.

21. See the excellent critical reviews of Fowler's work and his response in Craig Dykstra and Sharon Parks, eds., *Faith Development and Fowler* (Birmingham: Religious Education Press, 1986).

22. See Carol Gilligan, *In a Different Voice: Psychological Theory and Women's Development* (Cambridge: Harvard University Press, 1982); and the summary in Boys, *Educating in Faith*, pp. 158-69.

23. Parker Palmer, *To Know as We Are Known: A Spirituality of Education* (San Francisco: Harper & Row, 1983), pp. 17-32. More recent attempts to encourage this shift to spirituality can be found in Robin Maas, *Crucified Love: The Practice of Christian Perfection* (Nashville: Abingdon Press, 1989) and Susanne Johnson, *Christian Spiritual Formation in Church and Classroom* (Nashville: Abingdon Press, 1989).

24. James Fowler, *Becoming Adult, Becoming Christian: Adult Development and Christian Faith* (San Francisco: Harper & Row, 1984).

25. Paulo Freire, "Education, Liberation, and the Church," *Religious Education* 79(Fall 1984):524.

26. Allen Moore, "Liberation and the Future of Christian Education," *Contemporary Approaches*, ed. Seymour and Miller, pp. 104, 120-22. See also Moore, ed., *Religious Education as Social Transformation* (Birmingham: Religious Education Press, 1989).

27. Freire, "Education, Liberation, and the Church," pp. 524-45.

28. Jack Seymour and Carol Wehrheim, "Faith Seeking Understanding: Interpretation as a Task of Christian Education," *Contemporary Approaches*, ed. Seymour and Miller, p. 124.

29. Andrew M. Greeley, *The Religious Imagination* (New York: William H. Sadlier, 1981), p. 17.

30. Thomas Groome, *Christian Religious Education: Sharing Our Story and Vision* (San Francisco: Harper & Row, 1980); James N. Poling and Donald E. Miller, *Foundations for a Practical Theology of Ministry* (Nashville: Abingdon Press, 1985); Maria Harris, *Teaching and Religious Imagination* (San Francisco: Harper & Row, 1987).

31. See Samuel Amirtham and John Pobee, *Theology by the People: Reflections on Doing Theology in Community* (Geneva: World Council of Churches, 1985); Carlos Mesters, "The Use of the Bible in Christian Communities of Common People," *The Bible and Liberation*, ed. Norman K. Gottwald (Maryknoll, N. Y.: Orbis Press, 1983).

Part I—Tradition

Foreword

1. George Lindbeck, *The Nature of Doctrine: Religion and Theology in a Post-Liberal Age* (Philadelphia: Westminster Press, 1984).

Chapter 2—Tradition and Education

1. The theory and practice of biblical interpretation also has been varied. Historical-critical interpretation is an attempt to ascertain an original

263

meaning of the texts of Scripture, while other modes are more interested in illumining the meaning of the text for today. For fundamentalists, interpretation focuses on the inerrancy of the biblical text—that is, the direct correspondence of the Bible to external reality; they view historical-critical interpretation as an attempt to establish errors in the Bible. Among the most recent modes of interpretation is the contextual, predicated on such questions as how the church's sociocultural context influences its interpretation.

2. Robert B. Coote and David Robert Ord, *The Bible's First History: From Eden to the Court of David with the Yahwist* (Philadelphia: Fortress Press, 1989), p. 15.

3. "Torah," *Encyclopedia Judaica* (New York: Macmillan, 1971), p. 1235. See also Jacob Neusner, *The Way of Torah: An Introduction to Judaism*, 2nd ed. (Belmont, Calif.: Dickenson, 1974).

4. See R. H. Pfeiffer, "Canon of the OT," *The Interpreter's Dictionary of the Bible*, Vol. 1 (Nashville: Abingdon Press, 1962), pp. 498-520.

5. F. W. Beare, "Canon of the NT," *The Interpeter's Dictionary of the Bible*, Vol. 1, pp. 520-32.

6. "Oral Law," *Encyclopedia Judaica*, p. 1439.

7. See Harold Coward's treatment of the rabbis and the oral Torah in *Sacred Word and Sacred Text: Scripture in World Religions* (Maryknoll, N. Y.: Orbis Books, 1988), pp. 10-19. See also Jacob Neusner, *The Memorized Torah: The Mnemonic System of the Mishnah* (Chico, Calif.: Scholars Press, 1985), for reflections on the power and practice of the oral Torah.

8. Amos N. Wilder, *The Language of the Gospel: Early Christian Rhetoric* (New York: Harper & Row, 1964), p. 23.

9. Ibid., pp. 20-21.

10. Ibid., p. 21.

11. Coote and Ord, *The Bible's First History*, pp. 3-4, 2.

12. *Reception* has increasing significance in contemporary ecumenical conversation. After effectively being relegated to the historical record, the Word and its dynamic are recognized as integral to the life of a community of faith.

13. William G. Rusch, *Reception: An Ecumenical Opportunity* (Philadelphia: Fortress Press, 1988), p. 31.

14. See Yves Congars, "Reception as an Eccleciological Reality," *Election and Consensus in the Church*, ed. G. Alberigo and A. Weiler, *Concilium* 77 (New York: Herder & Herder, 1972), pp. 43-68.

15. Those who eventually lost the debate over the terms that should rightly shape orthodox Christianity.

16. Baptismal creeds usually were given to candidates during their instruction, and "regiven" in the personal form—"I believe . . . "—before the gathered congregation at the time of baptism. By contrast, ecumenical creeds usually were in the plural form, expressing the unity of the gathered body—"We believe . . . ."

17. J.N.D. Kelly, *Early Christian Creeds*, 3rd ed. (New York: Longman, 1972), p. 32.

18. Ibid., pp. 38-40.

19. Ibid., p. 98.

20. Some scholars underscore the distinction between the catechetical and

the liturgical use of creeds by clarifying that the Magisterial Reformation used confessions, not creeds as such, in giving instruction. Kelly's book emphasizes the liturgical setting of the ancient creeds.

21. Rusch, *Reception*, p. 53.

22. Andrew F. Wall, "The Old Age of the Missionary Movement," *International Review of Mission* 76(January 1987):26.

23. Aylward Shorter, *Toward a Theology of Inculturation* (Maryknoll, N. Y.: Orbis Books, 1988), p. 11.

24. Pope John Paul II, Letter to Cardinal Agostino Casaroli, Secretary of State, 20th May 1982, quoted from *L'Osservatore Romano*, June 28, 1982, as cited by Cecil McGarry, S. J., *Inculturation: Its Meaning and Urgency* (St. Paul Publications-Africa, 1986), pp. 7-8.

25. "African Church Seeks Ways of Inculturation," *National Catholic Reporter* 22(March 28, 1986):36.

26. "Native Drum, Song and Spear at Mass in Zaire," *National Catholic Reporter* 23(December 12, 1986):11.

27. Shorter, *Toward a Theology of Inculturation*, pp. 61-62.

28. In *An Asian Theology of Liberation* (Maryknoll, N. Y.: Orbis Books, 1988), pp. 53-54, Aloysius Pieris, S. J., from Sri Lanka, is critical of what he calls "Western models of inculturation: . . . Inculturation-fever might appear to be a desparate last-moment bid to give an Asian facade to a church that fails to strike roots in Asian soil because no one dares to break the Greco-Roman pot in which it has been existing for four centuries like a stunted *bonsai!*" He goes on to quote a Buddhist: "The so-called indigenization . . . appears to be a matter of tactics rather than one of appreciation and admiration of things indigenous. . . . It can be likened to the tactics of a chamelion which takes on the colour of the environment in order to deceive its prey."

29. Cain Hope Felder, *Troubling Biblical Waters: Race, Class, and Family* (Maryknoll, N. Y.: Orbis Books, 1989), p. xi.

30. Pieris, *Asian Theology of Liberation*, p. 109.

31. Itumeleng J. Mosala, *Biblical Hermeneutics and Black Theology in South Africa* (Grand Rapids: Eerdmans, 1989).

32. Eduardo Hoornaert, *The Memory of the Christian People*, trans. Robert R. Barr (Maryknoll, N. Y.: Orbis Books, 1988), p. 151.

33. James A. Sanders, *From Sacred Story to Sacred Text* (Philadelphia: Fortress Press, 1987), p. 181.

34. C. H. Dodd, *Apostolic Preaching and Its Developments* (London: Hodder & Stoughton, 1960), pp. 7-8.

35. Wilder, *Language of the Gospel*, p. 23.

36. Rebecca S. Chopp, *The Power to Speak: Feminism, Language, God* (New York: Crossroads Press, 1989), p. 27.

37. Nel Noddings, *Women and Evil* (Berkeley: University of California Press, 1989), p. 235. Also see Antonio Gramsci, *Selections from the Prison Notebooks*, ed. and trans. Quinton Hoare and Geoffrey Newell Smith (New York: International Press, 1978).

Chapter 3—Tradition and Sacramental Education

1. The following works provide a basic grounding in contemporary Catholic sacramental theology and history: Michael G. Lawler, *Symbol and*

Sacrament (New York: Paulist Press, 1987), esp. chap. 2; Bernard Cooke, *Sacraments and Sacramentality* (Mystic, Conn.: Twenty-third Publications, 1983); Kenan Osborne, *The Christian Sacraments of Initiation* (New York: Paulist Press, 1987); Joseph Martos, *The Catholic Sacraments* (Wilmington: Michael Glazier, 1983); Joseph Martos, *Doors to the Sacred* (Garden City, N. Y.: Doubleday, 1981); David N. Power, *Unsearchable Riches* (New York: Pueblo Publishing Co., 1984); Edward J. Kilmartin, *Christian Liturgy: Theology and Practice*, Vol. 1 (Kansas City: Sheed & Ward, 1988). Important earlier works include: Bernard Leeming, *Principles of Sacramental Theology* (Westminster, Md.: Newman Press, 1956); Bernard Cooke, *Ministry to Word and Sacraments* (Philadelphia: Fortress Press, 1976); Edward Schillebeeckx, *Christ the Sacrament of the Encounter with God* (Kansas City: Sheed, Andrews, & McMeel, 1963); Karl Rahner, *The Church and the Sacraments* (London: Burns & Oates, 1963). Recent Protestant works include James F. White, *Introduction to Christian Worship* (Nashville: Abingdon Press, 1980) and *Sacraments as God's Self-giving* (Nashville: Abingdon Press, 1983); Hughes Oliphant Old, *Worship* (Atlanta: John Knox Press, 1984); Marianne H. Micks, *The Joy of Worship* (Philadelphia: Westminster Press, 1982); Keith Watkins, ed., *Thankful Praise* (St. Louis: CBP Press, 1987). Extensive bibliographical essays that treat several aspects of worship are included in David Buttrick, *Homiletic* (Philadelphia: Fortress Press, 1987).

2. Medieval theology distinguished three stages, as it were, in the action of a sacrament. The completion of the ritual words and gestures (1) brought into being a lasting symbolic reality (2), which in turn signified and delivered the grace given by God (3). The instrumental causality of the rite was therefore twofold and transitive: The ritual itself (*sacramentum tantum*), brought into being the symbolic reality (*res et sacramentum*), and the latter in turn brought about the special grace of the sacrament (*res tantum*). Each sacrament has a different *res et sacramentum*, or intermediate sacramental reality. For baptism, it is the permanent reconfiguration of one's personal being which entails the responsibilities of church membership. For Eucharist, it is the real presence of Christ in the elements and in the church. The *res et sacramentum* is a potent and contagious symbol, not an end in itself. In modern terminology, we can regard it as a version of the Christic Paschal pattern which tends to replicate itself in the human realities with which it comes into contact.

3. For background on the historical development of this issue, see Lawler, *Symbol and Sacrament*, pp. 36-45.

4. God's love is not controlled by sacraments or held back by sacramental malpractice, of course. Yet given that God has entrusted the gospel to human communication, it follows that failures in communication do indeed block the delivery system which God intended. Christian teachers must do everything possible to ensure that all components of the traditioning process are in working order.

5. This listing is adapted from *Sharing the Light of Faith, the National Catechetical Directory for Catholics of the United States* (Washington, D.C.: U.S. Catholic Conference, 1979), pars. 112-39. The Eucharist belongs in all three categories, being much more than a sacrament of initiation, according to the *Directory*.

6. For a thorough discussion of this and other approaches, see Mary C. Boys, *Educating in Faith* (San Francisco: Harper & Row, 1989), esp. pp. 39-63. Helpful bibliographical essays are included.

7. The term *catechesis* is used also by the Orthodox and by some Protestant Christians whose traditions place particular emphasis upon sacramental experiences; see list of contributors in John H. Westerhoff III and O. C. Edwards, Jr., eds., *A Faithful Church: Issues in the History of Catechesis* (Wilton, Conn.: Morehouse-Barlow, 1981). Therefore the term identifies not a denominational bias but rather an interdenominational commitment to the ecclesial and liturgical location of Christian becoming.

8. See Daniel J. Sahas, *Catechesis: The Maturation of the Body*, trans. Alex G. Dedes (Brookline, Mass.: Holy Cross Orthodox Press, 1984), a collection of talks at Canadian conferences of clergy and laity in the 1970s, for the Greek Orthodox explanation of catechesis: "The process of 'turning together' the members of the Body of the Church; the thorough learning and practicing of the 'tone' according to which the Church 'chants,' that is, believes, worships, and expresses herself—these three together" (p. 17).

9. Because personal contact is essential in catechesis, one must be careful to maintain an atmosphere of dialogue and personal interaction when using media such as videotape or printed materials. Individual reading, research, and study must be brought into a dialogical context in the learning group.

10. According to the *National Catechetical Directory*, catechesis has one source and content: "God's word, full revealed in Jesus Christ." However, the *Directory* also mentions four "signs" which manifest this source: the Bible, the liturgy, the church (including doctrine and the witness of Christian living), and human experience and history (pars. 41-46). See also chaps. titled "Principal Elements of the Christian Message for Catechesis" (pars. 82-111) and "Catechesis for a Worshiping Community" (pars. 112-48).

11. See *Rite of Christian Initiation of Adults*, study ed., rev., prepared by the International Commission on English in the Liturgy and the Bishops' Committee on the Liturgy (Washington, D. C.: U. S. Catholic Conference, 1972, 1988). Now mandatory in all American Catholic parishes, the RCIA has also spurred some creative adaptation in Protestant congregations; see Dennis L. Bushkofsky, "Baptizing Adults: Preparation for the Christian Life," *Lutheran Partners* 5(January-February 1989):20-25.

12. In antiquity, however, Cyril of Jerusalem used the articles of the creed as an outline of his *Catechetical Lectures*.

13. *Rite of Christian Initiation of Adults*, par. 75.

14. *Sharing the Light of Faith*, par. 33.

15. *Sharing the Light of Faith* calls the bishop "chief catechist of the diocese." Among the services provided to parishes by diocesan staff are in-service training, newsletters, guidelines and resources for programming, selection of catechetical curriculum and textbooks, sponsorship of continuing education, a media lending library, training and certification programs for catechists, and liaison with other diocesan activities (par. 218).

16. A useful exercise with which to begin the goal-setting process: On a chalkboard or newsprint, set up five columns with the headings "beliefs, attitudes, behaviors, knowledges, skills." Ask participants to describe the adult Christian by suggesting some qualities such a person ought to have. List

each item in the appropriate column. When the group is satisfied with that list, move on to the kind of programming that could foster each of the desired qualities. Keep the lists on display for reference and revision. Let the group discover the paradox that while human efforts cannot "produce" a Christian, catechists must plan as if they could. Eventually the group notices that Jesus, Peter, and Mary would not fit the profile. This down-to-earth process entails theology in its purest form. Many parish RCIA teams have ventured to begin this kind of theology in planning. Based on this experience with the RCIA, it would be well to organize teams for planning reconciliation catechesis, and commitment catechesis as well.

17. The *CFI* includes a manual, answer sheets, workbooks, and scoring materials. Written by K. Boyack, R. Duggan, and P. Huesing, it was copyrighted in 1986 by Paulist Press.

18. For indications of this trend, see Susan Ross, "The Aesthetic and the Sacramental," *Worship* 59(1985):2-17; Stephen Happel, "Worship as a Grammar of Social Transformation," *Proceedings of the Catholic Theological Society of America* 47(1987):60-87.

19. See Maria Harris, *Teaching and Religious Imagination* (San Francisco: Harper & Row, 1987) for her helpful reflections on the view that art is the metaphor for all teaching.

20. This view of art and aesthetic education is owing to the philosophy of Martin Heidegger; some of the suggestions offered here are adapted from F. David Martin, "Heidegger's Being of Things and Aesthetic Education," *Journal of Aesthetic Education* 8(1974):87-105.

21. See James W. Fowler, *Stages of Faith* (San Francisco: Harper & Row, 1981); his adaptation and refinement of the developmental theories has had increasing influence upon religious educators, but has not been received uncritically.

22. See Marianne Sawicki, "Religion, Symbol, and the Twenty-year-old Demythologizer," *Horizons* 11(1984):320-43 and *The Gospel in History: Portrait of a Teaching Church: The Origins of Christian Educaton* (New York: Paulist Press, 1988), pp. 14-21.

23. See Isabel Briggs Myers, *Gifts Differing* (Palo Alto, Calif.: Consulting Psychologists Press, 1980). Myers' four dominant mental processes, somewhat misleadingly labeled Thinking, Feeling, Intuiting, and Sensing, would correspond to the four learning styles enumerated here. In characteristic ways, these processes are combined in the sixteen different temperament types. Myers based her work on that of Carl G. Jung, *Psychological Types* (Princeton: Princeton University Press, 1971). Educational applications of Myers' work are suggested by Gordon Lawrence, *People Types and Tiger Stripes: A Practical Guide to Learning Styles* (Gainesville, Fla.: Center for the Application of Psychological Types, 1982), on which my observations are based.

24. Penance is usually the first sacrament received by a baptized adult transferring membership to the Roman Catholic Church. In this case, the catechesis overlaps with that given for confirmation and Eucharist, but should be distinct from it. For children, it is especially important to provide separate catechesis for first Eucharist and first penance.

25. Confirmation is *not* a sacrament of commitment in this sense. While it is

true that initiation requires a degree of commitment appropriate a person's developmental level, children and teenagers are sealing their initiation into the church when they are confirmed. In the United States, two divergent theologies of confirmation have emerged in the debate between liturgists and religious educators: see Kieran Sawyer, "Toward an Integrated Theology of Confirmation," *The Living Light* 19(1982):336-43; "Reflections on Kavanaugh's 'Reflections on Confirmation,' " *PACE* 16(1985):77-82; "The Confirmation Debate Continues," *The Living Light* 22(1986):215-21; Aidan Kavanagh, "Reflections on Confirmation," *PACE* 16(1985):16-19; "A Further Reflection on Confirmation," *PACE* 16(1986):110-11.

26. The catechesis of commitment begins within the family and the preschool, as the basic structures of human relationality are being formed. For a magnificent theology of sexuality along with practical curricular guidelines, see *Education in Human Sexuality for Christians* (Washington, D. C.: U. S. Catholic Conference, 1981).

27. See Robert T. O'Gorman, *The Church That Was a School: Catholic Identity and Catholic Education in the United States Since 1790* (Washington, D.C.: Catholic Education Futures Project, U. S. Catholic Conference, 1987). Several articles treating the CCD movement are collected in Michael Warren, ed., *Sourcebook for Modern Catechetics* (Winona, Minn.: Saint Mary's, 1983). For background on the modern history of Catholic education in the United States, see Sawicki, *The Gospel in History*, "Nineteenth Century: Evangelizing a New Nation," pp. 257-84.

28. Although the parish is the primary unit, regional structures are needed for some aspects of sacramental catechesis. Seminary formation for Orders is provided at the diocesan or regional level, as is training for the Diaconate. Some components of Marriage catechesis are coordinated regionally through programs like Engaged Encounter and Marriage Encounter. In some dioceses, initiation catechesis begins with a welcoming or inquiry program in which several parishes cooperate. Regional activities also are offered for youths preparing for Confirmation, and the diocese may organize formal training programs to prepare and update parish catechists.

29. Christian Initiation brings responsibilities toward the society at large, as well as toward the church. Volunteering for church service can be a means of preparing for service to the wider community. Theology supports what experience bears out: Many people who minister to the church also give their time and energy to secular organizations for the common good.

30. See Kieran Sawyer, *Confirming Faith* (Notre Dame, Ind.: Ave Maria Press, 1982); Jim Bitney and Yvette Nelson, eds., *Welcome to the Way: A Confirmation Catechesis* (Valencia, Calif.: Tabor Publishing Co., 1989) includes separate editions for junior and senior high, with video- and audiocassettes; Bitney and Nelson, *Welcome Home: A Catechesis for First Reconciliation*, and *Welcome to the Table: A Catechesis for First Communion* (Valencia, Calif.: Tabor Publishing Co., 1987) include videos for children and parents, parent manual, parish manual, parent and teacher training video; Patricia O'Brien Fischer, *In the Lord's Peace: A Program for a Child's First Penance*, 2nd ed., and *Around the Lord's Table: A Program for a Child's First Communion*, 2nd ed. (Huntington, Ind.: Our Sunday Visitor, 1985). These materials can be used in a conventional weekly class or adapted for a children's catechumenate.

269

31. Proponents of the "liturgical" approach include the North American Forum on the Catechumenate, which organizes institutes and conferences on the RCIA for dioceses, and Liturgy Training Publications of the Office of Worship of the Archdiocese of Chicago, which publishes *At Home with the Word*, a yearly study guide and prayer book incorporating the Sunday lectionary readings. It also publishes *Catechumenate: A Journal of Christian Initiation* six times a year, which, together with *Worship* (from Saint John's Abbey in Collegeville, Minn.) and *The Living Light* (edited at the Catholic University of America), provide an arena for reflection on experiences of sacramental catechesis which can contribute to the development of sacramental theology.

Chapter 4—Feminist Theology and Education

1. See a review of much of this literature in Barrie Thorne, Cheris Kramarae, and Nancy Henley, eds., *Language, Gender and Society* (Rowley, Mass.: Newbury House, 1983), "Language, Gender and Society: Opening a Second Decade of Research," pp. 7-24.

2. Delores Williams, "The Color of Feminism: Or Speaking the Black Woman's Tongue," *Journal of Religious Thought* 43(1986):42-58; and "Women's Oppression and Lifeline Politics in Black Women's Religious Narratives," *Journal of Feminist Studies in Religion* 1(1985):59-71.

3. Blu Greenberg, *On Women and Judaism: A View from Tradition* (Philadelphia: Jewish Publication Society of America, 1981), pp. 105-23, esp. 118-20, and "Confrontation and Change: Women and the Jewish Tradition," *Women of Faith in Dialogue*, ed. Virginia Ramey Mollenkott (New York: Crossroads Press, 1987), pp. 17-28.

4. Susannah Heschel, *On Being a Jewish Feminist: A Reader* (New York: Schocken Books, 1983), pp. xxii-xxxiii.

5. See Delores Williams, "Womanist Theology and Feminist Theology: Shades of Difference in Perspectives," Bennett-Morton Lecture, February 1989, School of Theology at Claremont. Williams has built on African-American traditions and the exegetical work of Phyllis Trible in analyzing the issues surrounding the figure of Hagar; see Trible, *Texts of Terror: Literary-Feminist Readings of Biblical Narratives* (Philadelphia: Fortress Press, 1984), pp. 9-35.

6. The term is widely used now, but it was first introduced by Alice Walker, *In Search of Our Mothers' Gardens* (San Diego: Harcourt Brace Jovanovich, 1983). She defines *womanist* as: "From *womanish* (Opp. of 'girlish,' i.e., frivolous, irresponsible, not serious). A black feminist or feminist of color. From the black folk expression of mothers to female children, 'You acting womanish,' i.e., like a woman," p. xi.

7. Deborah Belonick, *Feminism in Christianity: An Orthodox Christian Response* (Syosset, N. Y.: Dept. of Religious Education, Orthodox Church in America, 1983), pp. 24-29; cf. pp. 35-36.

8. Julian of Norwich, *Showings*, trans. and intro., Edmund Colledge, O.S.A., & James Walsh, S. J. (New York: Paulist Press, 1978), pp. 181-87, 293-305.

9. Sallie McFague, *Metaphorical Theology* (Philadelphia: Fortress Press, 1982), pp. 1-29, esp. pp. 1-10. McFague's earlier work argues that the language of parable and metaphor is essential to the theological task of hearing the

270

gospel in our time; see *Speaking in Parables: A Study in Metaphor and Theology* (Philadelphia: Fortress Press, 1975), pp. 1-7.

10. Sallie McFague, *Models of God: Theology for an Ecological Nuclear Age* (Philadelphia: Fortress Press, 1987), pp. 3-28.

11. (New York: Harcourt Brace Jovanovich, 1982). This quote is reprinted in Alice Walker, "God Is Inside You and Inside Everybody Else," *Weaving the Visions: New Patterns in Feminist Spirituality*, ed. Judith Plaskow and Carol P. Christ (San Francisco: Harper & Row, 1989), p. 103.

12. Elisabeth Moltmann-Wendel makes a case that Martha often has been discredited by the dominant streams of interpretation; see *The Women Around Jesus* (New York: Crossroad Press, 1982), pp. 15-48, esp. 15-28.

13. Ibid., pp. 61-90.

14. Rosemary Radford Ruether, *Sexism and God-Talk* (Boston: Beacon Press, 1983), pp. 139-58; cf. Ruether, *New Woman New Earth* (New York: Seabury Press, 1975), pp. 36-62.

15. Moltmann-Wendel, *Women Around Jesus*, p. 67; cf. pp. 60-90.

16. Mercy Amba Oduyoye, "Be a Woman, and Africa Will Be Strong," *Inheriting Our Mothers' Gardens*, ed. Letty M. Russell, Kwok Pui-lan, Ada Maria Isasi-Diaz, Katie Geneva Cannon (Philadelphia: Westminster Press, 1988), p. 36.

17. Ada Maria Isasi-Diaz, "A Hispanic Garden in a Foreign Land," *Inheriting Our Mothers' Gardens*, ed. Russell et al., p. 99.

18. For one model of the God-world relationship developed by McFague, see *Models of God.*

19. This theme is developed by Valerie Saiving, "The Human Situation: A Feminine View," *Womanspirit Rising: A Feminist Reader in Religion*, ed. Carol P. Christ and Judith Plaskow (New York: Harper & Row, 1979), pp. 25-42; and by Sue Nelson Dunfee, *Beyond Servanthood: Christianity and the Liberation of Women* (Lanham, Md.: University Press of America, 1989), esp. pp. 105-30.

20. Isabel Carter Heyward, *The Redemption of God: A Theology of Mutual Relations* (Lanham, Md.: University Press of America, 1982), p. 1.

21. Ibid., pp. 2, 32, 36.

22. Ada Maria Isasi-Diaz and Yolanda Tarango, C.C.V.I., *Hispanic Women: Prophetic Voice in the Church* (San Francisco: Harper & Row, 1988), p. 31.

23. See Marianne Sawicki, *Faith and Sexism: Guidelines for Religious Educators* (New York: Seabury Press, 1979); Mary Elizabeth Moore, "Women and Men in the Social Order: Challenge to Religious Education," *Religious Education as Social Transformation*, ed. Allen J. Moore (Birmingham, Ala.: Religious Education Press, 1989), pp. 66-91.

24. Maria Harris, *Women and Teaching* (New York: Paulist Press, 1988), pp. 4-10.

25. Ibid., p. 90.

26. Two source books have given particular attention to these questions: Christ and Plaskow, eds., *Womanspirit Rising* and *Weaving the Visions.*

27. Mary Elizabeth Moore, *Education for Continuity and Change: A New Model for Christian Religious Education* (Nashville: Abingdon Press, 1983).

28. Rosemary Radford Ruether, "The Call of Women in the Church Today," *Women of Faith in Dialogue*, ed. Mollenkott, p. 79, cf. pp. 77-88; cf. Ruether, *New Woman New Earth*, pp. 80-81.

271

29. See esp. Letty M. Russell, *The Future of Partnership* (Philadelphia: Westminster Press, 1979), and *Growth in Partnership* (Philadelphia: Westminster Press, 1981). Similar themes are developed in Lynn N. Rhodes, *Co-Creating: A Feminist Vision of Ministry* (Philadelphia: Westminster Press, 1987).

30. Nelle Morton, *The Journey Is Home* (Boston: Beacon Press, 1985).

Part II—Church

Foreword

1. Leonardo Boff, *Ecclesiogenesis: The Base Communities Reinvent the Church*, trans. Robert Barr (Maryknoll, N. Y.: Orbis Press, 1986).

2. Catharine Albanese, *America: Religions and Religion* (Belmont, Calif.: Wadsworth Publishing Co., 1986), pp. 1-16.

3. Peter McKenzie, *The Christians: Their Beliefs and Practices* (Nashville: Abingdon Press, 1988).

Chapter 5—Education in the Quest for Church

1. Walter Brueggemann, *The Creative Word: Canon as a Model for Biblical Education* (Philadelphia: Fortress Press, 1982), p. 1.

2. Martin E. Marty, *The Public Church: Mainline-Evangelical-Catholic* (New York: Crossroad Publishing Co., 1981), p. ix; Wade Clark Roof and William McKinney, *American Mainline Religion: Its Changing Shape and Future* (New Brunswick, N. J.: Rutgers University Press, 1987), p. 25; Jeffrey K. Hadden, *The Gathering Storm in the Churches: A Sociologist Looks at the Widening Gap Between Clergy and Laymen* (Garden City, N. Y.: Anchor Books, 1970); Peter Berger, et al., *The Homeless Mind: Modernization and Consciousness* (New York: Vintage Books, 1973, 1974), pp. 82, 184-85; Robert C. Worley, *A Gathering of Strangers: Understanding the Life of Your Church* (Philadelphia: Westminster Press, 1976); Richard Sennett, *The Fall of Public Man* (New York: Alfred A. Knopf, 1977), cf. pp. 8, 18-19; Robert N. Bellah, Richard Madsen, William M. Sullivan, Ann Swidler, and Steven M. Tipton, *Habits of the Heart: Individualism and Commitment in American Life* (Berkeley: University of California Press, 1985), pp. 50-51, 115, 130-38.

3. Avery Dulles, *Models of the Church: A Critical Assessment of the Church in All Its Aspects* (Garden City, N. Y.: Doubleday & Co., 1974), pp. 8-9; Peter C. Hodgson, *Re-visioning the Church: Ecclesial Freedom in the New Paradigm* (Philadelphia: Fortress Press, 1988), pp. 11-19.

4. Maria Harris, *Fashion Me a People: Curriculum in the Church* (Louisville: Westminster/John Knox Press, 1989).

5. Craig R. Dykstra, "No Longer Strangers: The Church and Its Educational Ministry," *Princeton Seminary Bulletin*, New Series 6:3 (1985):189, 193.

6. The principle of covenantal confederacy may be seen in the Hebrew bonding of tribal houses into a common covenant of obedience to God. It emphasized the equality of those participating in the covenant. In contrast,

principles of monarchical hierarchy emphasize the vertical structure of society, usually centered on the dominance of a king or corresponding figure and embodying some kind of divine sanction. The anointing of Saul and David by the prophet Samuel reflects this distinction of setting apart and elevating leadership, as does the medieval doctrine of divine right. William Johnson Everett examines the symbolic power of these principles in *God's Federal Republic: Reconstructing our Governing Symbol* (New York: Paulist Press, 1988), pp. 22-25, 105-6. The pervasive acceptance of voluntarism in the United States was noted in the nineteenth century by such observers as Alexis de Toqueville, *Democracy in America*, trans. George Lawrence, ed. J. P. Mayer (New York: Anchor Books, 1969), and recently by Robert N. Bellah and his colleagues in *Habits of the Heart*.

7. Cf. Fayette Veverke, "The Ambiguity of Catholic Educational Separatism," *Religious Education* 80:(Winter 1985):64-100; Robert T. O'Gorman, "Foundation of the U.S. Catholic Church's Educational Mission and Ministry," *Religious Education* 80(Winter 1985):101-22.

Several Christian educators have begun to explore both the historical and contemporary issues in the educational experience of cultural minorities in the struggle to make sense of traditional educational structures and values in the midst of dominant European American perspectives and approaches to education. For studies that explore the persistence of cultural minority values and approaches see Charles R. Foster, ed., *Ethnicity in the Education of the Church* (Nashville: Scarritt Press, 1987), and Anne Greer Ng, "The Dragon and the Lamb: Chinese Festivals in the Life of Chinese Canadian/American Christians," *Religious Education* 84(Summer 1989):368-83. Still unpublished is the research of: William R. Myers on black church youth ministry; Mary Elizabeth Moore and her students at the School of Theology at Claremont on ethnographic studies of the education of several minority community congregations; and Jack Seymour on cross-cultural issues in Christian education.

For studies of the social and political negotiations of cultural minority Christian communities with dominant culture approaches to Christian education, see Grant S. Shockley, "Christian Education and the Black Church," *Christian Education Journey of Black Americans: Past, Present, Future*, ed. Charles R. Foster, Ethel R. Johnson, and Grant S. Shockley (Nashville: Discipleship Resources, 1985); Charles R. Foster, "Double Messages: Ethnocentrism in Church Education," *Religious Education* 82(Summer 1987):447-68; Taylor McConnell, "Oral Cultures and Literate Research," *Religious Education* 81(Summer 1986):341-55.

8. Hodgson, *Re-visioning the Church*, p. 63.

9. Max L. Stackhouse, "James Luther Adams: A Biographical and Intellectual Sketch," *Voluntary Associations: A Study of Groups in Free Societies*, ed. D. B. Robertson (Richmond: John Knox Press, 1966), p. 363.

10. Ibid., p. 364.

11. Bellah, et al., *Habits of the Heart*, pp. 28-31, 20.

12. Richard Rodriguez, *An Autobiography: The Hunger of Memory: The Education of Richard Rodriguez* (New York: Bantam Books, 1982, 1983), p. 110.

13. Catherine L. Albanese, *America: Religions and Religion* (Belmont, Calif.: Wadsworth Publishing Co., 1986), p. xix; Marty, *The Public Church*, p. 10.

14. Lawrence A. Cremin, tracing the shifting patterns of agency interdependence in American education, noted the ecological character of these relationships in *American Education: The National Experience 1783–1876* (New York: Harper & Row, 1980), chap. 12. Robert W. Lynn similarly explored the mutuality of educational agencies in *Protestant Strategies in Education* (New York: Association Press, 1964).

15. Sidney E. Mead, *The Nation with the Soul of a Church* (New York: Harper & Row, 1975), pp. 73-74.

16. C. Ellis Nelson, *Where Faith Begins* (Richmond: John Knox Press, 1967), pp. 59-60.

17. Stuart Langton, "The New Voluntarism," *Voluntarism in the Eighties: Fundamental Issues in Voluntary Action*, ed. John D. Harmon (Washington, D. C.: University Press of America, 1982), pp. 3-9.

18. Roof and McKinney, *American Mainline Religion*, p. 40.

19. Ibid., pp. 48-50.

20. William Irwin Thompson, *At the Edge of History* (New York: Harper & Row, 1971), chap. 1; George De Vos, "Ethnic Pluralism: Conflict and Accommodation," *Ethnic Identity: Cultural Continuities and Change*, ed. De Vos and Lola Romanucci-Russ (Chicago: University of Chicago Press, 1975), pp. 20-24.

21. Bellah, et al., *Habits of the Heart*, p. 55.

22. Arthur G. Powell, Eleanor Farrar, and David K. Cohen, *The Shopping Mall High School: Winners and Losers in the Educational Marketplace* (Boston: Houghton Mifflin Co., 1985), pp. 2-6.

23. The greatest challenge to the continuing usefulness of the voluntary principle for understanding the impetus to community may actually come from contemporary scientific research. Such discussion is beyond the scope of this essay, yet it must be noted that the popular appropriation of voluntarism as a social principle during the seventeenth and eighteenth centuries was undoubtedly reinforced by the increasing acceptance at the time of such scientific principles as "cause and effect." Insights from the new science of chaos point to the possibility that the structure of reality may actually involve the interplay of order and randomness. See for example the provocative discussion of this new science and an introduction to its social implications in Ilya Prigogine and Isabelle Stengers, *Order out of Chaos: Man's New Dialogue with Nature* (New York: Bantam Books, 1984).

In that literature, perhaps the closest contemporary discussion on the nature of community to the scientific exploration of randomness may be found in Victor Turner's description of "communitas" in *The Ritual Process* (Ithaca, N. Y.: Cornell Paperbacks, 1966, 1977), chap. 4.

24. Cf. Dykstra, "No Longer Strangers," pp. 188-96, and Charles R. Foster, *Teaching in the Community of Faith* (Nashville: Abingdon Press, 1982), pp. 30-34, for earlier uses of "participation" as an educational concept.

25. Nelson, *Where Faith Begins*, pp. 67-70.

26. Cf. John H. Westerhoff III, *Building God's People in a Materialistic World* (New York: Seabury Press, 1981); Matías Preiswerk, *Education in the Living Word: A Theoretical Framework for Christian Education* (Maryknoll, N. Y.: Orbis Books, 1987); Mary Elizabeth Moore, *Education for Continuity and*

274

Change: A New Model for Christian Religious Education (Nashville: Abingdon Press, 1983), pp. 59ff.; Harris, *Fashion Me a People.*

27. Brueggemann, *The Creative Word*, p. 17; Dykstra, "No Longer Strangers," p. 193.

28. Brueggemann, *The Creative Word*, pp. 14-15.

29. Ibid., pp. 23-25; Dykstra, "No Longer Strangers," pp. 193-96; Stanley Hauerwas, *A Community of Character: Toward a Constructive Christian Social Ethic* (Notre Dame: University of Notre Dame Press, 1981), chap. 1.

30. Moore, *Education for Continuity and Change*, chap. 3.

31. Parker J. Palmer has reminded us of the importance of practice in the educational process, cf. *The Company of Strangers: Christians and the Renewal of America's Public Life* (New York: Crossroad Press, 1981), chap. 7; Craig Dykstra, more recently, has identified illustrative central practices to congregational education that are crucial not only to the continuity of Christian community, but as an experiential impetus to renewed understandings for community life; see "No Longer Strangers," p. 197.

32. Cf. John H. Westerhoff III, *Building God's People*, as well as *Bringing Up Children in the Christian Faith* (Minneapolis: Winston Press, 1980), *Living the Faith Community: The Church That Makes a Difference* (Minneapolis: Winston Press, 1985), and *A Pilgrim People* (Minneapolis: Seabury Press, 1984), for extensive discussions of the importance of Christian education as integral to building community. This theme is also central to Hauerwas, *A Community of Character.*

33. J. Stanley Glen, *The Recovery of the Teaching Ministry* (Philadelphia: Westminster Press, 1960), chap. 2.

Chapter 6—The Church in a Racial-minority Situation

1. "Challenge to the Churches—Toward a Racially Just World," Report of The International Consultation on Racism and Racial Justice, U. S. Commissioners of the Program to Combat Racism, World Council of Churches, 1988, pp. 4-5.

2. Ibid., p. 5.

3. Ethnic identity differs from kinship groups by being a presumed identity, not a group with concrete social action. Ethnic identity does not necessarily constitute a group; it only facilitates group formation.

4. Winthrop D. Jordan, *White over Black: American Attitudes Toward the Negro, 1550–1812* (Chapel Hill: University of North Carolina Press, 1968), p. xiv.

5. Kwang Chung Kim and Won Moo Hurh, "Asian-Americans and the 'Success' Image: A Critique," *P/AAMHRC Research Review* 5(January/April 1986):7.

6. "Challenge to the Churches," p. 3.

7. Wesley Woo, "Socio-historical Starting Point for a Pacific and Asian American Theology," *Branches: Pacific and Asian American Journey of Theology and Ministry* 3(Summer 1987):11.

8. Ibid., pp. 4-5.

9. Ibid., p. 5.

10. World Council of Churches, *Racism in Theology, and Theology Against*

Racism. Report of a consultation organized by the Commission on Faith and Order and the Programme to Combat Racism (Geneva: World Council of Churches, 1975), quoted in *World Council of Churches' Statement and Action on Racism 1948–1979*, special issue of PCR Information Reports and Background Paper of the Programme to Combat Racism, ed. Ans J. Vander Bent (Geneva: World Council of Churches, 1980), p. 43.

11. Ibid., p. 38.

12. William Speer, *The Oldest and the Newest Empire: China and the United States*, quoted from *Proceedings of the Sixth Triennial Meeting of The National Conference of Christian Work Among the Chinese in America* (June 21–27, 1971), pp. 34, 35.

13. *Remembering: The Sojourners in Asian-American History*, Asian-American Christian Education Curriculum Project, Golden Gate Mission Area, Synod of the Pacific, Presbyterian Church in the U.S., pp. 37-38.

14. Ibid., pp. 37-38, 30-32, 1.

15. Ibid., p. 9.

16. The Chinese Methodist Center Corporation, an outreach ministry of the Chinese United Methodist Church, is located in the heart of Chinatown.

17. Maxine McKinney Langston, "Helping the Generations Build a Bridge Toward Each Other," *elsa* (April 1983):55.

18. From the Centennial Worship Celebration, Japanese Christian Mission in North America (October 9, 1977), quoted in *Remembering*, p. 2.

Part III—Person

Chapter 7—Education in the Image of God

1. Walker Percy, *The Message in the Bottle* (New York: Farrer, Straus & Giroux, 1975), p. 3.

2. Dorothee Soelle, *Death by Bread Alone*, trans. David L. Scheidt (Philadelphia: Fortress Press, 1978), p. 8.

3. Ibid., p. 10.

4. Gustavo Gutierrez, *We Drink from Our Own Wells: The Spiritual Journey of a People* (Maryknoll, N. Y.: Orbis Press, 1984), p. 37.

5. Material in the following section—selected portions, as well as the subhead title—is adapted from Susanne Johnson, *Christian Spiritual Formation: In the Church and Classroom* (Nashville: Abingdon Press, 1989).

6. Five distinctive streams of thought exist within modern psychology: traditional behaviorism (Skinner); classical psychoanalytic thought (Freud); humanistic, third-force psychology (Maslow); transpersonal, fourth-force psychology (Wilber); and structure theory (Piaget, Kohlberg). The third-force and fourth-force psychologies constitute the self-actualization approach to human change and growth.

7. Daniel Yankelovich, *New Rules: Searching for Self-fulfillment in a World Turned Upside Down* (New York: Random House, 1981), p. 14.

8. Don Browning, *Religious Thought and the Modern Psychologies* (Philadelphia: Fortress Press, 1987).

9. David L. Norton, *Personal Destinies: A Philosophy of Ethical Individualism* (Princeton, N. J.: Princeton University Press, 1976), pp. 5-6.

10. Browning, *Religious Thought*, p. 72.

11. Don Browning, "Images of Man in Contemporary Models of Pastoral Care," *Interpretation* 33(April 1979):144-56.

12. Scott Peck, *The Road Less Traveled* (New York: Simon & Schuster, 1978), p. 281.

13. Historically speaking, we are further mired in the privatized version of self from the eighteenth-century period of romanticism and enlightenment, when everybody began looking within—Quakers to the inner light; pietists to the inner testimony of the Spirit; rationalists to innate reason; romanticists to imagination and emotion.

14. Soelle, *Death by Bread Alone*, p. 4.

15. Craig Dykstra, "The Formative Power of Congregations," *Religious Education Investigations* 82:(Fall 1987):530-46.

16. Soelle, *Death by Bread Alone*, p. 9.

17. Stanley Hauerwas, *Truthfulness and Tragedy: Further Investigation in Christian Ethics* (Notre Dame, Ind.: Notre Dame Press, 1977), p. 12.

18. Soelle, *Death by Bread Alone*, p. 14.

19. D. Campbell Wyckoff, "From Practice to Theory—and Back Again," *Modern Masters of Religious Education*, ed. Marlene Mayr (Birmingham, Alabama: Religious Education Press, 1983), pp. 89-90.

20. Stanley Hauerwas, *Character and the Christian Life: A Study in Theological Ethics* (San Antonio: Trinity University Press, 1975), pp. 227 ff., 125.

21. Ibid., p. 223.

22. Craig Dykstra, "No Longer Strangers: The Church and Its Educational Ministry," *Princeton Seminary Bulletin*, New Series, 6:3(November 1985):195.

23. Dykstra, "The Formative Power," pp. 540-41.

24. Edward Farley, *Ecclesial Man*, (Philadelphia: Fortress Press, 1976), pp. 151, 169. *Ecclesia*, he suggests, refers to the interpersonal, relational, interdependent matrix of the church, whatever institutional form it may take.

25. Ibid., p. 170.

26. Here I am adapting a point made by Mother Teresa, see *Life in the Spirit: Reflections, Meditations, Prayers*, ed. Kathryn Spink (San Francisco: Harper & Row, 1983), p. 13.

27. David T. Abalos, "The Teacher as Guide," *Journal of Dharma* 11(January-March 1986):62-75.

28. Stanley Hauerwas, "The Gesture of a Truthful Story: The Church and 'Religious Education,' " *Encounter* 43:(Autumn 1982):319-29.

29. Roberta Bondi, *To Love as God Loves: Conversations with the Early Church* (Philadelphia: Fortress Press, 1987), p. 9.

30. Cf. Micah 6:8; Jer. 22:16; Isa. 3:13, 10:1-3; Pss. 101:1, 146:7-10).

31. Craig Dykstra, *Vision and Character: A Christian Educator's Alternative to Kohlberg* (New York: Paulist Press, 1981), p. 102.

Chapter 8—Education and Human Development

1. Gabriel Moran, *Religious Education Development* (Minneapolis: Winston Press, 1983), p. 24.

277

2. See Jean Piaget, *The Child and Reality* (New York: Penguin Books, 1976).

3. See Lawrence Kohlberg, "Education, Moral Development and Faith," *Journal of Moral Education* 4(October 1974):5-16.

4. James W. Fowler, *Stages of Faith* (San Francisco: Harper & Row, 1981).

5. H. Richard Niebuhr, *Radical Monotheism and Western Culture* (New York: Harper & Brothers, 1960).

6. Fowler, *Stages of Faith*, p. 176.

7. Stuart McLean, "Basic Sources and New Possibilities: H. Richard Niebuhr's Influence on Faith Development Theory," *Faith Development and Fowler*, ed. Craig Dykstra and Sharon Parks (Birmingham: Religious Education Press, 1986), p. 173.

8. Fowler, *Stages of Faith*, p. 102.

9. Ibid., p. 24.

10. Garnett Green, *Imagining God: Theology and the Religious Imagination* (San Francisco: Harper & Row, 1989), p. 53.

11. James W. Fowler, "Faith and the Structuring of Meaning," *Faith Development and Fowler*, ed. Dykstra and Parks, pp. 15-42.

12. See Wilfred Cantwell Smith, *The Meaning and End of Religion* (New York: Macmillan, 1961).

13. Douglas John Hall, *Imaging God: Dominion as Stewardship* (Grand Rapids: Eerdmans, 1986), p. 113; Erik Erikson, *The Life Cycle Completed* (New York: W. W. Norton, 1982), pp. 32-33; See Jane Loevinger, *Ego Development* (San Francisco: Jossey-Bass, 1976); Lawrence Kohlberg, "Stages of Development as a Basis for Education," *Moral Development, Moral Education and Kohlberg*, ed. Brenda Munsey (Birmingham, Ala.: Religious Education Press, 1980), pp. 66-72; Fowler, *Stages of Faith*, pp. 199-213.

14. Erik Erikson, *Identity and the Life Cycle* (New York: International Universities Press, 1959), p. 65.

15. Erikson, *The Life Cycle Completed*, p. 88.

16. Green, *Imagining God*, p. 133.

17. Ibid., p. 144.

18. Kohlberg, "Stages of Development as a Basis for Education," pp. 62-72.

19. Carol Gilligan, *In a Different Voice* (Cambridge, Mass.: Harvard University Press, 1982) p. 19.

20. Fowler, *Stages of Faith*, p. 199.

21. Green, *Imagining God*, p. 134.

22. Sally McFague, *Metaphorical Theology* (Philadelphia: Fortress Press, 1987), p. 33.

23. See Klaus Riegel, *Dialectical Psychology* (New York: Academic Press, 1979).

24. Fowler, *Stages of Faith*, pp. 184-98.

25. Maggie Ross, *Pillars of Flame* (New York: Harper & Row, 1988), p. xxiv.

26. Ibid., p. xxx.

27. Ibid., pp. xxx-xxxi.

28. Soren Kierkegaard, *Either/Or*, Vol. II (Princeton, N. J.: Princeton University Press, 1959), p. 348.

29. See William J. Wilson, *The Truly Disadvantaged* (Chicago: University of Chicago Press, 1987).

30. McFague, *Metaphorical Theology*, p. 104.

Part IV—Mission: The Church in the World
Foreword

1. H. Richard Niebuhr, *Christ and Culture* (New York: Harper & Row, 1951).
2. Jack L. Seymour, Robert T. O'Gorman, and Charles R. Foster, *The Church in the Education of the Public: Refocusing the Task of Religious Education* (Nashville: Abingdon Press, 1984).

Chapter 9—A World of Religious Pluralism

1. Simon P. David, "Can a Christian Celebrate Diwali?" *Case Studies in Missions*, ed. Paul G. Hiebert and Frances F. Hiebert (Grand Rapids: Baker Book House, 1987), pp. 84-85.
2. Elie Wiesel, introductory "epigram" from *The Gates of the Forest* (New York: Avon Books, by arrangement with Holt, Rinehart & Winston, 1966), pp. 6-10.
3. *Majjhima-nikaya*, Vol. I, 426ff. (62 *Cula-malunkya-sutra*), from *Buddhist Scriptures*, trans. E. J. Thomas (London: 1913), pp. 64-67, quoted in Mircea Eliade, *From Primitive to Zen: A Thematic Sourcebook of the History of Religions* (New York: Harper & Row, 1967), pp. 570-71.
4. Walbert Buhlmann, *The Coming of the Third Church* (Maryknoll, N. Y.: Orbis Books, 1978), p. 143.

Chapter 10—Ecumenical Learning in a Global Perspective

1. For a stimulating analysis of the educational implications of faith understood as a system shaped by the past that is to be defended and passed on, compared with faith formed in the thought-world of today and understood as a journey with continual surprises, see John M. Hull, *What Prevents Christian Adults from Learning?* (London: SCM Press, 1985). Readers of German have access to probably the first book in ecumenical learning, Klaus Gossman, *Okumenisches Lernen im Religions Unterricht* (Munster: Comenius Institute, 1987).
2. *Scripture, Tradition and Traditions*, "Report of the Fourth World Conference on Faith and Order," Montreal, 1963 (Geneva: World Council of Churches, 1963), esp. pp. 19-20.
3. See C. Ellis Nelson, *Where Faith Begins* (Richmond: John Knox Press, 1967), the seminal work in this regard. Also see John Westerhoff III, *Will Our Children Have Faith?* (New York: Seabury Press, 1976), which popularized the concept of the community of faith as the context of education.
4. Thomas H. Groome, *Christian Religious Education: Sharing Our Story and Vision* (New York: Harper & Row, 1980).
5. Gabriel Moran, *Religious Education Development: Images for the Future* (Minneapolis: Winston Press, 1983), p. 13.
6. *The Upsalla Report* (Geneva: World Council of Churches, 1968), p. 246.
7. See, for example, Hans-Ruedi Webber, *Experiments with Bible Study*

279

(Geneva: World Council of Churches, 1981). See also Robert McAfee Brown, *Unexpected News: Reading the Bible with Third World Eyes* (Philadelphia: Westminster Press, 1984).

8. Michael Taylor, "People at Work," *Theology by the People*, ed. S. Amirtham and J. S. Pobee (Geneva: World Council of Churches, 1986).

9. These definitions and descriptions were developed by the members of the World Council of Churches Working Group on Education, at the consultation at Bossey Ecumenical Institute in 1986. See also *Alive Together: A Practical Guide to Ecumenical Learning* (Geneva: World Council of churches, 1989).

Part V—Method

Chapter 11—Latin American Theology and Education

1. See Walbert Buhlmann, *The Coming of the Third Church* (Maryknoll, N. Y.: Orbis Books, 1978); Richard Shaull, *Heralds of a New Reformation* (Maryknoll, N. Y.: Orbis Books, 1984); Peter C. Hodgson, *Re-visioning the Church* (Philadelphia: Fortress Press, 1988). My own concept, "Transformation church," is my attempt to clarify this church as a new Reformation—that is, always reforming in light of God's acts.

2. Comunidad Ecclesial de Base (Basic Ecclesial Community); CEB is the common designation for these groups. Key to this designation is the word *ecclesial*. Latin Americans are clear that these groups are an expression of *church*, not movements or programs *of* the church; see Marcello de C. Azevedo, S. J., *Basic Ecclesial Communities in Brazil* (Washington, D. C.: Georgetown University Press, 1987).

3. I am indebted to my former colleague from St. Thomas Seminary in Denver, C. M. Kempton Hewitt, for this account, a summary from his unpublished journal. Dr. Hewitt is presently Riley Professor of Biblical Interpretation at Methodist Theological School in Ohio.

4. Azevedo, *Basic Ecclesial Communities*.

5. Ibid., p. 124.

6. J. R. Newbrough, of Peabody College, Vanderbilt University, in "Toward a Theory of Community for Community Psychology," address presented to the 22nd Interamerican Congress of Psychology, Buenos Aires, Argentina (June 29, 1989), says we are experiencing the "core problem of community, the relationship of the individual to the social grouping," or "the problem of the One and the Many." Assisted by the writings of Frank G. Kirkpatrick, *Community: A Trinity of Models* (Washington, D. C.: Georgetown University Press, 1986), Newbrough points to a stage in the development of community that is beyond the view of community as "organic," in which the Many smother the One, and beyond the view of community as social contract, in which the One reigns supreme over the Many, to a third stage—community as human social system, in which the tension of the One and the Many is brought into balance.

280

7. Virgilio P. Elizondo, *La Morenita: Evangelizer of the Americas* (San Antonio: The Mexican American Culture Center, 1980).

8. Since this was the only continental group with an intact association at the Vatican Council of bishops (Vatican II), it had a special influence on the council; cf. Edward L. Cleary, O. P., *Crisis and Change* (Maryknoll, N. Y.: Orbis Books, 1985).

9. Personal interview with François Houtart, October 1986. See also François Houtart, "La Contribution de L'Université Catholique de Louvain-la-Neuve au Développement de la Sociologie de la Religion en Amerique Latine," April 4, 1985, mimeograph of Centre de Récherches Socio-Religieuses, Section: Religion et Développement, Université Catholique de Louvain, 1348, Ottignies, Louvain-la-Neuve, Belgium.

10. On the influence of Latin American bishops on *Gaudium et Spes*, see Marcos McGrath, "The Impact of *Gaudium et Spes*," *The Church and Culture Since Vatican II*, ed. Joseph Gremillion (Notre Dame, Ind.: Notre Dame University Press, 1985).

11. In the English-speaking world, this document was called *The Church in the Modern World;* in the Spanish speaking world, *The Church in the World Today*, or more literally, *The Church in the Here and Now;* cf. McGrath, "The Impact of *Gaudium et Spes.*" At the council, Latin American bishops chose identification with the poor, rather than the accommodation with modernity chosen by the English speakers.

12. Interview with Houtart.

13. The movement known as Catholic Action permitted students only to see and judge, not to act. The development of a "Christian left" allowed them to act and yet retain their Catholic identity; see Cleary, *Crisis and Change* and Daniel S. Schipani, *Religious Education Encounters Liberation Theology* (Birmingham, Ala.: Religious Education Press, 1988).

14. Azevedo, *Basic Ecclesial Communities*, p. 85.

15. Ibid.

16. Schaull, *Heralds of a New Reformation.*

17. Carlos Mesters, "The Use of the Bible in the Christian Communities of the Common People," *The Bible and Liberation*, ed. Norman K. Gottwald (Maryknoll, N. Y.: Orbis Books, 1983). For a detailed analysis of Mesters' approach, see Schipani, *Religious Education Encounters Liberation Theology*, pp. 180-83.

18. Pope Paul IV, *Evangelii Nuntiandi [On Evangelization in the Modern World]* (Washington, D. C.: USCC Office of Publishing and Promotion Services, 1975).

19. Western technical rationality operates out of a three-level universe: At the bottom level, the underlying discipline or basic science upon which ministry should rest (foundational theology); next, theology elaborated in terms of the major religious themes of our experience—creation, redemption, resurrection, etc. (systematic theology); finally, the skills and attitudes that involve the actual performance of ministry (practical theology). See Robert T. O'Gorman, "The Search for a Usable Knowledge in Religious Education: Educating Reflective Practitioners," *Religious Education* 83 (Summer 1988):322-36; Samuel Amirtham and John S. Pobee, eds., *Theology by the People* (Geneva: World Council of Churches, 1986).

20. Centers include Valdivieso in Nicaragua; CEE (Center for Educational Studies), Mexico City; Bartalameo de Las Casas, Lima, Peru; Centre de Formation, Rio; La Sucre in Boliva; San Migalito in Panama; Golconda, Medellin, Columbia. Several of these are described in Cleary, *Crisis and Change*.

21. The movement for "participatory research" has gained much ground in this country and internationally. The Highlander Research and Education Center near Knoxville, Tennessee, is a major world center for this research; over a three-year period, 100 people in 80 counties in six Appalachian states produced a definitive research piece: Bill Horton, Dave Liden, and Tracey Weis, *Who Owns It?: Researching Land and Mineral Ownership in Your Community* (Prestonburg, Ky.: Appalachian Alliance [no date]).

In participatory research, the people are viewed as producers (subjects) of knowledge, not its objects. Accountability for what will be researched, and how and why it will be researched lies with the people, not with "research directors." Participatory research raises the question of what constitutes valid knowledge, the purpose of the knowledge, and who has the capacity to produce knowledge. It challenges the belief that the disenfranchised have no voice and are incompetent. Participatory knowledge affirms popular knowledge. It assumes a faith in the people's own experience as a basis for action. In contrast, classical research is based on the assumption that the disenfranchised are incompetent and should have no voice.

No participatory research exists on theology. Upon considering such research, questions arise: How is theology knowledge? If knowledge, what is its power? How is theology produced? How can the people produce it? These questions move us to ask what role theology plays in social reform—that is, how does it contribute to the needs of the people? Seen from the perspective of participatory research, theology is both action and reflection: The pre-text (the experience of the people) interacts with the text (the canonical Scriptures), and a new text (the context) is produced. This new text is action (acts, or a narrative) and, as such, is itself a text. Thus this whole process of bringing the experience to the text and producing more text through action can be seen as theology. In this outlook, theology becomes more inclusive: people, experience, canonical text, and action; see Amirtham and Pobee, *Theology by the People*, as an example.

22. Kirkpatrick, *Community: A Trinity of Models*, distinguishes between *community* and *society*. He reserves *community* to the third level of human development—the "personal"—whereas *society* refers to the lower levels of human organization—the "mechanistic" and the "organic".

23. Newbrough, "Toward a Theory of Community for Community Psychology."

24. Robert N. Bellah, et al., *Habits of the Heart* (New York: Harper & Row, 1985); Kirkpatrick, *Community: A Trinity of Models;* M. Scott Peck, *The Different Drum: Community-making and Peace* (New York: Simon & Schuster, 1987); Martin Marty, *The Public Church* (New York: Crossroad Press, 1981); Peter C. Hodgson, *Re-visioning the Church;* Jack L. Seymour, Robert T. O'Gorman, and Charles R. Foster, *The Church in the Education of the Public* (Nashville: Abingdon Press, 1984).

25. Amirtham and Pobee, *Theology by the People*, p. 29.

26. One example of an attempt to see CEBs as programs of the church comes from East Africa, where the Roman Catholic bishops tried to mandate the base communities. One pastor in Kenya said, "Well, we have four base communities in this parish, and there are four weeks in the month. Thus Base Community No. 1 will clean the church the first week, Base Community No. 2 will do it the second week, and so on."

27. "One can see a noticeable convergence between the larger Church, structured as a network of institutional services, and the Church as a network of grassroots communities. From the larger Church the latter gets the symbolic capital of the faith, its links with apostolic tradition, and the dimension of universality. The larger Church, in turn . . . gets concrete embodiment on the local and personal level, insertion among the common people and links with the most urgent causes revolving around justice, dignity, and participation. . . . They are not two Churches. They are one and the same Church of the Fathers of the faith, made concrete at different levels of society and confronting specific problems." (Azevedo, *Basic Ecclesial Communities*, p. 238)

28. Pedro Casaldaliga, *Prophets in Combat* (Oak Park, Ill.: Meyer-Stone Books, 1987), p. 62.

29. Amirtham and Pobee, *Theology by the People*, p. 6.

30. Brazilian philosophers have never developed a "systematic" philosophy; their epistemological mode is different from major Western thought, and this difference shows up in the way *knowing* operates in the base communities.

31. David Tracy, *The Analogical Imagination* (New York: Crossroad Press, 1981).

32. Leonardo Boff, quoted in Amirtham and Pobee, *Theology by the People*, p. 8.

33. Hodgson, *Revisioning the Church*, pp. 78-80.

34. Amirtham and Pobee, *Theology by the People*, p. 13.

35. *National Pastoral for Hispanic Ministry*, (Washington, D. C.: USCC Publications, 1988). See also *The Theological Education of Hispanics*, a study commissioned by the Fund for Theological Education, February 1988.

36. Hodgson, *Re-visioning the Church*, p. 17.

Chapter 12—Teaching as Practical Theology

1. While such reflection frequently is located at the beginning of a theological system, it often is the final section, completed after the actual theological work has been done. See Paul Tillich, *Systematic Theology*, Vol. I (Chicago: University of Chicago Press, 1951), p. 34.

2. See Edward Farley, "Interpretating Situations: An Inquiry into the Nature of Practical Theology," *Formation and Reflection: The Promise of Practical Theology*, ed. Lewis S. Mudge and James N. Poling (Philadelphia: Fortress Press, 1987), pp. 1-26. More extensive interpretation can be found in Norbert Mette, *Theorie der Praxis* (Dusseldorf: Patmos-Verlag, 1978).

3. A helpful account of differences between Roman Catholic and Protestant understandings of ethics can be found in James Gustafson, *Protestant & Roman Catholic Ethics: Prospects for Rapprochement* (Chicago: University of Chicago Press, 1978), chap. 1; see also Bernard Haring, *Free &*

Faithful in Christ, Vol. I (New York: Seabury Press, 1978), pp. 45-61.

4. The "cases of conscience" literature of the English Puritans is particularly important; see William Ames, *The Marrow of Theology*, 1st. ed. (Latin, 1623); William Perkins, *A Discourse of Conscience* (1596), reprinted in *William Perkins, 1558–1602: English Puritanism*, ed. Thomas Merrill (Netherlands: 1966).

5. Voetius, *Disputationes*, trans. (in part) John Beardslee, *Reformed Dogmatics: Seventeenth-century Reformed Theology Through the Writings of Wollebius, Voetius, and Turretin* (Grand Rapids: Baker Book House, 1965), pp. 265-334.

6. Voetius developed his understanding of practical theology in conjunction with his teaching of people preparing for the ordained ministry.

7. Edward Farley, *Theologia: The Fragmentation and Unity of Theological Education* (Philadelphia: Fortress Press, 1983), chaps. 3-5.

8. See Schleiermacher's thought in *Brief Outline on the Study of Theology*, trans. T. Tice (Richmond: John Knox Press, 1966), and *Christian Caring: Selections from Practical Theology*, ed. J. Duke and H. Stone (Philadelphia: Fortress Press, 1988).

9. Those who collapsed practical theology into pastoral theology lost contact with Schleiermacher's broader understanding. See Phillip Schaff, *Theological Propaedeutic: A General Introduction to the Study of Theology—Exegetical, Historical, Systematic, and Practical, Including Encyclopedia, Methodology, and Bibliography—A Manual for Students* (New York: Charles Scribner's Sons, 1893); Karl Hagenbach, *Theological Encyclopedia and Methodology on the Basis of Hagenback*, trans. G. Crooks and J. Hurst (New York: Phillips & Hunt, 1884); Alexander Vinet, *Pastoral Theology: Or the Theory of the Evangelical Ministry*, trans. and ed. T. Skinner (New York: Harper & Brothers, 1853); Alfred Cave, *An Introduction to Theology: Its Principles, Its Branches, Its Results, and Its Literature* (Edinburgh: T & T Clark, 1896).

10. Some continued to define practical theology in a broader fashion, using the rubric "pastoral theology" to refer to theological reflection on clergy functions. Others limited the focus of practical theology to ministerial activities or substituted pastoral theology for it altogether.

11. George Albert Coe, *The Psychology of Religion* (Chicago: University of Chicago Press, 1917, reprint 1979); *A Social Theory of Religious Education* (New York: Arno Press, 1927, reprint 1969); *What Is Christian Education?* (New York: Charles Scribner's Sons, 1929); Anton Boisen, *Out of the Depths* (New York: Harper & Brothers, 1960); *The Exploration of the Inner World: A Study of Mental Disorder and Religious Experience* (New York: Harper & Brothers, 1936); Seward Hiltner, *Preface to Pastoral Theology* (Nashville: Abingdon Press, 1958).

12. For Coe, see Richard R. Osmer, "Practical Theology and Contemporary Christian Education: An Historical and Constructive Analysis," Vol. 1, "Christian Education in Crisis: An Historical Examination of John Dewey, George Albert Coe, H. Shelton Smith, and James Smart" (Ph.D. diss., Emory University, 1985), chap. 2.

13. James Smart, *The Rebirth of Ministry* (Philadelphia: Westminster Press, 1960); *The Teaching Ministry of the Church* (Philadelphia: Westminster Press,

1954); H. Shelton Smith, *Faith and Nurture* (New York: Charles Scribner's Sons, 1948); "The Gospel for an Age of Good Works," *Advance* 128(October 1936):107-11; "The Supremacy of Christ in Christian Nurture," *Religion in Life* 12(Winter 1942-43):31-40; "Let Religious Educators Reckon with the Barthians," *Religious Education* 29(January 1934):45-51.

14. For Marx's influence on liberation theology, see Jose Miguez Bonino, *Christians and Marxists* (Grand Rapids: Eerdmans, 1976). See Alasdair MacIntyre, *After Virtue* (Notre Dame: University of Notre Dame Press, 1981) for a reinterpretation of the Aristotelian tradition. That influence has been largely mediated by Stanley Hauerwas, *A Community of Character: Toward a Constructive Christian Social Ethic* (Notre Dame: University of Notre Dame Press, 1981).

15. Farley, *Theologia*, has played a major role in clarifying this custom. The base-community movement in Latin America also has raised questions about confining theological reflection to academic settings; see S. Torres and J. Eagleson, eds., *The Challenge of Basic Christian Communities* (Maryknoll, N. Y.: Orbis Books, 1981).

16. See James Poling and Donald Miller, *Foundation for a Practical Theology of Ministry* (Nashville: Abingdon Press, 1985). Without question, the foremost representative of hermeneutical practical theology is Charles Gerkin, *The Living Human Document: Re-visioning Pastoral Counseling in a Hermeneutical Mode* (Nashville: Abingdon Press, 1984), and *Widening the Horizons: Pastoral Responses to a Fragmented Society* (Philadelphia: Westminster Press, 1986). For somewhat different understandings, see Don Browning, *Religious Ethics and Pastoral Care* (Philadelphia: Fortress Press, 1983); Dennis McCann and Charles Strain, *Polity and Praxis: A Program for American Practical Theology* (Minneapolis: Winston Press, 1985).

17. See Richard Palmer, *Hermeneutics* (Evanston: Northwestern University Press, 1969).

18. See Rudolf Makkreel, *Dilthey: Philosopher of the Human Sciences* (Princeton: Princeton University Press, 1975); see also English trans., ed. H. Rickman, *Pattern and Meaning in History: Thoughts on History and Society* (New York: Harper & Row, 1961).

19. See Martin Heidegger, *Being and Time*, trans. Macquarrie and Robinson (New York: Harper & Row, 1962); Hans-Georg Gadamer, *Truth and Method* (New York: Continuum, 1975); Paul Ricoeur, *The Conflict of Interpretations* (Evanston: Northwestern University Press, 1974).

20. Prejudice is not a negative concept, but reflects the historicity of all understanding; see Gadamer, *Truth and Method*, pp. 235 ff.

21. Thomas Kuhn, *The Structure of Scientific Revolutions* (Chicago: University of Chicago Press, 1962).

22. See Gadamer, *Truth and Method*, pp. 235-73 for discussion.

23. Gadamer describes this in terms of the moment of negativity in all true dialectic, when understanding becomes aware of its limitations, bringing about a restructuring of understanding.

24. See Gerkin, *Living Human Document*.

25. Paul Holmer, *The Grammar of Faith* (New York: Harper & Row, 1978); George Lindbeck, *The Nature of Doctrine: Religion and Theology in a Post-liberal Age* (Philadelphia: Westminster Press, 1984).

285

26. Roman Catholic theology would view theological interpretation somewhat differently, placing greater emphasis on the official teachings of the church to set the initial parameters for investigation of Scripture, tradition, and present existence; see Karl Rahner, "Replik. Bemerkungen zu: Hans Küng, Im Interesse der Sache," *Stimmen der Zeit* 187(1971):145-60. In spite of this difference, the essential structure is basically circular. Certain Roman Catholic scholars develop their understanding of theology as hermeneutical in ways that are analogous to that suggested here; see Edward Schillebeeckx, *The Understanding of Faith: Interpretation and Criticism*, trans. N. Smith (New York: Seabury Press, 1974).

27. See Lawrence Cremin, *Public Education* (New York: Basic Books, 1976).

28. See William Frankena, *Three Historical Philosophies of Education* (Chicago: Scott, Foresman Co., 1965), intro., regarding moral dimension of education. Alasdair MacIntyre, *After Virtue*, points to the narrative character of a community's moral vision.

29. Charles Melchert, "Understanding and Religious Education," *Process and Relationship*, ed. Iris Cully and Kendig Cully (Birmingham, Ala.: Religious Education Press, 1978), pp. 41-48; Sara P. Little, *To Set One's Heart: Belief and Teaching in the Church* (Atlanta: John Knox Press, 1983), pp. 23-25, and "Religious Instruction," *Contemporary Approaches to Christian Education*, ed. Jack Seymour and Donald E. Miller (Nashville: Abingdon Press, 1982), pp. 43-45.

30. Ronald Hyman, *Ways of Teaching* (New York: J. B. Lippincott, 1974), pp. 10-11.

31. These categories, as well as the definitions of education and teaching, are derived in part from philosophical and social scientific reflection on the practice of teaching. Though the theological significance of these dimensions and definitions is explored, this does not mean that education and related disciplines set the basic terms which theology then reflects upon. Rather, the philosophical perspectives and social scientific understandings of education engaged as dialogue partners are chosen in part on theological grounds. For example, perspectives that acknowledge the normativity of education are preferred to those that bracket out the underlying ethical basis of education. This is based on a theological understanding of the faith dimension inherent in all sustained communal activities, as explicated by H. Richard Niebuhr, *Radical Monotheism and Western Culture* (New York: Harper & Row, 1943). Theology provides the basic assumptions upon which nontheological resources are engaged.

32. There is a wide range of ways in which theology and nontheological resources can be related. Contrast the correlational method of Paul Tillich, *Systematic Theology*, Vol. 1, pp. 3-70, and the even more extreme revisionist approach of David Tracy, *Blessed Rage for Order: The New Pluralism in Theology* (New York: Seabury Press, 1979), chaps. 2-3, with the sort of Barthian analysis found in Eduard Thurneysen, *A Theology of Pastoral Care*, trans. J. Worthington (Richmond: John Knox Press, 1962), chaps. 7, 10-11. For a brief indication of my position, see Note 31 above.

33. Obviously, this is one of the important points that practical theological reflection opens out to other moments in the larger process of theological interpretation. Comprehensive accounts of Christian truth are typically articulated by systematic theology.

34. See Richard R. Osmer, *A Teachable Spirit: Recovering the Teaching Office in Mainline Protestantism* (Louisville: Westminster/John Knox Press, 1990).

35. See Don Downing, *Generative Man: Psychoanalytic Perspectives* (New York: Delta Books, 1973) and *Religious Thought and the Modern Psychologies: A Critical Conversation in the Theology of Culture* (Philadelphia: Fortress Press, 1987).

36. See Sara Little, *To Set One's Heart,* in which she draws in part on Bruce Joyce and Marsha Weil, *Models of Teaching* (Englewood Cliffs, N. J.: Prentice-Hall, 1972).

37. See Louis Rubin, *Artistry in Teaching* (New York: Random House, 1985).